WHERE DO YOU WANT THIS LOT?

By BOB RUST

GINGERFOLD PUBLICATIONS

ACKNOWLEDGEMENTS

Peter Davies for the front cover design and photographs duly accredited in the captions. Arthur Ingram for his photos. Steve Wimbush for proof reading my text and giving me encouragement to finish this work after putting it on hold for a few years. All three men are long-serving stalwarts of the Commercial Vehicle & Road Transport Club (C.V.R.T.C.) and I duly record my thanks and appreciation to them. Many others have also assisted me in recollecting events and names from the past. You know who you are and I am grateful.

Photographic Credits

The Transport Archives Series is produced and published by Gingerfold Publications.

This title was first published in March 2007 by
Gingerfold Publications, 52 Lentworth Drive, Walkden, Manchester M28 3EX.
Tel: 01204 573806 Email: gingerfold@ukonline.co.uk
Website: www.gingerfold.com

ISBN 1-902356-20-09
ISBN(13) 978-1-902356-20-4

Printed and bound by The Burlington Press, Station Road, Foxton, Cambridge, CB2 6SW.

CONTENTS

WARNING

Some sections of this book do contain strong language. The chapter entitled 'Ladies of the Road' also contains some sexually explicit details and is not considered suitable reading for juveniles under the age of 18 years. Neither the author nor publisher can accept responsibility if any readers are offended by the contents of this book.

FOREWORD

"Where do you want this lot?" Anyone who has been at the sharp end of haulage has asked that question many thousand times. I thought it an apposite title for the story of forty-two years in the game.

A warning to enthusiasts! In this book you will not find long lists of fleet and registration numbers. It is written by a driver who has always regarded the wagon as a tool. A wheel on each corner and a seat at the front, some good, some bad, comfortable or more often, uncomfortable. I certainly can't tell this year's from last by the shape of the sidelight.

This is more a story about the job. After one of those days, when I have been either soaked to the skin, frozen solid, bored stiff, even scared to death, I have often thought, "I ought to find myself another job". I have been in that situation many times in forty-two years, but always ended up with the thought "What else would I do? There is no job like it!!"

In my family, if you exclaim, "That's funny!" you will be asked, "Peculiar or ha-ha?" Shades of an old wireless programme. Some of the incidents and characters fall into one category some into the other, a few into both. I have always been interested in history so I have tossed in a bit here and there where appropriate, either transport or general. It is the way I learned in that great University, "Life." This tale is like the after dinner conversation that used to take place in digs. With "Off at a tangent" as a route often pursued. It is the bits that have stuck in my mind.

When I started you had to know your way about. Places like Milton Keynes and Telford did not exist, while Basildon and Crawley were rural villages. The motorways have made the roads like the Hilton Hotels. You only know where you are by the name on the signs. Today, if it is not on a motorway you can't get there. In those days, there were two million cars on the road. A 'trucker' wheeled a barrow on a parcel bank and a 'rig' was an incompletely castrated horse. 'Just in Time' meant finding a cafe' for dinner. It ends with thirty million cars on the road and a wagon carrying nearly twice as much, three times as fast!

For most of my time it was the driver who was full of chips, now it's the wagon. The philosophy has changed from "If it's not broke, don't mend it" to "If it's broke you can't mend it".

Enjoy reading the story. I have enjoyed writing it and living it. Try not to frighten the family with bouts of uncontrolled mirth.
Bob Rust, Basildon, September, 2006.

DEDICATION
Dedicated to my wife Leslie who endured all those years of being married to a driver.
(Her Dad didn't know there were two spellings).
My friends Steve and Alan who encouraged me to write this book.
My friend the late Dave Tarbuck who personified the best of BRS.
Not forgetting all the restorers who have kept the momories alive.

CHAPTER 1
SETTING THE SCENE

In February 1997 I collapsed with an attack of vertigo. The Doctor diagnosed extremely high blood pressure of the 'Lucky you're not dead' kind. He brought it down with tablets, but thought I should not go charging about with a lorry, as stress could bring it up again. On his advice, the DVLA withdrew my LGV licence on 11th July1997. Thus ended forty-two years, four months and one week of employment in the road haulage industry.

My involvement in transport goes back sixty-three years and five months, to my first trip from London to Broadstairs at the age of three weeks. This was on the front seat of a Baico-Chevrolet, with a soap carton for a cot. My family has been in transport a long time; farm horses, coachmen, carters, steam wagons and motors.

Great Granddad was a coachman, finishing his career at Barkby Hall near Syston in Leicestershire. Granddad was born near Kings Lynn, as a young man he moved to London probably when his father changed jobs In the late 19th century London was growing apace and with it the demand for horsemen, it was about 1901 when Granddad moved eventually he married the daughter of the lodgings. My Dad was born in 1909, when Granddad was 34.

I always knew of Granddad's Norfolk ancestry and thought we were descended from the invading Saxons. But thanks to DNA technology, I have found out we are descended from the Iceni, the original inhabitants of Norfolk.

Granddad collected cheese from the famous 'Bell' at Stilton on the Great North Road, in a packet van, which was the Ford Transit of its day. Built by a coachbuilder, not a Cartwright, to a very high standard. Drawn by a pair of Cleveland Bays or heavy hunters running in tandem, it was the express delivery vehicle, the Transit of its day. He also drove horse trams and was, for a time, in charge of the tram company's trace horse (also known as a cock horse or steamer) at Highgate Hill, before the advent of electric traction, he went on to be an electric tram driver. He finished his career driving a Ford AA two-tonner, with an early pantechnicon body, which was covered from the waist rail up with tarred hessian, which was repainted with hot tar at the gas works each autumn.

On a historical note, a trace horse, generally a big Shire or Clydesdale was called a steamer because after working a heavy load up a hill assisting the shaft horse or team, he stood and steamed with perspiration. This explains the pubs at the top of hills being called 'The Steamer', which have a picture of a horse on the sign. There is one at Old Welwyn just north of Hatfield. They were sometimes called cockhorses because they were entires i.e. uncastrated males (stallions are breeding horses) which are generally stronger.

My Dad made a big impression in my life. Between leaving school at 14 and starting in road haulage he had done many jobs. He had worked in a Bakelite factory, the earliest type of plastic. He had been a tennis racquet stringer and still had a groove at the base of his little finger 35 years later. Whilst working for a painter and decorator he learned to make his own paint, buying all the oils and colours from the oil shop. While I was small we had the first 'magnolia' kitchen in the area. He was a self-taught cabinet maker and French polisher, a skill he passed on to me and which was to become very useful to me when I did furniture carriage. In addition he was a fitter and turner and motor fitter.

Dad's brother was a toolmaker for 45 years working for M.K. Electric. (We had the first ring main with 13amp square pin plugs in Wood Green, all M.K. prototypes). His hobby was radio from its earliest days. He was friendly with many of the big name radio manufacturers, A J Balcombe of Alba, Cossor, Eric Cole of Ekco and Bulgin the component maker. He built his own TV using the Baird principle and after the war a 405 line-CRT

TV using ex-RAF airborne radar parts. I followed in his footsteps, the ultimate DiYer, I would still rather mend something than replace it.

Dad followed in Granddad's footsteps with single and pair horse, but going quickly to steam and motors. Around 1931 in conjunction with Mr Adams who owned a tiling and asphalting business he operated a Sentinel under-type, a 2½-ton over-type Foden with trailer, and a model T Ford. He carted all the green roof tiles for the estate opposite Wembley Stadium from Richardson's Metallic Tiles of Newcastle-under-Lyme. The tiles were delivered by the driver to the tiler on the roof, no 'to the tailboard' deliveries in those days! Incidentally, when I loaded out of Richardson's in 1968 via BRS Tunstall, the same man that had loaded Dad loaded me, and they still had 'Wembley Greens' in the corner of the tile yard!

When the 1933 Road & Rail Traffic Act came into force Mr. Adams sold the vehicles, sending Dad back to casual driving. He (Adams) did not like the idea of restrictions and unnecessary form filling, "keeping the Whitehall parasites" he said.

When I had my first ride, on 21st February 1934 he was driving the Baico-Chev. for W.T. Noble & Sons. a removal contractor newly into motors. Old Tom Noble had been a greengrocer and did light removals with his pony and market van. When he found that light removals with horse and van paid better than greengrocery he sold the shop and bought a horse pantechnicon, quickly followed by the Chev. Incidentally, that trip from 7.30am to 4.30pm earned Dad 10/- (50p).

By the time I can remember clearly, the horse van was the tackle store and dog kennel and the Chev. was on blocks being used as a loading bank and warehouse. It was a strange looking machine; it had been built at Luton as a 30cwt and then converted by Baico to a six-wheeler with trailing axles and a very long rear overhang. It had the same part timber; part painted hessian pantechnicon body as Granddad's Ford with a very small Luton head just over the cab roof and a very long bonnet, as the entire six-cylinder engine was ahead of the dashboard.

It made the national press when it was being used to bring a prototype capstan lathe from Sheffield to a machine tool exhibition at Wembley. The huge turret saddle worked loose and made its way to the end of the bed, which was right at the end of the overhang. A quick gear-change on a hill south of Worksop resulted in the wagon standing on its tail in the middle of the road and a five bob (25p) fine for Dad for having an unsafe load. A picture of this vehicle featured on the firm's stationary until about 1950.

This was a time of great uncertainty and a lot of drivers were employed on a regular casual basis, my Dad included. Sometimes he drove for another removal firm called Fuller's. It was quite a regular thing for Fred Fuller to pawn his piano on a Friday to get cash to pay his men. Dad also did a bit for a firm called D & O Transport which specialised in pianos, one of the partners was German and was interned in 1939 as an enemy alien.

Dad still worked for Mr. Adams, delivering tiles from railway trucks shunted into Adams' yard at Noel Park. (I don't know if Mr. Adams bought another lorry or hired one). As I said Adams also did tarmacing and employed a one-legged steamroller driver 'Peggy' Scott a WWI veteran. I have fond memories of 'Peggy' although as a very small boy his peg leg scared me when I first met him.

His other employers included Stan Illett, for whom Granddad worked. George Thornton, the father of one of my teachers, and Bert Blower, a haulage contractor turned scrapman who is mentioned from time to time in books on transport history. He was working for Bert the day I was born, 7am to 8pm for 10/- (50p). His gross earnings for 1934 were £135.3s.

He also did some driving for the United Dairies out of its Wood Lane depot, (he went from Wood

Green on a belt driven motor bike), this was with chain-drive Scammells and box trailers on bulk crate deliveries.

Dad went on full time with Noble's sometime in 1938. Things were tough even then. These were the days of the cumulative week. This meant that no overtime was paid until 48 hours work had been completed. Thus it was possible to work 12 hours a day, Monday to Thursday and then be told "Don't come in Friday, no work", only to find out that a casual had been brought in for Friday and Saturday. Alternatively to do eight hours a day including a full day on Saturday, for no extra.

By the time I started school in April 1939, Noble's operated two Bedfords, a 1937 WTB and a 1934 WB. Dad drove the WB, which had a 1500 cu.ft. coach built body covered with Plymax (aluminium faced plywood) with skirt panels to hide the chassis. It was a full Luton body, by which I mean that the Luton head extended to above the radiator. It had no front stay-irons so that entire six feet of Luton cantilevered off the first body frame behind the driver's seat.

As the WB was a coach chassis it only came in chassis-scuttle form so the cab was integral with the body. It had PSV refinements; polished drop and steering arms, a hoop under the rear prop-shaft, a long exhaust pipe to discharge on the offside, a drip tray with a copper drain pipe under the carburetter, and a dry powder fire extinguisher with spare cartridges under the nearside bonnet. The back end of the body had a drop-well built on to the coach chassis' long tail, there was a 4ft 6in tailboard and a top hinged shutter completed the rear closure. It was registered EMP 563.

This van had originally been built for the Luton straw-hat trade. The firm that had ordered it went broke and it was bought by ex-professional footballer Jimmy Dimmock who had gone into the sports goods business. He drank himself into bankruptcy as he had drunk himself out of football. Thus, Noble's got the vehicle for a song.

One funny story regarding EMP. As it was a coach chassis the carburetter had to have a drip tray with a pipe leading right away from the engine, over the years this had got blocked with dirt. Inevitably the float stuck and the carburetter overflowed filling the drip tray, then the whole lot caught fire. The fitted fire extinguisher looked like a Very pistol with the barrel a 2in. x 10in. tube filled with bicarbonate of soda. You aimed it and cocked it just like a pistol and an explosive charge blew the powder over the fire. Dad grabbed this thing which had never been looked at in 16 years, he cocked it and fired it two or three times: nothing! He was holding it loosely by his side when it suddenly went off. We were covered from head to toe in white powder and the extinguisher flew over the hedge! At that moment a coach pulled up and the driver ran over with a modern Pyrene extinguisher. He said to Dad "Need an extinguisher mate?" to which Dad replied "No thanks, I've just had one" and chucked a bit of furniture wrapper over the last of the flames.

Pantechnicon and Luton warrant an explanation. 'The Pantechnicon' was a huge warehouse and carriage store in Motcomb Street, SW1. A man called Seth Smith built it in 1830. At that time, the 'gentry' would leave their town house and go to their country house for the summer. All their furniture and possessions would be put into store. To do this Seth Smith employed a fleet of large volume horse drawn box vans. These were canary yellow with the firm's name in green on the side. In the way that all vacuum cleaners tend to be called Hoovers, any high capacity box vans came to be called a pantechnicon. In 1996 'The Pantechnicon' still existed, now at Turnham Green (the original warehouse burned down in 1867) run by one of Seth Smith's descendants. The name still exists in 2003.

The original Seth Smith was a meticulous man who set high standards. In the 50's I worked with an old furniture porter who had worked for 'The Pantechnicon', if you bumped the furniture or broke a piece of china he would say, "That would never do for Seth Smith". 'The Pantechnicon' also had a reputation for packing, dating back to the start of the Empire when the great and the good moved abroad to run things. I am told that even at the end to qualify as a packer you must be able to pack a case of china so that it could be kicked off the loading bank without anything being broken.

It was Seth Smith's search for perfection that really brought about the unique feature of the pantechnicon. It had a low floor, which meant that heavy, intricate, and valuable furniture could be 'walked' in, not lifted up to a high floor. This was first done with small wheels. Abel's of Watton have a preserved example but this gave a rough ride on cobbles. Fitting a 'u' shaped rear axle which allowed standard 4ft 6in wheels to be fitted solved the problem. 2ft 6in front wheels were still needed to allow the lock (or fore-carriage) to turn.

The Luton or Luton head stems from the high volume required by the straw-hat trade for which that town was famous. In the days of rail transport, the best hats were packed in hampers and the cheaper ones wrapped in hessian in long rolls which, looked like rolls of lino. When motors came into use the first box vans were built like the old horse vans with thick diagonal planking which produced a very heavy van. This was then reduced to high sides with wooden hoops covered in tarpaulin or tarred hessian. Then someone realised that for things as light and bulky as straw hats, there was a big space above the cab and engine, which could be enclosed and filled. Thus the Luton head was born.

The Construction & Use and Motor Vehicle Speed Limit Regulations posed a challenge to body builders. The aim was to keep the wagon classified as a Light Motor Car, under 3 tons unladen weight thus allowing it to travel at 30 mph. The advent of Plymax had allowed van bodies to be built on a frame and panel design.

Furniture was getting lighter and bulkier and the demand for bigger volume bodies was growing. The problem of 'lozenging' as vans got higher and longer but more lightly built was solved in many ingenious ways. The most common being to take the side uprights below the level of the floor and then bracing them diagonally to the cross bearers which led to the characteristic 'furniture van' appearance with the chassis and running gear hidden behind skirt panels.

The Jensen was probably the ultimate in lightweight Luton van building. As much as possible of it was aluminium. I was told that its designer, who also designed aircraft, had called the monocoque principal into van building. The main chassis runners were wide aluminium plates with angle ally riveted to both sides of both edges, to make an 'I' beam, the cross members were made the same way. Cross bearers, body sticks and roof hoops were extruded top hat sections, the tying raves were ribbed extrusions and the floor was square section corrugations with wood strips inserted to make it flat.

They were put together with thousands of pop rivets, just like an aircraft. The early ones suffered electrolytic corrosion when salt water got into all those riveted joints on the chassis. This was overcome by inserting fibre strips in all the joints to eliminate metal-to-metal contact. The early ones carried the curved line of the cab front right up to the roof, which gave a small odd shaped Luton.

Later ones had a squared off Luton, which overhung the cab slightly. When I started, the biggest van was about 1,500 cu.ft. The Jensen was the first genuine 2,000-cu.ft. van at an unladen weight of 2 tons 19cwt 3 qtrs. 20 lbs. It shared one fault with Pickfords' all ally body, the ribs on the tying raves raised small 'bruises' on the edges of furniture tied to them. It was never safe to put a new piece 'face in', no matter how much wrapper you put in; the ribs concentrated the entire load on to narrow strips and caused 'rave burns' or wrapper imprints. Anyway, enough of the history lessons, back to the story.

In September 1939 Hitler started all the trouble, by the spring of 1940 the evacuation of London was in full swing and Noble's Bedfords were under the direction of the Ministry of War Transport (MoWT).

There were so few children about that schools were closed and EMP became a second home along with the air-raid shelter.

As a very small boy I saw the sun set behind Stonehenge and brewed tea on a Primus in the lee of its stones. I had seen the white horses of Uffington, Calne and Westbury before they were camouflaged; Silbury Hill; the Clifton Suspension Bridge and the Lowry landscapes of Manchester, Bury and Bolton all before my seventh birthday. I found out about 'cabbing it' and 'sleeping in the back' with furniture wrappers for bedding. I had nights out at Tiny's in Honiton, Paris' in Exeter, Mrs Howard's next door to the Fleet Air Arm at Yeovilton; the Ace at Weedon; Sid's Wood Farm in Daventry, Bob's at Stretton; The Aero at Doncaster; The Bridge in Gloucester and Woodley's at Rode Heath.

There were also the cafes, many of which I used when I started driving. To name just a few: The Blue Hut at Basingstoke, The Ridgeway at Beckhampton, Tubby's at Willoughby, The Bungalow at Marks Tey, Mac's at Alconbury, Tony's at Grantham (the old one at the top of Spittlegate Hill); The Sentinel at Dunstable, The Pullman in Fenny Stratford, The Jungle on Shap, The Beacon on the A66 near Penrith, Kay's Cottage - the first house in Devon, Bill Spittle's 48 mile at Loughton on the A5 universally known as The Glue Pot and Morley's Farm Hut at Riverhead, where goat meat was served during the war because it was not on ration. We will return to the subject of cafes later.

One of the jobs we did was the evacuation of Jeremiah Rotherham's textile warehouse in Shoreditch, the stock being dispersed to safer locations around the country. Hitler must have known!

We delivered to the Co-op warehouse in Spon Street, Coventry on the afternoon of 14th November 1940. We stopped for the night at Bob's and had a ringside seat at the Coventry blitz. The next day, we had to wait for permission to move from the police. The A5 and A45 were both closed except to fire fighting and rescue vehicles being sent from the south.

The 'jinx' followed that job, we delivered to Bristol, Exeter and Plymouth and had stopped at Melksham, Honiton and Ivybridge only to see the city behind us blitzed and all the stuff we had delivered was destroyed! Ironically, Rotherham's warehouse in Shoreditch survived the London blitz with nothing more than broken windows! As this was a MoWT job, we got a fuel allowance that, came in two-gallon cans. It was stale aircraft fuel, full of lead, and after the first trip using this fuel, we carried a spare cylinder head as it burned out valves like nobody's business. Roadside head changes were routine and I soon learned all the right words for when you hit your knuckles as a spanner slipped!

Despite the cold, pins and needles in the bum, walking in front in the fog, acting as a lookout in the blackout, the romance of transport had gripped me. I loved the road and travelling. When the schools re-opened I was still off with Dad whenever possible. When I was 14 I even did a couple of journeys as a fully paid porter on long distance removals, one to St Austell, the other to Clyst Honiton. I got an official week off school in 1948 to help Dad change the old 27hp 'W' engines in both vans to the then modern 28hp 'O' type. My headmaster thought it would be useful work experience. In April '49 I left school to start an apprenticeship as a motor mechanic

In 1952 it was into the Army. After a short spell learning to drive Centurion tanks with the Royal Armoured Corps, I transferred to the Royal Electrical & Mechanical Engineers (R.E.M.E). It was back to Bedford's - MW, OW and QL Plus K2 and K4 Austin's, K-type Karriers, Morris Quads, AEC Matador gun tractors and Scammell Pioneer's (the latter always known in the Army as diesel Scammells). From Swindon workshops I went to Hong Kong to the AFV shop of the Command Workshop overhauling Comet tanks. These like the earlier Crusader and later Centurion tanks used Rolls Royce Meteor engines, which were really naturally aspirated Merlins with a magneto rev limiter. In 1954 many of the recons. we got back from the RAOC had done their time in Lancasters during the war. These engines were designed for maximum use, 500 hours from new in a fighter, then a rebuild and two 500 hour tours in bombers, then after another rebuild which included removing the supercharger, fitting different inlet and exhaust manifolds and a normal carb. to finish their useful life in tanks. The downrating reduced them from 1,020 to 540 horsepower.

My last year in Hong Kong was spent as a mobile vehicle inspector, touring the island and the New Territories. The colony was the land of the Bedford, a few W and early O-models, which had survived the Japanese occupation, lots of OLBD's, some S's and a few A's. They were all dropsiders, although some had a locally built tilt of lashed bamboo poles and a tarpaulin that was normally rolled up to roof height like a furled sail, except in the monsoon. There was a local rule that a motor wasn't loaded until it was full which produced some spectacular loads.

A cab high load of bagged cement on a 5-tonner! Or three six-foot diameter teak logs about 30ft long. Without doubt the most spectacular was spoil for a landfill - a 22ft. dropsider filled to the top of the sides with loose earth and small stones, then more carefully pyramided up and tamped to a 40-degree slope right down the length of the load. On arrival at the site, the vehicle was reversed diagonally towards the tipping face until the offside rear wheel dropped and the diff. grounded. This usually left the nearside front wheel about a foot off the ground and put about 30 to 35 degrees of twist in the chassis. This move facilitated shovelling off; there were no tippers! The next loaded vehicle towed the empty one back on to level ground!

My time was up with HM Forces. Just after Christmas it was on a troop ship to Singapore to wait in a transit camp for a flight back to Britain. The Army had just started to use air trooping. We flew in an aircraft which had rearward facing seats and turbo-prop engines (a Viscount I think). We flew via Colombo, Calcutta, Bombay (where we had a night out). Nicosia (another night out) and after a breakdown in Athens, landed at Blackbush at 02:00 on 2nd February 1955, my 21st birthday. After another night out in the Goodge Street Movement Centre, formerly a deep air raid shelter (heavily infested with bed bugs), it was off to Aldershot to await demob on 1st April. Then it was home to start in the road haulage industry.

As someone interested in the road haulage there is something I had seen all my life, right on my own doorstep, taking it very much for granted. On a purely historical note I will slip it in here before finally leaving my childhood and youth.

Wood Green Borough Council had one of the most advanced refuse collection services. It had fully enclosed rear loading artics. These had a manually operated moving floor. As the rubbish piled up just inside the back the driver put a handle in a hole in the side and 'wound' the rubbish forward. The trailers were moved from house to house by a horse, supplied by Mr Nicholls, the Horse Contractor.

There was a little rubber tyred bogie with shafts, which was fitted with a modified Scammell coupling. The coupling hooks were on the end of a long screw, the bogie was backed up to the trailer until the hooks engaged, then the driver wound a handle which drew the trailer jockey wheels up the ramps. Once the outfit reached a certain point on the round a Scammell Scarab would come along to meet them with an empty trailer. Winding the handle the other way dropped the loaded trailer, and then the Scarab hooked up and took it to the 'dust destructor'.

The adjoining Borough of Hornsey used Shelvoke & Drewry side loading tipping carts with the semi-circular slide up lids, whilst Islington & Holloway used the same type of body but this was carried on a Ford chassis and demounted with a system similar to the Rolonoff. Once on the ground it was dragged along on little iron wheels by a trace horse. Robert Deards Ltd., of Finchley supplied the system under contract (as it did the men).

CHAPTER 2
INTO ROAD HAULAGE

My early days of employment in haulage revolved around two companies, both very typical of the haulage scene of the early 1950's - a time when the country was starting to come out of wartime austerity. This was supposed to have been marked by the 1951 Festival of Britain, which nearly sent the nation bankrupt. The nationalisation of the industry in 1948 played a part in events coupled with the Carriers' Licencing system. After nationalisation, small removers although on 'A' licences were not involved. They were allowed to carry on unhindered with local removals. However, long distance removals required a permit from the Road Haulage Executive (R.H.E.) which often required a back load of van traffic to be picked up to its instructions. This might even be a removal under the control of Pickfords - the nationalised removers.

Old Tom Noble had died and the firm was under the control of his son Bill. Bill had two sons, neither of whom was interested in the business. The eldest was an artist and the younger had gone back to the family trade of greengrocery. Bill was getting fed up with all the paperwork generated by the R.H.E. so he formed a limited company. The yard in Westbury Avenue, London N.22 was on a bend on a main road bus route. The insurance policy insisted that the vans be reversed in so that they could be driven out unassisted. If they were driven in, the Insurers would not pay out, as they were 'rendered potentially unrecoverable'. Reversing in was getting steadily more hazardous; traffic was beginning to grow, even in 1951. You would never get it as an Operating Centre on an 'O' Licence. With denationalisation in 1952, Bill suddenly had a valuable asset - 6 tons of 'A' licence for two vehicles with a normal user of 'General Goods - Great Britain' a legacy of working for MoWT during the war, plus a freehold house and a yard big enough to build another house. He put the firm up for sale.

Nearby was Aitkin's Transport which, started off before the war as a father and son firewood merchants delivering with a pony trolley. When the pony died they bought a motor and started doing a bit of haulage during the summer on a 'B' licence. When Aitkin senior died, Harold Aitkin moved into full time haulage. He had his old Bedford WLG which until it was scrapped kept its firewood body. This had fixed sides at the front with 'park railings' extensions on top and dropsides at the back half. Also a Bedford OW which came out of Luton with civilian 'O' model axles fitted, on an 'A' licence and two semi-forward control pre-war Dodge's later converted to Perkins P6 power. One of these was on a 'B' licence restricted to 'Three Hands disinfectant anywhere in Great Britain and General Goods within a 12 mile radius of Wood Green Post Office', the other was on a 'Contract C' licence for Benjamin Electric Ltd., of Tottenham.

In the post-war period, Harold's mate Gill Cousins came out of the forces and used his gratuity to start Bruce Grove Transport in a small yard behind the houses in Bruce Grove, Tottenham. It became B.G. Transport; when it outgrew its yard it moved to the top of Harold's yard in New Road, Wood Green. B.G.'s original vans were on a restricted 'B' licence and thus escaped nationalisation.

With an eye to expansion, Harold bought W.T. Noble & Sons Ltd., and another small remover, Joseph Harvey Ltd. The fleets were merged and joined by an ex-Pickfords Removals Bedford OLBZ with a special Pickfords integral cab and an all-aluminium body. There was a much stretched and Perkins engined OLBC, a WLG, a WTB and a very smart OLBZ - these four being ex-BRS New Furniture Delivery Service. The four vans were on 'S' licences via the 1952 denationalisation. The WTB was 'nationalised' with Defferies Transport Ltd., of Balls Pond Road. I had worked on it in 1949 while apprenticed to Coaches & Components at Stamford Hill. The OLBZ was an acquisition from Henry Bayes, HYL 352 and it appears on page 26 of "*BRS The Early Years 1948 – 1953*". There was also another OLBZ and a very ancient WLG, the result of buying out one-man band removal businesses for their 'A" licences. Also a very luxurious coachbuilt van on a Bedford OB chassis ex a bankrupt three-piece suite firm, which had been added to the original Noble's 'A' licence. Shortly after came two brand new Ford Thames's, - a 4D and a 6D, - which were also added to the 'A' licence which, was starting to be consolidated. The 6D bore a special livery designed by the fitter's wife. The words **"Note Our Better Everyday Long Distance Services"** were written singly one above the other so that the initial letters formed the name Nobles. There were plans to do the entire fleet, but these never came off.

We were heavily (not quite the right word!) into new furniture (including soft suites, as upholstery was known) at that time. Stonehills, Austinsuite, Gainsborough, Golden key, Put-U-Up, Epstein, Ferroflex. Also Prestige kitchen cabinets. Those were the days when furniture was a big plywood box full of wind. We also did televisions for Pye and Ekco, upholstery padding for Rapido and the original Aitkin traffic of disinfectant and industrial lighting. With both firms sharing one yard there was a great deal of co-operation and traffic sharing. I well remember one of the P6 Dodge's - it had holes cut in the internal 'bonnet' to facilitate the changing of exhaust manifold gaskets which often blew and No.6 injector pipes which broke even more often, there was always a bundle hanging in the cab.

We carried Neon signs for Claudgen Lighting of Wembley. My Dad had the job of delivering the new illuminated sign made by this firm to the Peek & Freen Biscuit factory in Bermondsey. These were loaded vertically on the ex-B.G. Bedford OW and stood 17ft high. Dad was left to plan a route from Wembley to Bermondsey without going under a bridge. He had to do it in the very early hours while the trolley bus wires were switched off. It took four nights, two for each word. He did go under one bridge, Highgate Arch.

One other historical note: Golden key Furniture employed David Kosoff (the actor) as a furniture designer, the first ever designer for mass-produced furniture. This firm contracted to make a vast number of Lee-Enfield rifle boxes during the War; these were to be delivered at a fixed number per week. When the War finished it had not fulfilled the contract, so well into the 50's the weekly quota of boxes were made, inspected by a man from the Ministry of Supply and then burnt under his supervision!

With B.G. Transport also buying ex-BRS vehicles, the New Road yard was overfull. While I was in the Army, B.G. Transport moved to a new yard in Mayes Road, Wood Green (now under the north end of Shopper's City).

In April 1955 I came out of the Army and started work for B.G. Transport. My first load was TVs, record cabinets and Spears Games, about twenty drops in Birmingham and Wolverhampton and a reload of conduit fittings out of G.E.C. at Witton. Just inside G.E.C.'s gate was 'The Large Generator Shop'. On my first trip I stood and watched a 100-ton load being put on to a Pickfords low-loader.

My Dad was still working for Aitkin's Transport, mostly as a driver but from time to time assisting Harry Corney the fitter. A vacancy for a driver came up and I left B.G. to work for W.T. Noble, it was five minutes walk from home and was the first of many moves between the firms. Both were run and owned by their respective 'Guvnors'. Typical of the time, young, thrusting, trying to expand and make their mark. Many liberties were taken and rows were common, it was also common for drivers in a fit of pique to swop companies, even to go and work somewhere else for a time.

These were the days of the 100-hour week, two or three log sheets and a time sheet for the guvnor. The 'official' log sheet, which was handed in for filing always, showed between 44 and 48 hours on which tax was calculated. The time sheet went into the 'secret' file; it showed the true hours. The difference between the two was paid as expenses, plus five nights out at 10/6 (52p).

Saturday in the yard was a sight to see! On Friday's every available van went and loaded from the various customers. Then, on Saturdays, we unloaded the lot and mixed it together and made it into vanloads for geographical areas. This meant packing together dining sets, bedroom suites, soft suites, and televisions in cartons, cartons of disinfectant, fluorescent lighting, china and cocktail cabinets all without damage and in the right order for delivery.

This was the heyday of the tailboard load. There was a saying that 'the costs are in the body, the profit is on the tailboard'. As the tailboard did not count for overhang or overall length, most were huge and often extended with three scaffold boards and a sheet of plywood! Good quality vans had properly shaped top and wing sheets, others just had a very long back curtain. A good packer could get five or six double bedroom suites or eight to ten dining sets on the tailboard. The rate in those days was between 9d and 1/3d a cubic foot according to distance, with, perhaps an extra 3d or 4d for destinations north of Edinburgh or west of Plymouth.

We were supposed to leave at various times on Sunday according to destination. In reality nobody went until Sunday night, each driver calculating his start to arrive outside his first drop at 9am Monday morning as the shop opened. Around midnight Sunday, the A10 became alive with the 'Scotch' traffic, C-licence vans from every furniture maker in north and east London, our vans and those of the well known new furniture carriers, - Merchandise Transport, Guest Carriers, Wades, Alexandra, Dormer's and D & H.

Charlie Dormer had been Eddie Defferies' road foreman prior to nationalisation and in 1954/5 bought back the old Balls Pond Road depot. Later, he sold out his van fleet to Merchandise Transport and set up again as C.E. Dormer Ltd., with tankers. His men knew Charlie as 'Chunky', he had won the £75,000 first dividend on the pools, giving quite a lot of his winnings to his men. When he set up his tanker operation it was in a street of rented houses and he had a lot of complaints from his neighbours, when he got the chance he bought the lot. He then gave the tenants the option of shutting up or moving!

From about 4am Barnet High Street would see the same exodus to the Midlands and North: first the Manchester's, then the Potteries', the Derby's and the Leicester's followed by the Birmingham's. Swansea and Cardiff were also 4am starts, earlier if the van was too high for the Chepstow arch. Exeter and Plymouth would go about the same time. If the tachograph had been introduced in 1955 half the country would have been sleeping on the floor, sitting on orange boxes and watching wallpaper!

One job we did was empty to Pye's Cambridge on Monday morning for 'load and away'. A 1500 cu.ft. van held 240 x 17-inch tabletop televisions and as supply could not match demand these were generally allocated one per dealer (Co-op's, Binns and other similar large stores had three). A typical run would be Doncaster, York, Newcastle, Edinburgh, Stirling, Glasgow, Carlisle and about 30 round the cotton towns and Manchester.

Van deliveries around the Manchester area were fun. All the 'furniture bumpers' would congregate on the Piccadilly car park (the bus station is there now). We would pool our deliveries so that the man with the biggest lot for a particular store would take everyone else's stuff for that shop. It was often possible to end up with two or three big drops instead of fifteen or twenty small ones. Some firms even supplied envelopes so that 'proof of delivery notes' (PoD's) could be returned to the right haulier or manufacturer.

We always slept in the vans (a luxury if 'Z-bed' was in) and washed in the underground convenience, but the old boy in charge would not allow shaving so we used to shave using the water in the puddles on the car park, the water providing a useful 'mirror' as well. The great cry was "Don't wash your razor, I'm doing the bit under my nose". From Manchester we back loaded cloth through Daces Motors, usually on a Friday, so it was a case of get loaded, have a wash and shave and a good dinner and down through the night to help with the Saturday morning trans-shipping.

Another regular run with industrial lighting was to leave early in the morning, do two drops in Bristol, one in Swansea, one in Cardiff (no Severn Bridge in those days!), one in Hereford and be in G.E.C at Witton before a quarter to five for overnight loading. This meant backing on to the bank and sleeping in the cab while the 2-to-10 shift loaded the van. The 10-to-6 shift clerk would do the notes and wake you when they were ready. Then it was down the road and get backed in to the G.E.C warehouse in Kingsway ready for them to open at 7am or, if it was a load of exports, it was straight into the Royal docks to get as near the front of the rank as possible.

After another row I left Noble's as it had by then become and went back to motor mechanics, working for Capital Motors the Vauxhall main dealers in Hornsey. I had only been there about six weeks when Abdul Gammell Nasser nationalised the Suez Canal. I was on the paid Regular Reserve and at the end of August 1956 I was called up, on the day I was going on holiday. It was off to the REME depot at Arborfield, then via a WWII Dakota to Tripoli, to the Base Workshop.

We were on stand-by with the 11th Hussars and 7th Royal Tank Regiment. We were to go via the coast road (Monty's old route) to reinforce the troops who had landed at Port Said. The whole thing fizzled out and we passed the time building a mobile officer's mess complete with cocktail bar. It even had a carrying box with cut outs for all the various shapes of drink bottles. We eventually got on one of the old 'Empire' troopships, the first big ship to enter Tripoli harbour since the RAF's attention during the war. It was back home in time for Christmas.

I went back to Noble's which had moved once more to another yard in Granville Road, Wood Green, the bottom of the road in which I lived! This yard had a long transport history. It had been the depot of 'Ruggles' a tipper operator who went back to two wheeled, one horse 'tumble' carts. Next door had been the yard of Bert Blower, the scrapman/coalman/haulier mentioned earlier.

Over the years the fleet was changing. The Bedfords were being phased out according to age and the first B.M.C. 5KFED's arrived - their two-piece sloping bottom windscreens and 'grinning' grills always reminded me of the cartoon character 'Droopy'. Then came the KFF, with the one-piece curved windscreen, I never liked the B.M.C. The work was beginning to change, away from new furniture and TVs to Vita-Foam bedding and Range boilers. The old freebooting spirit was going and an air of respectability was creeping in (Harold Aitkin had joined the R.H.A) so I left just after Christmas 1956 by which time my Dad was off the road and working as a full-time night fitter.

There are some events which have stuck in my mind from those early days and which I think are worth telling as they include some rare coincidences. The first goes back to my third day on the road. I was doing a load of deliveries in the West End of London, and as I was going down Marylebone Road and got stopped by the lights at Baker Street, the first pedestrian to cross in front of me was Major Blunt, my C.O in Hong Kong.

I had delivered to Nottingham and got a back load through Tower Hill Transport. Government surplus to be loaded at Syston Aerodrome. I parked at the hanger and eventually two elderly men came to help me load. One looked the van over and said "I see you're from Wood Green in London; a chap from the village moved to Wood Green and he got married". I said to him "That must have been Albert Rust". He looked dumbfounded and said "How on earth did you know that?" so I said "His Dad was the head coachman at Barkby Hall, he married one of the housemaids and his mates called him Alf". I thought the old boy was going to have a fit, he kept saying to his mate "What about that?" To calm him down I said, "It's easy, he was my Granddad, he died a couple of years ago!"

I was doing Bath and Bristol deliveries and had some stuff for Boundary Road, Filton. I got into the middle of the town and saw a Bus Inspector. Naturally, I thought he was the one to ask for directions.

He said "No good asking me mate, I could direct you to Boundary Road, Wood Green, I only moved here from Gladstone Avenue, Wood Green about six weeks ago.

Then I was doing central Nottingham I found the back of the shop, but there was a builder's wagon in the way. I asked one of the builders if he could get the driver to move up a bit, he shouted into the job and out came Brian Talbot my old drinking mate and who slept in the next bed to me in Tripoli.

I was again doing the Midlands round with TVs and the first drop was at Bunny, between Loughborough and West Bridgeford. I had gone up through the night and left too early so just south of the town I stopped for a sleep. When I woke up it was dark when I expected it to be light. I saw a chap on a bike so I asked him the time he replied, "Just gone seven", I said "It's not dark at seven in the morning" to which he replied "No, but it is at seven at night!!" Yes, I had slept through a whole day.

When I was with Nobles the second time, we had a contract for a van with Rapido's who made upholstery padding. I had done about a dozen drops; the final one was about 10 rolls of pure cotton felt for Babydream cot mattresses. It was about 4.00pm when I pulled up. I went and found the man in the white coat and said "Good afternoon, Rapido's". He said "I don't give a f--- who you are, we're finished for the day". I walked out, got in the van and was about to drive away, when I saw him running out of the gate. I thought 'sod him if he can't be civil' and drove off. He started hammering on the side of the van but I ignored him.

When I got back to the yard Harold was standing outside the gate. As I got out he said, "What the hell have you done to the Foreman at Babydream? I've had Oscar (Rapido's transport foreman) on the phone in a right old state, he says the Babydream bloke is in hospital, did you hit him?" I said "You know me better than that Harold, I'm like my old man, polite to the customers and don't go round hitting people. Even ignorant, rude sods like that foreman". I then told him what had happened, he said in the same position he would have done the same. He got back to Oscar and relayed my side of the story. It transpired that after he had been abusive the Babydream foreman had realised that my felt was needed for first thing in the morning. When he hammered on the van to try and make me stop the back wheel had run over his foot. Although I did the Rapido job several times after that, their own driver always did Babydream.

After the great Saturday trans-shipment, we all went over to the local for a couple of pints, Guvnor and office staff as well. It was a typical driver's gathering with everyone relating the happenings of the week and Harold buying the beer and circulating, trying to discover the latest money making dodges. One Saturday the big talking point was Billy, who had gone to sleep and run off the road somewhere north of Kingussie. It was certain he was asleep, because the driver of the Noble's van running about 10 minutes behind found him still asleep lying on the passenger door of the van, which was on its side. The accident wrote off the body and its load of Admiralty furniture and severely damaged the nearly new B.M.C. chassis.

We were somewhat surprised when Harold called for silence. He said, "You all know what happened to Billy and I don't want any more accidents like that, we can't afford them. All right the insurance will pay for the repairs and the G.I.T. will pay for the load, but the premiums will go up. The dealer reckons three weeks to a month to get the van back on the road so that is all that income lost. Billy will expect his wages (there was no vehicle hire in those days!). The company had to pay for the recovery, clearing up the mess and bringing the chassis home. All in all I reckon two grand. It you find your eyelids drooping, pull off and go to sleep. Even if you have four hours, we all know it will go on the time sheet and I don't care because that would only have cost about ten bob (50p). So think about it! Now, who wants another pint?"

Back in '58 Brian (Billy's mate) broke down in Dunstable, Dad went out with the old 30cwt MW to tow him home. Coming into Redbourn, down the hill they began to pick-up speed as Brian had a heavy load of GEC fittings on. Dad braked but nothing happened, Brian had dozed off, he braked harder and the MW spun round. The jolt woke up Brian who then braked and stopped them both. The towing pole now had a 45-degree bend in the middle. Dad remembered from his steam days that there used to be a blacksmith behind the High Street. He put the pole over his shoulder and went to look, the forge was still there and the light was on in the cottage. After some negotiation (involving the Governor of the Bank of England) the fire was drawn up and the pole straightened plus four lengths of angle iron beautifully welded on to stiffen it. The tow home was completed successfully, with Brian full of adrenaline and very much awake.

Billy, who was involved in the overturning incident, was also involved in one of the most peculiar accidents I have heard about. It featured an OLB Bedford converted to Perkins power. On the old A10 was the Orange Cafe, it lay on the right going north and if you wanted to use it you parked in a kind of lay-by, leaving the car park for southbound wagons. A driver went in and asked who was the Noble's driver? Billy put his hand up and the driver said "I bumped your van as I pulled in, there does not seem to be any damage, we'll go and have a look when you've had your breakfast and I've had a cup of tea". They sat for two or three minutes, then there was a terrific crash, then another, the cafe window caved in and there was the bonnet of Billy's van. Billy had backed into a space and left his van on a full right lock, he had left it in bottom gear, as the handbrake was not too good. When the other vehicle had bumped it the engine had started. It had chugged on tickover out of the lay-by across the two lanes of the A10 (no dual carriageway then) in a semi-circle; it had demolished the cafe's garden wall and stalled when it hit the building.

When I was very young I learned how to nick sugar. Parting the weave of the sack with a pencil, putting a piece of highly polished petrol pipe in the hole, taking out a 2lb jam jar full (no more or the sack went slack!) and closing the hole with a sharp slap. While driving one of the Dodges I learned another little trick. Sometimes we unbolted the hoops and used them as dropsiders. Kinloch's the grocery wholesaler for whom we delivered packet sugar from Tate's to the Stamford Hill depot with the Dodge as a tilt, asked if we could do some Polish bacon out of Mark Brown's wharf in Tooley Street. This was crane work so it was off with the hoops.

Mark Brown's was a Victorian warehouse with drop boards and loopholes and a hydraulic crane right at the top of the building which served all floors. A rope running the height of the building at the side of the loopholes controlled it. The crane driver leaned out of the hole to watch the load; he pulled the rope down for down, up for up, and somewhere between was an unmarked neutral which 'held', it was erratic to say the least. This type of crane was common throughout the Victorian wharves and warehouses right down as far as the West India and Millwall Docks; even some old office blocks had lifts which used the same system. They were powered by high-pressure water supplied through a network of mains operated by The London Hydraulic Power Company. When all the old wharves closed down so did the company, selling its mains as ducting for a fibre-optic network for TV and computers.

Right! Back to the bacon. This came three sides sewn up in a hessian 'Bacon cloth', the outer two had the gammons one end, and the centre one was reversed. When one of the old hands heard I was going to do bacon, he went to his cab and got a sack needle, saying, "You'll need this". I asked why? He said "For your free bacon hock. When you load up make sure that you put two bales at the bottom of the back row with the thick end to the nearside. On the way back to Kinloch's find a quiet side street, pull up the sheet, pull out the bale and unpick the sewing for about two feet. Push up the top gammon and cut the hock off the middle side, let the gammon drop and sew up the bale with the original string and my needle". Being a bit green, I said, "Why two bales?" After he stopped laughing he said, "You're going to need two hocks, my needle and advice don't come free".

That job certainly needed some perks. You had to draw up close alongside the building, as the bacon came down on the crane it dripped brine and fat all over you. When the dockers handled the bacon they wore old overcoats kept for the job. I was told that when the wharf was redeveloped the 'bacon coats' were found standing up by themselves in a corner!

There was another time I was driving that Dodge on my way home from Leeds quite late at night. Coming down the main road about a quarter of a mile from the depot, in the road on my left I saw a single deck bus approaching the junction. It seemed to be coming fast so I flashed the main beam but he took no notice and came straight out in front of me. I hit him full tilt just behind the driver's cab. It was an A.E.C. Q-type with an underfloor engine, which I hit straight on the cylinder heads. When I got out there was bits of bus everywhere, underneath was a mass of broken rocker gear and a cylinder head all laying in a great puddle of oil.

The Dodge needed a front bumper, rad. shell, rad., headlights and a broken driver's door window. We had to take the steering box off and straighten the chassis top flange, but it was back on the road in two days. The bus was a write-off because the chassis was bent about two feet.

I mentioned that we carried Prestige kitchen cabinets - in the late 50's the ultimate! Costing about £12. Today one in good condition with original paint would set you back about £220. I was given the job of taking an exhibition van to Glasgow. This was fitted out with all the different kinds of cabinet the firm made, and the idea was to go round with one of the reps to take orders from furniture shops.

The Ford 4D at 950 cu.ft. was big enough so that is what we used. I set off on Sunday morning with a bed booked at Penrith, intending to be in Glasgow to meet the rep. about mid-day on Monday. One of my mates was going on a cycling holiday so I was giving him a ride to Stamford.

Away up the A10, on to the (original) A14 at Royston, around Arrington there was a funny little noise from the engine that soon died away. As I passed Caxton Gibbet the noise came back, louder than before, and then died away again. The oil pressure was OK, temperature normal, but I stopped and checked the levels in case. Going through Papworth the temperature shot up, there was a hell of a clatter and the engine stopped! The phone box needed coins and both of us had only notes. Being a Sunday there was only the watchman in the yard and he would not accept a transfer charge call.

I called about every half-hour hoping another driver had come in or the Guvnor had dropped in on his way to the pub as he often did. I made so many calls that the operator finally agreed to give the watchman a message to walk up the road and get Bert the fitter (my Dad). After half-an-hour I called again (the operator would not pass on my number) and got my Dad. He turned out with the old Bedford MW we used as a breakdown and towed me back.

By then it was dark but we set to and stripped the engine. On number 3 cylinder we found that the clamp bolt on the gudgeon pin had broken, the pin had moved sideways and neatly shaved a rectangular slot out of the liner right through to the water jacket. On Monday, the day fitter, Harry got on to the Ford dealer whose first reaction was to tell him off for not reading the recall notice, the clamp bolt was undersize for the job and had been uprated. They sent a piston liner and a new set of con. rods PDQ. Dad was got out of bed and he and Harry rebuilt the engine. He got me out of bed about 6pm and I set off to go straight through to Glasgow, arriving at mid-day on Tuesday - twenty-four hours late.

That same 4D gave me a fright at Rugeley. It broke a number 4 injector pipe (a common fault and we carried spares). The 4D had an alligator bonnet held up by an 'over-centre' stay. I stood on the bumper and leaned over the radiator to change the pipe. Unfortunately the spanner slipped and I hit the stay with my shoulder. Down came the bonnet, with the radiator grill part sliding down behind my backside,

I was trapped! I tried everything but could not move the bonnet. This was late on a Friday night on the lay-by outside Sunley Transport. Every time I heard a wagon I waggled my left leg which was the only bit I could move. After about an hour I thought I was there for the night. I heard a wagon pull in behind mine, I thought, "He's going to have a pee or a kip and pull out without seeing me". Fortunately, it was one of Dace's going down to do an urgent Saturday drop. He walked round to see which Noble's driver it was and let me out.

With that 4D I took my brother for a ride to the Midlands. My return load was tea chests of toilet soap weighing 4t 19cwt from Ashby de la Zouch to Lenthric in Tottenham. We loaded these in a block down the centre of the floor to keep the weight even. I went down through Hinckley on to the A5 at the 'Hinckley Knights' where I decided to fill up. When I went to get out I could only open the door about 6 ins. My brother tried his side which was the same. When we looked closely we found that the Luton had come down and the bottom frame was overlapping the doors. I decided to get out of the window.

About half way out I heard my brother break into loud laughter. Once I was out he told me that a man had come round the roundabout in a sports car, he had spotted me climbing out and turned right round to watch. He then entered the A5 on the wrong side of the road, swerved too sharply back to the nearside and mounted the verge. It took him about 300 yards to sort himself out. Once we had unloaded the fitter got underneath to look and found that the chassis had bent, right under the front cross bearer. It was a body off straightening job.

In my last week with Noble's, I was going down Braunstone Hill following a Pickford's van. As he went under the railway bridge an eight-wheeler passed him coming up the hill. Just as he came up to the right hand bend over the canal bridge he ran off the road and turned over. When I got down into the cab, he was lying at the bottom stone dead. It turned out at the inquest that he had been stabbed through the heart by a sliver of mirror! When the police examined the van they found a long thin sliver missing from the centre of the driving mirror. It was concluded that the eight-wheeler's load had clipped the mirror as they passed close under the bridge. The piece of glass went through the open window of the door, then went through the open neck of his shirt and between his ribs. The pathologist said that the wound was so small (about 1/4 inch) that he had not found it until he had made a very detailed examination of the body. Even then he did not suspect it as the cause of death until he did the autopsy. This goes to show you never know when your luck has run out!

One final note about Nobles, the first motor I drove in 1955 was EMP 563, which was made in the year I was born. I did Scotch with it and it finally went to the knackers while I was in the Army in 1956. Twenty-two years for a cheap and according to Bedford 'short life vehicle'. One final note on my Dad. He was blind in his right eye from birth (as was Harold Aitkin). In 36 years of driving he had only one accident, a very minor one with a 5cwt Fordson service van.

From Noble's I went to Wm. Aldridge & Sons Removals at Southgate, but by now I was engaged to be married and nights out were not so attractive. Another fleet of Bedfords ranging from a 1935 WLG to the latest coachbuilt 'S' model. From there to a builders' merchant driving an ex-WD Bedford MW converted to run on Calor Gas (in 1957). Next it was to the exhibition division of Cyprien-Fox and a 5-ton Commer Superpoise boxvan. This job involved too much sitting about outside exhibition halls, so I went back to Noble's, but by this time it had totally changed, nearly all the old hands had left and there was no laughter in the job, so after a short while I left again, never to return. During this spell with Noble's I got married, on 29th March 1958 - a date you only forget on pain of being nagged to death.

There was an incident involving my (then) future wife and a Noble's van about which I had totally forgotten for over forty years. That is, until I was given a present of a book, while typing this one. I turned to page 27 and there facing me was HYL 352, which I mentioned as the "very smart OLBZ" on page 11 above and which I have since found out to be an OB. It was not my regular van but had been fitted to carry a special filling station canopy full of fluorescent lamps, which was 29 feet long. Its regular driver did not want he job so I volunteered to do it.

I said to my girlfriend, "I have got an all night job, I've got to queue up outside Earls Court and when they get to it, collect some material from an exhibition stand. Would you like to come and keep me company?" To which she readily agreed. Eventually as the queue moved along, a large hoarding advertising Playtex bras came into view. I said to her, "You women must be contortionists getting both hands up your back to do up those hooks and eyes". With that she put both her hands up the back of her jumper and unhooked her bra, saying, "Like that?" Then she said, "Would you like to put your hand up the front and feel what we keep in our bras?" That was the first naked female I had felt and a few minutes later, seen. Very forward and quite an experience in 1956.

By the time I left Noble's it was totally involved with Vita-Foam and not long after was bought out to form the core of Blue Dart Transport, something which grew out of a chance meeting! Noble's ran a lot to the Northwest and had a back loading arrangement with Dace's Motor Services in Manchester, well known for its fleet of yellow Seddon box vans. Also with Timporley Transport of Altrincham, who ran a fleet of Jensen's and did a lot of work for Kellogg's. When neither could provide, it was out with the notebook and a pile of pennies and into a telephone box.

On one such occasion, a driver called Harry Kendrick was in a box when a man knocked on the glass and asked if he wanted a load for his van. This was George Minshall, Transport Manager for Range Boilers which produced back boilers and hot water cylinders, as a result we did a lot of work for them. George had a lot of contacts in Manchester, among them Vita Foam. This was a new and expanding company, I believe founded by Ukrainians or Latvians. In the beginning the chemicals to make the foam were mixed in old cast iron baths taken from houses being modernised. This was the dawn of the foam mattress era so this traffic grew apace. The demand was so great that the mattresses were made up and loaded before the reaction that made the foam had finished and the loads used to heat up.

George Minshall left Range and set up the Manchester depot of Noble's at Ashton-under-Lyne. The London depot in Granville Road was quickly outgrown with the demand to store mattresses for delivery in the south. Thus in 1960 there was another move to the recently vacated premises of Lynne, Frank & Wagstaff - the Morris main dealer - just by the Hornsey gate of Alexandra Palace.

My first lorry, a Baico extended Chevrolet similar to that refered to on page 6. This picture was used in a 1932 Wood Green newspaper advert and is reproduced here by courtesy of the Bruce Castle Museum. (Haringey Libraries, Archives and Museum)

CHAPTER 3
MY DAD

My Dad has been mentioned quite a bit in my story and as I said earlier, he had a profound effect on my life. Before relating the rest of my career here are one or two tales about my Dad.

First is a story, which I was told when I was about 10 or 11 and showing an interest in the haulage game.

Back when Dad operated Mr. Adam's wagons he used to do a job for the Pickadite Glass Co. of Southgate, London N11 taking the famous square HP Sauce bottles to the Aston Vinegar Company in Brum. He had a mate Alfie Brett who worked for another firm on the same job. Dad knew Alfie as 'Wonky'; he was so cross-eyed Dad swore he watched the nearside kerb with his offside eye. On this job they used to leave on Monday morning and it took about 14 hours to get to Sid's Wood Farm Cafe at Daventry for a night out. In those days Weedon Hill was water-bound Macadam. On Tuesday, it was into Birmingham to tip and reload empty crates, then back to Daventry or the Ace at Weedon for the second night out. I think Dad had another name for this cafe, the building was a wooden one at the south end of the existing site and the digs were downstairs at the back where the end of the site had been raised. On Wednesday it was back to Southgate for the night shift to reload for Thursday and another three-day trip.

Those were the days of solid tyres with a speed limit of, I believe, 12mph. The police regularly operated a speed trap in the Towcester area and Alfie was such a regular attender at the Magistrates Court that he was known by name. The Bench would enquire about the health of his wife and children, before fining him 5/- (25p), almost a day's wages. Alfie Brett got tied up with a Brummie girl and moved from London.

On this same job, Dad was doing an urgent load on a Sunday; going down Stowe Hill he threw a front wheel tyre. He crept up to the Ace where he took off the wheel. He then rolled it down the hill to the canal, where he got a lift to Wolverton on a narrow boat. He rolled the wheel to Stony Stratford to what is now the London Road Garage where they had a tyre press, the proprietor turned out on a Sunday evening to press on a new tyre. Dad then retraced his steps via the canal back to Weedon where he refitted the wheel and made his delivery on time on the Monday.

The Pickadite Co. became The Standard Bottle Co. and was demolished not that long ago to make way for the Middlesex Polytechnic. It stood at the side of Bounds Green Road, which formed part of the main route out of North and East London to pick up the Great North Road at Whetstone.

I can well remember this next event; I had not long left school. It was the nearest I had ever seen my Mum to being worried about Dad being late home. Going south on the old A21 into Tonbridge is Hildenborough, in one of the houses on the left lived a MoT examiner. He had a nasty habit of getting the village Bobby and setting up a checkpoint. My Dad was coming home from Hastings when he got stopped in one of these. It was discovered that the rim of the steering wheel was loose and he was given an immediate GV9. It did not matter that it had been like that since 1941 and it was now 1950. The WB coach chassis had a sprung four-spoke wheel, the flat spring steel spokes were screwed to captive nuts welded inside the rim and the whole lot had been originally coated in celluloid. The welds had broken and the rim moved slightly.

The local Bedford dealer, E. J. Baker Ltd. of Tonbridge came out with a new steering wheel, but it was a solid three spoke goods wheel and would not fit (the coach steering column was a bigger diameter). The motor was 16 years old and not many coach chassis were built and there was no spare available. In the finish the fitter cut a trap door in the rim above each fixing, got the screws out, re-welded the nuts and tightened the screws. He then brazed the trap doors back into place and filed it all smooth, all on the side of the road. He did a first class job, which lasted 'til the van was scrapped in '56. All that could be seen was a little line of brass in a three-sided square on the rim of the wheel.

In his old workshop in Noble's yard he had some bits left over from his Foden steam days. There was an exceptionally long engineer's tap for firebox stays, a tube expander for smoke tubes and a pair of high-speed sprockets for an over-type Foden. These involved winding the back axle forward on the chain adjusters, lifting off the chain and sliding the extra sprocket over the existing one, then replacing and readjusting the chain. The effect was the same as raising the back axle ratio on a modern diff. It was used for empty running and light loads and according to Dad saved a lot of coal and water. With all the moves, these together with his lists of water holes and coal merchants were lost. With his Sentinel he did beer for Whitbread's at Tottenham through C. D. & T. He was the first to do a load of beer to Brighton and back with empties all in one day! He had several fines for picking up water from fire hydrants and cattle pounds and one for throwing sparks while going up Barnet Hill.

My Dad was a very placid man who was brilliant with animals. He and my Granddad could 'whisper' horses. A talent of which my daughter has shown signs. My Granddad told me a story about when he and Dad worked for a firm of horse carters. They had an 'entire' called Charlie a really cantankerous beast. He had 'biting bars' on his loose box and had to be worked in a muzzle. He had nearly killed a stable lad. Granddad had trouble with him, but Dad could walk straight into his box, tack him up and take him to work. They used to use him on internal work at Standard Telephones at Southgate. It needed a strong horse as it involved continually starting off a heavy wagon.

One funny thing, Standard's water came from an artesian well and was slightly chalky. Charlie would never drink it so Dad had to take a churn of water from the stable.

When Noble's and B.G. were in the yard in New Road there was an old yard dog. One day one of the early starters opened the gate and Buster went for him and would not let him in. Other drivers arrived and could not get in. The lady next door said there had been a commotion in the early hours and since then Buster had been howling and barking. They could see there was something wrong with the dog's leg so the Vet was called. He could not get near Buster but he could see that the dog's leg was badly broken and he must be in agony. Harold agreed that the dog should be put down so the Vet poisoned some meat, which he threw to Buster, who proceeded to eat it. Nothing happened so the Vet put a bigger dose in more meat, which again the dog ate. Then the Vet said that there were some dogs that were not affected by cyanide, which was the only poison he had (no hydrochloric acid in their stomach). He said the dog would have to be shot and phoned the police.

He was told that when they needed a marksman for situation like this they could call on the Guards at Knightsbridge Barracks. This was done but they could not send anyone until at least early afternoon. Harry the fitter turned up, was told the story and said, "Where's Bert? He's your animal man he can do anything with that dog; he was the only one who could treat the carbuncle he had on his back". Dad was in bed; he was going to do an overnight engine change. He was sent for and told the story. He asked the Vet what he wanted; the Vet told him he wanted the dog caught and held so that he could him a lethal injection. Dad said, "Fill up the syringe tell me where to stick it and I'll do the job." He walked straight into the yard towards Buster who hopped over to meet him. Dad talked to the dog and stroked his head after a couple of minutes Buster lay down and rolled on his back. Dad just kept on stroking him and talking to him and put the needle in his shoulder.

When we got in we found that an attempt had been made to break into one of the vans. On the top of the corrugated iron gates were several bits of torn clothing and half way down trapped behind a wooden cross bar was a lot of Buster's skin and fur. He had obviously chased the intruders over the gates, which were about 8ft high, then tried to go after them trapping his leg behind the bar in one of the corrugations. When the Vet had a look poor old Buster had broken his leg in several places and almost torn his paw off.

The woman across from the yard had a Siamese cat that was daft enough to walk up the yard. Buster chased it into its own garden and up a tree. Harold went over to soothe the woman's hurt feelings and that turned this event into a bit of long term hanky-panky!

I mentioned that my Dad was a very placid man. He was also patient and long-suffering, but could be very stubborn.

I came back from a journey and found he had a brand new three-speed record player just then coming on to the market. I asked him what it cost; he said "That's part of my compensation". Apparently he had gone to load a full load of these things. As is usual with carton work he put a row across the van, and a row down the side to find out how many in a tier, then divided that into the total to find out how high to go. The cartons were being sent down rollers as they were packed. When he got to the back it needed three cartons to complete the row. When they did not come he went on to the bank, the foreman asked if he'd come to sign up, he said he was waiting for three more. The foreman then made a wrong move, he said "You're on the fiddle driver, you've had the lot". With that Dad pulled out into the middle of the yard and set out to unload the lot (about 400 cartons). He put them in piles of five all over the yard. When he had got the lot off he called the foreman and made him count them. Yes, he was three short.

He said to the foreman "Send some of your blokes out and we'll reload them". The foreman then made his second mistake, he said, "You took 'em off, you put 'em back". My Dad said "The van's empty, I'll take it back to the yard and tell them you don't need it". Just then it spotted with rain, and the foreman stopped the entire factory and got everyone loading. Dad delivered the load to a distributor and was sent back to load a second load. When he got to the back he was three short again. The foreman did his nut; he said that after yesterday's fiasco they had double-checked. Dad said "Count the top layer, and see for yourself, or we'll have them off again". The foreman gave him three more. I asked him, "How is that compensation?" he replied, "That's one of the three. You know that old van has a slack body? We always put the stay iron across when we do bulk. Well, when I reloaded I left the stay out and got an extra carton in the middle row of the second, third and fourth tier. I wanted compensation for being called a fiddler and unloading that lot myself".

Another Dad story concerns him setting off one Sunday morning for Scotland. His first drop was Carlisle so he was "going through," to sleep outside the warehouse. He reckoned with his drops, a reload out of Hamilton's with a couple of drops on the way home, he should be home Saturday afternoon. Saturday came and went, so did Sunday no sign of Dad. On the Monday I did a one-drop job in Birmingham with a GEC reload. I was coming down the A5 north of St Albans when I saw a Noble's van pulled off the road (no lay-bys then, you pulled half on the verge). I pulled up and saw it was my Dad. After waking him up I asked him where he had been. He said, "It was bloody windy up north, look at my arms!" His arms from wrist to elbow were about twice normal size.

He told me he had run into a headwind north of Boroughbridge, which had got steadily worse. When he turned into the A66 it was on his offside and he had a job to keep the van on the road all across the moors. He had got to Carlisle just before they shut on Monday. All the way to Glasgow he had been mostly in third gear. He had picked up a 'runner' and managed to do his drops round Glasgow although his arms were painful. Hamilton's had given him a mixed load, mostly London, but some for Doncaster and some for Leicester. The wind was still blowing and he flew down to Penrith. Then he turned onto the A66 and the wind was on the nearside and he had to fight to keep on his own side of the road. Then it started to lift the nearside drive wheels. He saw a GUS van parked up on his right by a big stone gable wall so he crept in close alongside him. As he stopped a gust of wind blew his van against the GUS van, which leant on the gable wall. Without the wall, they would both have been over. They were leaning against Dotheboys Hall (of *"Nicholas Nickleby"* fame).

They sat there until early afternoon the next day (Saturday) when the wind dropped. He then he made it to the 'Tudor Cafe' at Catterick, by which time he could hardly move his arms. Next day he made his way to Doncaster from cafe to cafe.

He did his drop in Doncaster on Monday morning, came down through Newark into Leicester, then down through Northampton on to the A5 at Hockliffe. He was yet again resting his arms when I saw him.

Wind was the enemy of the van driver. I was told when I started that you weren't a furniture man until you were blown over! One winter about fifteen London furniture vans were over at the same time on the Catterick Straight. The aerial photograph in the Daily Express looked like an advert for the London furniture trade. In those days you did your own repairs and changed your own wheels, a sensible van man kept all his heavy tools in a sack tied to something solid in the nearside of the cab. There was a London driver who was killed by a falling jack. He was blown over onto the nearside, falling onto the passenger door. The jack, which had been behind the driver's seat, fell on his head!

The job I had been doing that Monday was not strictly a drop and reload as it was the same load! We used to take a load of very big conical industrial lampshades from Benjamin's at Tottenham to GEC, Landor Street, Birmingham. When you reported to the foreman, he would say, "Hop in the back and take the top shade off of three different stacks". He would then take them away to be inspected. He would bring them back after about half-an-hour with a set of notes. If they passed you brought them back to GEC's export packing division at North Woolwich. If they failed they went back to Benjamin's.

Over the years Noble's had progressed from a pony, to two horses, Baico-Chevrolet, through W, O, S and A model Bedfords, 4- and 6D Fords, KFED Austins to FFK B.M.C.'s. It had stuck to the original orange and cream livery (chosen by Tom Noble's wife). My Dad developed cancer of the lung in December 1961 and died at mid-day on 24th March '62 his fifty fourth birthday. So I lost direct touch with the firm. I can remember Blue Dart being set up from a picture in *'Motor Transport'* of Harold Aitkin (by then its Managing Director) standing in front of its fleet all lined up on parade

A Baico extension of what could be a Morris Commercial chassis. A better class of furniture van with all panel construction body. Note the full Luton with stay irons for support.

CHAPTER 4
THE NEXT STEPS

After parting with Noble's, I signed on at the Labour Exchange in Medina Road, Holloway. I had lived in Holloway since getting married. This was the first proper Labour Exchange (built in 1935) in England. At that time Holloway was beginning to attract a large West Indian community. When I asked the clerk about a benefit problem, she said, "Come back at 2pm. Outside you will find a big white car driven by a Jamaican gentleman. Ask him, everyone goes to him for advice, he knows more about the benefit system than our Manager". He had been a Barrister back home, not only did he give me good advice, but also introduced me to another driver who did casual shunting. This driver had it all organised, he got jobs where you could get back to Medina Road to 'sign on' (twice a week in those days!). Drawing benefit while working is not an exclusive fiddle of the nineties!

Through one of his jobs, I was re-introduced to A. M. Walker Ltd. of Leicester, with whom I had had a passing acquaintance while working the Noble's Dodge as a dropsider. Even reading the name makes my back twinge. Alice Walker was the 'Queen of the Paving Slabs', a legend in her lifetime, a formidable figure. An ex-driving instructor with the ATS she regularly drove eight-wheelers when the steering was bio-powered. She resurrected her father's old firm with de-nationalisation. She used to have a full sized paving slab by her office door. When a driver applied for a job she would pick it up and 'press' it over her head two or three times saying "If you can't do that, your no good to me."

Many years later when BRS started to take back loads from 'reputable' hauliers, I still dreaded the words 'Go to Alice's for your backload', and then be sent to Mountsorrel. There must be vast holes in Leicestershire that used to be full with the millions of slabs and kerbs hauled away by Alice's fleet. All loads were put on handball, none of this banded pallet nonsense. In her late 60's she married an old gent of 96.

One Thursday (signing on day) my acquaintance asked me to do one of his regular Monday jobs for the next two weeks as he was going on holiday. On Monday morning I met an eight-wheeler from Scotland at the Archway Tavern. All I had to do was drop the driver at his digs in Tufnell Park and deliver the load, then drop the wagon back to the digs and collect my fiver (good money in those days!). The job was a doddle; all packets of paper, with a loading plan showing the top and both sides. It was a dropsider loaded just to the top of the sides with a small fitted sheet. You looked at the plan, untied a bit of the sheet, dropped the side and there was the delivery.

It was twenty-two years afterwards that I found that this job was completely unofficial and illegal! I was talking to my mate on Morton's and mentioned this job. He told me his Uncle was the Transport Manager for that firm and had always suspected that the 'London' driver was up to something. He should have left on Sunday and run to Boroughbridge, then to London on Monday. Pick up a casual porter and deliver the load Tuesday, then spend Wednesday and Thursday running back to re-load Friday and Saturday morning. He was obviously running straight through Sunday and Sunday night, going straight back up Monday night and Tuesday and having Wednesday and Thursday at home!

I did a few casual days for W.H. Bowker Ltd. of Blackburn, which had a reloading office just off the Seven Sisters Road. I also did some furniture portering for Neale's of Stoke Newington who had one of the oldest fleets of AA Fords in London. Then I heard from an ex-Noble's driver, Jack Spears, who was the foreman driver for Hamilton's (Long Distance) Transport. Billy Calder ran its London depot an ex-Lebus 'Scotch' driver who was in fact a Scot living in London. Jack Spears' life story would make a book on its own; he was out of my Dad's era but was as extrovert as my Dad was introvert. Jack divorced his wife, married his sister-in-law, divorced her and remarried his ex-wife then left her for a bit of stray he'd picked up. He was the ultimate womaniser. I had to take over a South Wales exhibition run for Prestige after he got himself stabbed in a pub fight over a girl.

I started with Hamilton's (Long Distance) Transport of Cambuslang, Glasgow as a casual driver and porter at its London depot at Harlesden. The fleet was mixed - two ex-WD Maudslay Moguls, an A.E.C. Regal, two 'twin stick' Matadors, three Jensens, one Dennis Max (this had overdrive engaged by a spring loaded dog clutch). and an Albion Chieftain (whose engine had a tendency to run backwards). There was also a 5-ton Austin uprated to an 8-tonner by fitting heavier springs and bigger tyres (the 9.00 x 20's on the front somewhat limited the lock!).

This was used for the express delivery of Decca and EMI records to Glasgow and Edinburgh. The traffic was televisions, new furniture, removals, pianos (there was a boom in 6-octave mini pianos) and all the Scottish traffic for Morphy-Richards and Electrolux. We did many loads of televisions from Ekco at Southend to a Glasgow warehouse, as it was cheaper to pay the haulage charge to Scotland than to store them in Southeast England! It was while I was on Hamilton's that I took my son on his first lorry ride at two weeks old - 15th March 1959.

Willy Hamilton was a character, and an ex-marine engineer. We had an A.E.C. that cracked a block when it froze. Those were the days of draining off. Willy took the block home and repaired the crack with 'boiler makers stitches'. A tricky job, which involved drilling two 3/16" holes on each side of the crack at a slight angle. These are then joined together with a 1/8" chase cut by hand with a narrow cold chisel; this is done about every inch along the crack. The stitch is a piece of hard steel about 1½" long and ¾" wide with four ribs which coincide with the holes. This is hammered into place and draws the crack closed its good up to 100 psi. He also designed and made what must be the first underlift for towing. It could be fitted to any of the vans, which had been modified to take it. Lifting was achieved with a small hand winch mounted on two sleepers that pulled a cable up through a hole in the floor of the van.

Eventually I became Road Foreman and then London Manager. By then the London depot had shrunk to a back-loading office and eventually I worked from home. Glasgow was becoming more and more involved with IBM on electric typewriters and the first generation computers; these were delicate machines requiring dust free transport so this customer paid both ways. The vans were vacuumed out and lined with Sisal-Kraft paper and for their prestige customers, washed and Simonised all over.

When it became just a clearing office I had a lot of dealing with J. & W. Watt's of Carlisle. It ran a lot of four-wheel Seddon boxvans plus insulated boxes on the home killed meat trade. That was the days before Cumberland and Westmorland were amalgamated and their lambs did not glow in the dark! There was a tie-up with Blue Band Motor Services of Lockerbie. Blue Band's vans can still be seen about in 2000, still with a Lockerbie address. I consigned many thousands of Morphy Richards irons and toasters to the Borders in Watt's vans. At that time it shared premises with Road Services (Caledonian) Ltd in Lots Road, Chelsea (right next to the London Underground power station). The operator there was Pauline, a very efficient young lady and the first female operator I had come across in general haulage, in those chauvinist times.

Hamilton's employed a lot of London Fire Brigade men as casual porters. When the back loading work dropped to a trickle, one of the firemen's wives agreed to do the job. As it did not warrant a full time London Manager I was once again out of collar.

Looking back over this part of my life has just brought to mind something which should make modern 'parcels' men think. I mentioned that Hamilton's had an express van to deliver new records. We lost that job early in 1959 when Tartan Arrow (then owned by the Cooper Brothers) started a new service. Smalls delivered to their depot at King's Cross before 5pm, were delivered in Glasgow central by 8am and in Edinburgh before noon on the following day and visa-versa with inner and outer London; or the customer got his money back! This service was done with two 1400cb.ft. B.M.C 3KFED vans with *four cylinder* engines.

The drivers were Tommy Moore senior and junior, they did the run straight through in opposite directions in thirteen hours. This was before motorways, bypasses and dual carriageways and until I lost touch with them in 1962 they had only missed five deadlines even in the 1961 winter when they had to go round the East Coast to get into Scotland!

Through a trade contact I heard of a vacancy for a Manager with Harry Green Ltd., of Derby and started as Manager of their London depot at Swiss Cottage. This was the weirdest firm I have ever worked for. It appeared to be constantly involved in litigation and retained a barrister full time! It did local removals in London and Derby and general van haulage to Derby and the Midlands. Harry Green's fleet was entirely of Guy manufacture; from an early 4LW powered Vixen through an Otter, five Warriors to an Invincible plus an early Warrior platform. When this needed to be weighed for tax purposes, it had to be weighted with ballast to exceed the 4-ton unladen weight required in the late '50s to qualify for an eight-foot wide body.

One of the Warrior vans was fitted with an experimental Meadows engine. This was a modified marine unit, and had counter rotating balance shafts inside the crankcase. Somewhere it generated some very high frequency vibrations and all the ancillaries bolted to the crankcase worked loose and fell off with alarming regularity. It spent more time in Guy's depot at Paddington than it did on the road! This was the first fleet of Luton vans I had ever seen with a door halfway down the nearside so that they did not need to load in strict drop order. This was a feature Harry shared with Porter's of Derby, his main rival. Harry ordered a new van on a Guy chassis from Guy's at Silvertown. Through some mix up it was not ready on time, and being so well known for his litiginousness, Guy's actually delivered him one that had been completed for Porter's. There was a slight visible difference in that Porter's had a bow front on its Lutons. It raised the blood pressure of Porter's board no end when they saw one of 'their' vans running round Derby with Harry's name on the side!

We had one regular lady customer. She was always buying and selling bits of furniture and having things moved in her house. Harry told me that some years ago he was moving her house, and as he lifted the cornice on a big old swivel door wardrobe the door complete with its huge bevel mirror, fell out just as she came into the room. It hit her across the face and broke her nose. She sued him for a packet. But every time she 'phoned, she always said, "I always come to Mr Green, he gives such good service". When I finally met her, she had a nose like a prizefighter.

Harry Green was an owner-driver who should never expanded. He wanted to do everything himself. He commuted between depots by driving one of the night trunk vans (we had two regular contracts, Pirelli slippers down and Mary Baker cake mix up). When in London he would do the books, estimate removals, flit round all the removal jobs doing a bit of packing here, a bit of portering there, before dashing off to load the overnight van and get back to Derby! Lord knows when he ever slept! This job did not last long, as his son wangled his way out of the Army where he was doing National Service, to become London Manager. Harry certainly kept it in the family; his daughter was depot clerk in London and his wife acted as Company Secretary in Derby.

I made one major mistake when I worked for Harry Green. I did the wages; one week I paid everyone their gross pay instead of their nett. No one said a word, but some months later I met one of the drivers in a cafe. He had the good grace to come over and thank me for the unexpected but most welcome bonus!

After leaving Harry Green I went back to driving, with Osborne's Transport (Hornsey) Ltd. Another fleet of B.M.Cs. plus a 6D Thames and an elderly Albion Chieftain which was 14ft 6in tall and had soft back springs so that on a camber you had to keep well over to the centre of the road or you bent or beheaded lamp posts! They did some general van haulage, mostly for Marks & Spencer, subbed through the Finchley depot of Alfred Bell of Newcastle. But the main emphasis was on new piano carriage and piano haulage. When I joined it was owned and run by Old Man (Tom) Osborne and his daughter Gert, a formidable lady (a lá Alice Walker) who had been known to 'back' a 7cwt Steinway up a flight of stairs. She always wore a collar and tie and had cropped hair. There were whispers, but being 'gay' was not talked about openly in 1960.

For the uninitiated 'backing' was used for pianos and pieces of heavy furniture on narrow stairs or those with bad turns. It involved a small person getting on their hands and knees, the piano was then stood on its end on their back and they crawled up or down the stairs. We did a regular job for the Royal College of Music. When 'big' musicians went there they would insist on a certain piano in a particular rehearsal room. This would mean putting a grand piano on a special 'shoe', standing it on its edge and taking all the legs off. We then carried it up several flights of stairs. Two or three hours later we would go back and put it back where it was. A concert Steinway could weigh 9 cwts.

There was also regular work for Miss Bloom who hired pianos. She had the basement under Park West Mansion and every piano had to be lifted about 4ft to the pavement. We took a concert Bechstein to the Wigmore Hall when the hall's piano wasn't good enough for the pianist! Part of the performance was a short ballet and the dancers were rehearsing. Freddy Jones, our foreman was a really rough handful and as we went in he said, "Look at all them 'poofters' prancing about, a days work would kill 'em?" One of the male dancers detached himself from the group, danced over and gave Freddy a right hook, which laid him out! The dancer then gave us a hand to lift the piano onto the stage and danced back to continue rehearsing.

We had delivered a beautiful black 'boudoir' grand to Shepperton Studios for use in 'The Avengers'. When we went to collect it, it had been given a coat of white emulsion paint. The TV Company happily paid a large sum (£500+) to have it repolished (all handwork). I watched the programme, the piano appeared for 17 seconds.

We did so many pianos that on journeywork we always took a porter. Mine was an Irish lad always called "Maginty" (he went to London Piano Services). We were going to Coventry and he wanted to see his sister in Leamington so I arranged to drop him off, spend the night in Leamington and pick him up in the morning. When I got into the town there were no digs, I tried a couple of hotels but they would not take drivers. There was no room in the van and you could not lie across the Albion cab.

I went to the police station. In the lobby I met a Sergeant and explained the problem to which he replied, "It's easy lad. Go back to your lorry, take all your money out of your pockets and hide it. Then come back here, go to the desk and say you're on your way through Leamington, you've got no money and nowhere to sleep. The constable will them deal with you under the Vagrancy Act of 1785. He will take you round all the registered inns until you find one with an empty bed. Under the Innkeepers Act they are obliged to 'put up' and feed a vagrant at the request of a constable. Not only will you get a bed and be fed but it will be at the ratepayers' expense. I know that both those 'snobby' places that turned you down have got beds so take your pick. Don't tell anyone I told you and remember this for the future". Not only did I get two slap-up meals and a very comfortable bed, but also a couple of the resident's bought me a beer because, I looked 'Down on my luck'.

I mentioned that we did a lot for Alfred Bell of Newcastle. This was another old removal firm going back to horse-pantechnicons. Like so many high volume van firms, it had diversified into general haulage van work as the demand for furniture carriers dropped off. It had a large removal storage warehouse in Finchley that was used as a break-bulk depot for Marks & Spencer's sweets and Irish Butter Fruitcake. There was also a depot at Kingswinford that received this traffic in bulk ex-Ireland via Liverpool. There was also a collection of M&S brand clothing from contracted manufacturers.

The Irish fruitcake came in cartons; among all the marks was one that said 'Do not stack more than four high'. Space was tight and they were stacked twelve high. Some keen eyed young QC man from M&S challenged the foreman about this. The foreman said "No Guv! There's only four in a stack. Look, count up four and you'll see a bit of ply sticking out, if you could see on top of that it says 'Stack One', count up another four there's another bit of ply, that's Stack Two' and above that there's a bit of cardboard hanging down. You can see for yourself that it says 'Stack Three'. So there's only four in each stack". The M&S man walked away scratching his head.

In 1960 the senior management of M&S had a very 'hands on' approach. It was common to find Mr. Simon Marks at the depot at 7am ready to go out for the day on a delivery round and have a look at his shops from the back door. While the driver was delivering he would walk round the store, checking on the displays and the attitude of the staff. He was with me when I delivered to the Chatham store, which had a very surly back-door man. As usual he took about 10 minutes to answer the bell, gave me a load of verbal and said I would have to wait 'til he was good and ready to unload me.

When I got back to the van Mr. Marks was gone, soon to reappear at the back door with the store manager, the deputy manager and the stock room supervisor. These three were given a rucking for not controlling the staff properly and the manager was told to apologise to me. The back door man was given his cards and the management ordered to unload me. As we drove away Mr. Marks said, "I've heard the drivers talking about that man. I don't want people like that working for me. Drivers are entitled to be treated with courtesy and respect, the organisation would not function without you chaps". When you went into a cafe for breakfast, mid-morning tea, lunch and afternoon tea, all at cafe's of his choice, he would pay the bill and would also pay for any other driver on M&S work who happened to be in the cafe.

Sir Isaac Woolfson of Great Universal Stores did a similar thing, although he did not go out with his vans. If he was passing a cafe and saw a GUS van or that of one of its subbies (GUS always put a sticker on the side under the haulier's name, saying 'Delivering on behalf of GUS'), he would go in, find the driver, and introduce himself. Then he would have a cup of tea or a meal with the driver, paying the bill not only of 'his' driver but also of any of the driver's mates sitting at the table. GUS had a large 'C' licence fleet. In the fifties and sixties it was still making its own furniture. Sir Isaac started as a glue boy working for his cabinetmaker father.

Back to Osborne's. One morning we were met at the gate by two men in black jackets and bowlers who informed us that we were all in imminent danger of being arrested for not paying our tax and stamps. Enough of us were able to produce payslips showing the relevant deductions to convince them that the fault lay elsewhere. The following Monday morning we were met by a very arrogant little Scot who told us that Osborne's were in the slammer and that the firm now belonged to Bell's of Edinburgh (later to be absorbed into Road Services Forth) who would be sending down a new Manager. He then asked who was the foreman, and when Freddy Jones stepped forward, gave him a rucking for not wearing a tie and being scruffy! Freddy responded by threatening to chuck his poncy trilby-hat down the railway embankment without taking it off of his head.

Later in the week Freddy and two of the porters made Bell's an offer for the 6D, which was fitted out with piano shoes, trolleys, window tackle, ladders and padded covers and had an ultra-low floor. As it was on a '25-mile radius of Kings Cross' B-licence, Bell's accepted and North London Piano Services was born. The new undertaking soon made the papers. Putting a 9ft 6in Steinway concert grand into a penthouse of a block of luxury flats by taking it up the outside, six floors at a time, on the window tackle, renting each front room for two hours while they did the job!

Bell's new Manager was a recent trainee who only knew the academics of running transport. He knew nothing about handling men and even less about estimating! This put me in a unique position, as the lads had elected me as Shop Steward because of the work I had done with the change of ownership and conditions, while the company appointed me estimator and foreman to help out the 'green' manager. It was too good to last however and one Thursday I was told to take the old Albion to Edinburgh where it was to be re-sprung and the engine overhauled. I was to bring back a replacement van from their Scottish fleet. When I arrived I was told I would have to work local in Edinburgh until the Albion was ready, about a fortnight! I said 'on yer bike' and got the train home. On the Monday I got my fare money and my cards.

A quick telephone call to my Union branch secretary resulted in an appointment for an interview at the British Road Services Ltd., depot at Hampstead where he was a shunter. Thus ended the van haulage and removals phase of my career. Before embarking on my story of BRS experiences, I have indulged in a quick look back at those formative years.

Ready for the off! Night trunkers waiting to roll from BRS Hampsttead Branch, Cressy Road. I believe that this is a still from a BTC promotional film, given to me by an old driver. Note the Scammell R8.

CHAPTER 5
A LOOK BACK AT THE EARLY DAYS

Although I had been regaled with flat wagon stories since childhood, all my practical experiences had been in the 'furniture van' trade. To some extent I was steeped in van transport lore. In those days there was a tradition in cafe's, - we stopped more often in those days, - that van men sat together, as did general haulage men, tipper men and tanker drivers. Different from today when everyone tries to sit on their own and not talk.

In the fifties and early sixties north and east London was the home of mass-produced furniture. Names that come immediately to mind include Beautility, Austinsuite, Stonehill, Bee'n'eez (Bluestone & Elvin), Gainsborough, Spanglett, Golden Key and Lebus. All ran 'C' licence fleets of varying sizes. There were many specialist van hauliers catering for the new furniture trade including Dormer's, Wades, A & E Bristow, Alexandra, John Duncan's, Alfred Bell, Ralston's, Blue Bell, G W McIntosh, Regal Transport, Smiths of Maddiston and, of course, Noble's, Hamilton's and Osborne's for all of whom I worked. There were also numerous furniture removers who did a bit of 'new' furniture delivery when removals were slack. For a very short time there were even two nationalised carriers, BRS New Furniture Carriage Group and Pickfords New Furniture Delivery Service.

Bedford was the linking factor for many of these names - the WB, OB and SB chassis lent themselves very readily to the building of high volume Luton bodies. Beautility favoured Guy Vixen's and Otter's, while A & E Bristow of Hackney, which specialised in East Anglia, ran a fleet of Albion's with original half and half bodies. Most of the Scottish specialists relied on A.E.C. coach chassis', although Geordie McIntosh was true to his country and ran Albion's. John Duncan was, as far as I know, unique in running Daimlers.

Duncan's main depot was in Haddington; its Tottenham depot now lies under Monument Way near the High Cross. It was nationalised into BRS Haddington. In Nick Baldwin's book *'The Pictorial History of BRS'* there is a picture of BU36, a Luton van on an A.E.C. chassis a direct descendant of the Duncan nationalisation. I had long thought that Duncan's had gone for good, but in May '94 I was going through Croydon, when in the distance I saw a van whose colour I recognised. It can only be described as 'muddy plum'. The sort of colour you get by mixing together all the leftovers in the shed! As I got nearer I could see the red diamond and the lettering, admittedly it was on a Leyland T45, but otherwise just as I remembered it from my youth!

Page 21 of Arthur Ingram's book *'London Lorries'* illustrates the ingenuity of London's new furniture carriers. The much-modified OW Bedford in BRS livery was nationalised from Eddie Deffries with his Balls Pond Road depot, which continued as a New Furniture Carriage Group depot. In the same picture is a Commer van belonging to Rapido's Padding, which I mentioned earlier.

Pitt & Scott was a large organisation that did removals, new furniture and exhibition work. It had an offshoot, MAP Transport, that was deeply involved with Belling Cookers from its works at Ponders End and was one of the earliest users of swop-bodies. The large map of the world on their vans distinguished both firms. In recent times Pickfords bought out Pitt & Scott, Belling closed its cooker factory at Ponders End and this was demolished to make way for Pickfords' 'state of the art' removal warehouse.

Freeborn's of Holloway was another old family removal firm, a fleet of canary yellow Bedfords. It would do new furniture for Lebus and some piano work subbed from Osborne's. Georgie Freeborn was a Japanese PoW; the stress gave him alopecea universalis, which meant he did not have a hair on his body, which was very disconcerting when you first met him.

Whilst talking of vans, there is one removal man I would like to mention. He had a pre-war forward control 2½ ton Dennis half-and-half Luton van. He had a tiny yard about four doors up from Noble's yard. Occasionally he would do odd bits for Noble's, but he was a removal man through and through. He never started before 8am and was always done by 5pm. If he could avoid it, never went outside Wood Green, Hornsey and Tottenham. Bob Spinney was a devout Salvation Army man, a gruff, likeable and thoroughly honest man, who went through life generally unremarked. I thought I would put him on record.

Lebus has had several passing mentions. This was the largest new furniture maker in north London. Anyone who has travelled east out of London through Walthamstow must have passed through its vast factory at Ferry Lane. It had its own timber yard, sawmill and a huge lorry park backed by a loading bank which I seem to remember had thirty doors. Packers loaded vans piece by piece, it could take all day. I don't think that there is a new furniture driver in north London who has not at sometime or another done a load for Lebus. It had its own enormous 'C' licence fleet and in latter days an 'A' licence operation called Merchandise Transport, the setting up of which generated one of the largest public enquiries ever held by the Metropolitan Licensing Authority and was really a 'Who's-who' of London van haulage! I was manager for Hamilton's at the time and sat next to a very old manager from Hallet Silberman. I can always remember his words to me. He said, "Look at all of us. The Road & Rail Traffic Act and 'A', 'B' and 'C' licences were drafted to protect the railways from us, now we are using it to fight one another".

Lebus had a legendary traffic clerk, Percy. If you gave him your notes for anywhere, he would put them in order. In a big city you could go from drop to drop coming the right way for a back entrance or if it was a front door job, coming up the street so that the job was on the nearside. If the staff wanted to contact a driver they would ask Percy, he would look up the run, look at the calendar, then look at his watch. He would say "He should be delivering at so and so's, if he's already done it try this one and this one". He was always right; it made him very unpopular with Lebus's own drivers who called him Vassal (after a Russian spy much in the news!).

Lebus built all its own plywood from veneers and had bag presses that could make curved plywood. Its technology was used to build the Mosquito bomber (the flying wardrobe). In the run up to D-Day it made long range jettison fuel tanks for fighter aircraft out of plywood; my Dad delivered many loads of these to airfields in southern England. Sadly Lebus at Tottenham is no more. The old factory and timber yard is now posh housing estates on the banks of the River Lee. The warehouse and loading bank were used as a distribution centre for the Greater London Council and the Inner London Education Authority. The last time I was by it appeared to be deserted. The Lebus name still exists through its upholstery division at Woodley (Reading) as part of Courts.

There is another van firm from the late '60's and early '70's worthy of inclusion, Wilkinson's Transport (Rochdale) Ltd. It had a fleet of large Lutons on Austin/BMC, Dodge, and Leyland Comet chassis. These could be seen regularly each night in convoy on the M1 motorway. Their Road Foreman who was also a fitter drove the last vehicle. He carried tools and spares to deal with minor breakdowns en-route. As a last resort his vehicle's front bumper could be removed to serve as a tow-bar and get the casualty into Rochdale on time. At about the same time Plackett's were doing a similar job in the same way. Although they were furniture vans they were just being used as high volume general freight vans.

Walker Brothers of Birmingham always operated pantechnicons (apart from Motor Transport's small ads I must be one of the last to make the distinction!). I first came across this firm in 1955 at GEC Witton, Birmingham. In '93 I went to the LIFT at Stratford with a young driver and as we got out I spotted a van loading right up the other end of the depot. I said to him "There's one of Walker's up there, I haven't seen them for years". He replied, "You're pulling my leg, I can only just see it". So I bet him a tea and a cake, he walked all the way down and back (about half-a-mile) and said "What sort of cake do you want?" and as we were drinking the tea he asked how I was so sure. I told him "It's easy, that must be the last firm to run pantechnicons and in the 38 years I've known it, the colour scheme hasn't altered. Unpainted ally body and mid-brown cab, did it have gold lettering?" I understand that this is another old firm that has recently gone to the wall.

Throughout BRS it was possible to come across a Luton van operating as part of a general haulage fleet. People were often confused that it was all green and thought it had something to do with BRS Parcels. In fact, green was the colour for vans. If you traced its history back through the various depots and groups you would find a haulier who had been nationalised who had a Luton van on the fleet, the previously mentioned BRS Haddington van being a prime example. The acid test was that the firm was not exclusively new furniture so did not go into the New Furniture Carriage Group. BRS Cambridge had what was reckoned to be the only Jensen Luton it was driven by Jack Bawling, we often ran together when we had both loaded from Pye's at Cambridge. Jack was a pigeon fancier who always had a basket of birds to release when he had just come out from home. He taught me a gypsy trick for overcoming toothache.

There is one other purely removal firm for whom I did a bit of portering - Bent's. This was run by the governor Sid Bent, it ran a fleet of AA and BB Fords some half-and-half and some all panel Luton's. This fleet was as immaculate as Neil's identical fleet was scruffy. It carried on with the addition of a couple of 7Vs until its demise with the collapse of the domestic removal trade.

In that era there were no plated weights, just maximum gross weight depending on the number of axles. You had to exceed 14 tons on a four-wheeler to be 'done' for overloading. When furniture vans started loading back with general goods it was quite possible to find what the manufacturer sold as a five tonner actually carrying eleven tons. This produced a strange anomaly when the speed limit was raised to 30mph for vehicles over 3 tons. Operators began to use more robust bodies and heavier chassis, which meant that what was nominally a 5-ton Bedford could carry eleven tons, whereas a late A.E.C. Regal chassis with a goods body could only carry 9 tons, when loaded to maximum gross vehicle weight.

I've done it again; I was supposed to be telling you about starting with BRS! So here goes.

This is a fine example of an early Bedford Luton van with a 'half and half' body of the type mentioned on page 6. It was operated by an owner driver from behind a private house.

CHAPTER 6
BRITISH ROAD SERVICES

The Superintendent, Doug Smith, conducted the interview at BRS. He was the son of a family firm that had been nationalised and there was still resentment in his voice when he talked about it at the Classic Commercial Motor Show at Cranfield in 1982. He became Branch Manager at Kentish Town and then went to Tunnel Cement at Pitstone only to return to BRS as Manager of the container depot at Bromford Lane (Birmingham) from which post he retired in 1984. To make room for the containers, the general haulage moved over the railway bridge to Bromford Mill, this later became a Ford consolidation depot.

Harry Skelton, the Vehicle Foreman, took the driving test. It was in an A.E.C Mammoth Major III boxvan - fleet number 1A333 loaded with 14 tons of Mars bars. As we went out of the gate Harry started to roll a cigarette. We went round South End Green (terminus of the 24 bus for over 100 years), past Constantine's (the showmen) winter quarters, up East Heath Road, round the Whitestone Pond, through the Spaniard's gate, along Hampstead Lane to Highgate village. Down Highgate Hill into Dartmouth Park Hill, Mansfield Road and under the round arch bridge at Gospel Oak station (14ft 6in but "keep 'yer eyes open its only 10ft 6in at the sides!"), back into Cressey Road and the depot. As we turned into the gate, Harry licked his cigarette paper and as I ratcheted up the handbrake he lit up. I subsequently discovered that this was his unvarying routine for every driving test.

Hampstead's fleet consisted of A.E.C. and Bristol eight-wheelers, Bristol artics, A.E.C. Mercury artics and a few Seddon four-wheelers. We changed over with depots in the North Western District- Queensferry, Kitt Green, Greenheys (Manchester), Studholme Street (Liverpool), St Helens, Bolton, Blackburn and Preston. The rigid changeovers produced a wide variety of vehicles, Fodens, E.R.Fs, Albions, Leylands, Scammell artics (which, of course, do not uncouple), an Atkinson, A.E.C.s and the inevitable Bristols.

When I started at Hampstead the speed limit for Heavy Motor Cars had been raised from 20mph to 30mph. BRS used this as an opportunity to reduce the average working day from 11 hours to 10. To make use of the extra speed, runs were rescheduled to do 11-hour runs in 10 hours. Existing employees were paid a lump sum to compensate them for loss of future earnings, until a satisfactory agreement could be reached. This resulted in a payment of 15% bonus on top of wages. For me, on nights, on 3s 4d (16.5p) per hour this worked out as follows: -

40 hours at basic hourly rate of 3s 4d	£6. 13s. 4d
10 hours at time and a half (5s)	£2. 10s. 0d
50 hours 'dark money (20% of basic i.e. 8d per hr.)	£1. 13s. 4d
	10. 16s. 8d.
Plus 15% 30mph bonus	£ 1. 12s. 6d
	£12. 9s. 2d.

This was for a 24 tons GVW rigid or artic. The 10-hour day was a two-way affair, BRS agreed to provide 10 hours work, the workers agreed to do it. There was one exception, if you reported for work and were sent straight home, you would only be paid 8 hours, but if you did any work, even only an hour, you were paid the full 10 hours.

There was a special arrangement for Sunday night work. Each Friday night a three-part list was put up. The first part showed all those drivers for whom there was definite work. The second part was for drivers (or their representatives) to phone the depot before 12 noon Saturday to see if they were needed. The third part was people who could receive a last minute Telegram calling them in for work. For making the phone call, or receiving a Telegram, you received one hour's pay. On Weekdays if you were asked to report to work before or after the normal starting time of 8pm you received a Penalty Payment.

The first hour each way was free and then it was 2s 6d (12 ½ p) for each half-hour - i.e. if you were asked to come in at 11pm for a late arriving load, that was 10s (50p). We had one trailer from Manchester that had been built for cable drum work and was fitted with a winch. This was rusted solid, but as the trailer was fitted with a 'mechanical means of loading' that was another 2s 6d (12 ½ p.).

My first changeover was at The Malt Shovel at Stonebridge. A Seddon four-wheel boxvan up and a Foden FG back. Knowing no better, I put the Foden in low reverse and spent the next five minutes getting it out again! My regular changeover came to be at Bromford Lane, with Bolton, Bury or Preston. This produced some elderly vacuum braked Leyland Octopuses (or should it be Octopii?) uprated by legislation to 24-tons gross. Fully laden with lino, the brakes were not man enough for the task. They were already hot when we took them over and we were very glad of the Beale Street workshops in Dunstable who took them up as tight as possible before coming into London, Barnet Hill and the Archway Road always smelled very strongly of hot Ferodo!

The first time I changed over at Bromford Lane I had a Bristol eight wheeler. These were built to BRS design, they had a fuel tank that only held 32 gallons. To keep unladen weight down, the designers had worked out that that amount of fuel would take them between any two BRS depots in the country. Unfortunately they forgot about Bull Hill on the way to Bolton where, if the fuel were low it would run back and uncover the stack pipe. This meant that they had to be refuelled en-route. Having filled up, I went into the fuel issuers office to sign up, as soon as the fuel issuer saw my name he said, "Are you anything to do with Bert Rust?" I told him he was my Dad. He said, "Next time you see him tell him 'Wonky' Brett was asking after him, we used to run together on Pickadite's with the HP Sauce bottles." He was the one always getting 'done' for speeding at Towcester, who is mentioned elsewhere.

There were four real characters on the northern end of that changeover.

The Bolton man was Billy Wilding, small, very jolly, always with a tale to tell, every southerner's idea of a northerner. He smoked a mixture of black shag and twist in a pipe. Above the driver's seat of his wagon was a round black tarry patch, while the whole of the cream cab interior was a walnut shade. It was said that when the wagon went in for its biennial repaint it took strong caustic soda solution and a lot of work with a steam cleaner to make it paintable.

The Blackburn man was Bobby Mirescough (pronounce Mis'coff). He was the opposite of Billy, quiet, always weighed his words, and had a very dry wit. He was the typical gentleman night trunk driver. Three-piece suit, stiff collar and tie and a flat cap that really was flat, as though it had just come out of the shop.

Preston supplied two wagons and drivers, as opposite as chalk and cheese. Tommy Farrell was a 'Cockney'. Many years ago while doing a straight through day service he had met a Preston girl married her and moved to Preston (like Wonky's wife she didn't want to leave her Mum). He could talk the hind leg off a donkey. Some years later he was involved in an accident and bit the end off of his tongue. He went home early from work one night (his job wasn't running) and caught a burglar coming out of his back entry. He hit him so hard it killed him. The other driver, Joe Dalton, was quiet and dry like Bobby. He is the only man I have ever met who could tie a "dolly" with one hand. A trick he had learned as a boy from an old horse cart driver.

Joe told me a story about Alf Barlow whose firm had been nationalised as Greenheys Branch. In the beginning the bigwigs from London were touring the main provincial depots. After a morning of paper work Alf invited them to his favourite eatery (the café across the road from the depot). He led the way and ordered six lunches. The London men were taken aback to get a basin of pig's trotters and a bread cob each.

I met a lot of characters on the night shift at Hampstead, older men from the early days. Some I remember really well. There was Bill Carrington and Sid Cummins, ex-General Roadways men. Under their old employer they were issued with free uniforms and overcoats. This had been carried on by BRS under what was called a 'pre-acquisition agreement'. At that time BRS were negotiating with them to buy out this 'perk' for a lump sum, £200 as I remember. Bill Brace, who went back to steam and had worked for Archie Redburn.

Bill Doyle, generally known as "The Moonman", he went a bit odd at the time of the full moon! He was killed in a collision with a mobile fish and chip shop that pulled out of the Watling Street Cafe right in front of him. Jim Spring, who lived in Berkhamsted and came to work by train every night. He was killed outside the 'Pack Horse' pub on the A5, when a drunk pulled out of the Whipsnade Road and knocked him off the road, 14 tons of carrots bound for Heinz at Kitt Green (Wigan) fell on him. Thirty-six years later the dead tree and bushes were still in the hedge where his motor landed.

Harry Sturler was another old timer. After I left Hampstead he had a stub axle break at Dunchurch, he lost his nerve and I came across him much later in my career working as a gatekeeper at Muswell Hill Parcels depot. The night foreman was Jimmy Hasler; he was about 5ft 2in tall and about the same round. One night I was working in the depot, we were loading bundles of clothing which BRS was carrying free for a charity (I think it was the Lady Hoare Thalidomide Appeal). A jacket fell out of a bale and Jimmy picked it up and for a laugh put it on, it was a perfect fit. We rummaged in the bale and found the matching trousers, which were also a perfect fit, considering he was a tailor's nightmare an incredible coincidence. He said "I'll have that and get it cleaned, it's better than my best suit". Then there was 'Ginger' Oviat, who suffered terribly with piles (an occupational hazard for drivers, I can't spell the posh word) he used to carry a small inner tube to use as an air cushion.

Bill Fenn, who got to the changeover and pulled the fifth wheel release before doing anything else. The trailer promptly slid off the unit breaking the airlines and smashing the landing legs. He was also involved with a Manchester based Atkinson with which he was supposed to change trailers. The fifth wheel would not uncouple despite the fitters being called out. So the whole wagons were exchanged and again the following night. Going north back in the hands of its own driver the trailer uncoupled itself at Knutsford and hit a pub!

We had a regular monthly union meeting, Jack Fowler was Chairman and Johnny Rolfe (he later became a cabby) was the Branch Secretary. These were always lively meetings, well worth 'going in' early for. At these one of the shunters, Dave Parsons, was always complaining that when he got an empty trailer to load the sheets were always rolled in a ball instead of being folded and he wanted 'the Management' to do something about it. All the shunters would privately say that Dave Parsons was the culprit.

Johnny Rolfe set it up with the Vehicle Foreman Harry, for Dave to get a trailer due for service each day of the next week, so that he would bring it back to the depot empty. The following week he was given the same five trailers to load. At the next meeting Dave really went off the deep end, every trailer the previous week had had the sheets screwed in a ball. Harry had been invited to the meeting and produced the Ops 8s (operating record sheets). He read these to the meeting, "Monday" x-date trailer number TlAxxx brought in empty by Dave Parsons for servicing ---", and so on through the week, then he got the next sheet "Monday x-date, (one week later) trailer number T1Axxx taken out for loading at xxx by Driver Parsons". By Wednesday's Dave realised he had been thoroughly 'had over'. We never heard another word about screwed up sheets.

The London District Manager at the time was Bernard Ridley, when he came to the depot for a meeting he looked like a stockbroker, bowler, black jacket and pin-striped trousers.

In those days there was not the 'rush and tear' of today, we used the A5 and A45 in preference to the Ml. I often stopped at 'The Bridge' pub by the canal in Stony Stratford for a couple of pints and a game of darts. We also went through the centre of Coventry up the Holyhead Road for a change. There was an old driver, Bill Thornywell, always known as Strawberry Nose, for very obvious reasons. When he was coming home he used to stop at Coventry by the Lady Godiva statue where there was a nice park. On a fine night he would sit on his bumper and smoke his pipe.

I saw him there and pulled in behind him and went to sit with him and have a smoke. After a while a Police car pulled up. The Sergeant asked him if he had seen anything happen there the previous morning, as they knew he often stopped there. Bill said "Nothing out of the ordinary" and the Sergeant told us they had picked up three yobs at that spot, two had broken arms and one was unconscious in the gardens. Away they went, Billy said, "I wasn't going to tell them it was me. Three 'herberts' came up and started taking the mickey, then one of them snatched me pipe. I knocked him out and chucked him in the garden, his mates decided to have a go so I broke both their arms, picked up the pipe and drove off". Now Bill was in his late 60's, built like a matchstick with the wood scrapped off, but what the yobs didn't know was that Bill was a 'fourth dan' Black belt at Judo. That pipe also caused him some trouble with a Bristol, he knocked it out down the handbrake slot, and the 'dottle' set fire to the bristle draught excluder and the toffee papers and fag packets that used to accumulate on top of the handbrake housing.

The depot fuelling system was a constant pressure electric pump through a meter. It worked like a shower pump, when you pulled the trigger the drop in pressure started the pump. One of the other holiday reliefs 'Johnny the College Boy' (I never knew his surname) was manoeuvring to get out and knocked the meter right off the pipe. The pump started and diesel flowed out. The pump controls were down a manhole with the shut off valves. When the yard man went to turn it off there was a trailer leg standing on the cover, so he had to run up the yard and get a Tugmaster to move the trailer, by which time the depot was awash. The following night Johnny came to me in the Blue Boar and asked for my assistance in filling in the Accident Report. He had to see Harry and hand it in when we booked on the next night. When I saw him on the changeover I asked how he had got on? "Well" he said "Harry read the statement you'd written, then he read it again, then he read it for a third time. He then said to me, 'I don't know who helped you with this, but I had to read it three times to make sure that the fuel meter hadn't deliberately thrown itself under your wheels, you owe him a tea for a month', then he went away chuckling. I'm going to take his advice, see you at Brickhill".

That Tugmaster caused a big headache for Harry Greenwood (the yard marshal), it was the only one in BRS. When the Continental Ferry Service started out of 4 Berth Tilbury Dock, BRFS had a grand inauguration ceremony. Everybody and his brother were going to be there, press, TV, the lot. To load the first ship, BRFS borrowed the Tugmaster (it had a lifting fifth wheel) and Harry to do the job. He picked up the first trailer and started to back it down the ramp into the ship, cameras rolling and flashing. Half way down the ramp the trailer fell off of the fifth wheel and dropped on its knees. Whoops!!!

Among the characters was 'Gus' Gusterson, a really nice fellow; he had been doing the Manchester run for donkey's years long before changeovers. I was told "If it's a foggy night follow Gus, he knows all the cats-eyes by their first name". There was a story that if the fog was very thick and he wasn't sure where he was, he would stop and look at flowers in gardens or types of bushes in hedgerows. (You can't do that on a motorway!). He had been on nights for forty years and lived beside the old A6 at Barnet. He had a mate Charlie Quarington, who had been employed at BRS London Colney, when it was closed he was made redundant. His last job was to deliver his wagon to Hampstead, when he arrived there Harry asked him if he liked BRS? Charlie said "Yes", so Harry said "Report for work on Monday morning".

Two of the shunters were twin brothers - Len and Stan Bird, ex-General Roadways' men. They were very small, Lenny was leaving the depot in a Scammell when a woman phoned to say that one of the lorries was going down Prince of Wales Road with no one driving it! I had the pleasure of reliving old times with Stan at the C.V.R.T.C.'s Classic Commercial Motor Shows in the 90's. I was very sorry to hear that he had died early in 1997. Another link lost with the beginnings of road haulage, although I understand Chris Salaman has got a lot of his reminiscences on tape.

One night I had the job of going to the King George V Dock with a driver called Ruby Pratt. We had orders to sit outside the gate and keep two places in the queue for the shunters who would take over the wagons to load oranges. Ruby was a bit of a dandy, lots of rings and silk cravats. He had a trick of filling paper bags with lots of torn up newspaper. He would wait until you were overtaking him then tip one of the bags out of the window; suddenly you were driving through a blizzard of paper scraps.

As I said earlier, there was not so much haste in those days. If we were going to Rowley Road Depot, Coventry, (the shortest run) we would leave London via Swiss Cottage and the A41 either picking up the M1 at Berry Grove (now Junction 5) to go to Friars Wash (J9) to rejoin the A5. Or right up the A41 via Aylesbury and Banbury to pick up the A423 through Southam to rejoin the A45 by the Ryton Bridge Hotel. In either case we would stop at the Busy Bee Cafe at Watford for tea and a snack. On one of those nights a couple of us were sitting chatting whilst eating small steak and kidney pies.

A young man came over and asked if we ate there regularly. He told us he was from the Watford Public Health Department and was doing a snap inspection. The next night we were going across the car park when the same young man came dashing across to us, all out of breath. Without so much as a 'Good Evening' he asked, "Have any of you had any stomach trouble", to which my mate Bernie replied "Don't be daft, we're drivers, we've all got galvanised pipes. Why?" The Public Health man said, "I noticed you were eating steak and kidney pies. I took some of those away for examination. Without doing cultures we have found that the harmful bacteria are at least 500% above the infective level, maybe even up to toxic once we've grown them. When I told the lab man I had seen men eating the pies, they thought I was pulling their leg. They said if I were to come back tonight I would not find any of you, you'd all be in hospital". I told him that I was 27 and had eaten pies out of that hot cabinet off and on since I was 5; the only things that gave me stomach trouble were cucumber and rhubarb. One of the men who was regularly on Coventry said he had had a hot pie every night for months. To quote Stainless Steven, "Collapse of stout party".

Going up one night I was following one of the other holiday reliefs, Tom Spencerly. We were just passing a big lay-by known as Sleepy Valley when Tom braked really hard and swung left. I just had time to think "what the hell", as I could not see anything, when the air was full of dust and flying debris. A car had run into the offside front corner of Tom's Bristol, which was about two-thirds onto the verge. Tom said to me "I never saw him 'til the last minute, he was coming down the wrong side with no lights on". The car driver was trapped and we could smell the drink through the broken window. The police and the ambulance came and between them they got the driver out. The inspector came over as they were loading the driver into the ambulance; he had a look and said that's Mr. So and So, obviously a prominent local. Tom and I made statements, but that was the last we heard of that. Tom made the national press about a year or so later, he was almost stabbed to death by a bloke he caught nicking the milk off his doorstep.

On an even more memorable occasion I was taking up an old Albion four-wheeler of Preston's allocation loaded with eight tons of apples, overstowed with cartons of cucumbers. Coming into Hockliffe I was catching up with a 30-cwt Bedford van when it pulled up outside the 'White Horse', the driver's door opened. I pulled out to pass, the door promptly shut and the van took off turning sharp right across my bows!

My front nearside wheel rode up on his front wing and bonnet and over I went. When the dust had settled I was lying on the offside door with the engine (suddenly a horizontal) ticking over above my head and I could not see. I soon realised that my overcoat (essential in those pre-heater days) had fallen off of the bonnet and was draped over me. I got a hand out and pulled the strangler.

When the engine had stopped I could hear lots of running feet, like the sound effect from the 'Goon Show'. I got clear of the coat and through the windscreen I could see a mass of faces, some with noses pressed flat on the glass which was still intact. Somebody opened the nearside door, which was now above me allowing me to climb out like a submariner, what a sight greeted me! There was a bloke in underpants and an overcoat, a couple in pyjamas, some in vest and trousers, even one holding a hand of cards still fanned! They were drivers on a night out at the Manor House Cafe close by and some of the early starters had been in bed. They had heard the bang, which they said was like a bomb going off and had come out to help. We stacked the load on the kerb and the A5 Garage stood the wagon up and towed it away. It turned out that the van belonged to the local greengrocer who was doing a right angle turn up a narrow drive.

I had an experience, which gave me a very queasy feeling, bearing in mind that I am generally regarded as a callous unqueasy individual. I was coming down the A45 (pre-dual carriageway) approaching the Blue Boar and thinking about a cup of tea, suddenly I saw headlights on my side of the road. As I stopped I could see a BRS A.E.C. at right angles across the road. Facing me was a Blamire's wagon and on the other side was a trailer with its headboard right up to the side of the BRS wagon. Under the trailer I could see the lead up ramps and jockey wheels of a Scammell coupling. I had a really horrible feeling as I walked towards it, I thought "If all I can see is the coupling, the cab must be right under the eight wheeler and somewhere in it will be the driver". When I summoned up the courage to look all I saw was a drawbar. The Blamire's wagon had been pulling a Scammell trailer on a converter dolly. When the A.E.C. emerged from the Blue Boar, Blamire's driver had braked hard and swung left. The mechanically operated brakes on the trailer being what they were, the weight of the trailer had pushed the wagon round so that it went back end first into the eight wheeler and of course the trailer had gone in head first. We sorted it all out with a chain and got the lot onto the Blue Boar car park.

After six years of 'private enterprise', BRS was a revelation. Vehicles were serviced regularly, all the tyres had treads and defects were repaired almost on demand. No more trekking from garage to garage to get DERV, trying to find one where your firm was not on the blacklist. Whatever went wrong there was always help, be it accident, breakdown, puncture or shot load. I was later to find out when I went on day tramp that this security extended to always having a bed booked in decent digs, being able to park without worry, even in Liverpool, and no longer being at the mercy of clearing house sharks.

I was so impressed by BRS, that when I became surplus at Hampstead, at the end of the holiday season. I decided to stay in the fold. Once again my Trade Union contacts came to my aid. Johnny Rolfe the Hampstead Branch Secretary sat on the same committee as Bill Carter the Senior Shop Steward at BRS Parcels, Muswell Hill Branch. Thus I got a job as a checker-loader with BRS Parcels; at its Coppetts Road depot (formerly Fisher Renwick), home to the legendary "Show boats". The Depot Superintendent was Bill Watkins an ex-Bouts, Tillotson man from Stratford. This suited me quite well; it was only about ten minutes from where I lived. This was the depot at which Parcels had just commissioned the first floor level 'carousel' conveyor. It was a very cold and draughty autumn and winter, although we did get an issue of very good donkey jackets and free cocoa.

CHAPTER 7
THE COPPETTS ROAD DAYS

The fleet there was mostly the old square cabbed Leyland Comets (in all my time with BRS this was the only vehicle that the company operated irrespective of the fact that it nearly always emitted black smoke). Some LAD Comets, a few BMC 5KFEDs (mostly used on inter-depot shuttles in the London area; and an ex-WD Bedford OW yard shunter. In those days all Parcels artics were fitted with Scammell automatic couplings. There was one fifth wheel, a Leyland Beaver, which was used with a tandem axle trailer on the Edinburgh trunk, which was a multi-changeover operation. We also had an A.E.C. Mammoth Major and dangler, which was used on a shared service with Waterden Road, this was a straight-through (or lodging service in Fisher, Renwick parlance) with one depot providing the wagon and the other the dangler (and mate) on alternate nights.

The driver on this service was Charlie Ley. The local press had a field day and ran a very cynical article, when someone pointed out that Charlie had 'L' plates on the moped on which he came to work. They published a picture of Charlie arriving for work 'L' plates and all, and then booking out with the wagon and drag. He never did pass the motorbike test.

I worked loading the Norwich service with a mad Irishman called Arthur. This was a road-rail service; we used to get the empty insulated boxes which brought meat into Smithfield, when we had filled them they were shuttled down to Broad Street Goods Yard to be craned onto the train. They often came in with blood and fat on the floor and it was a running battle between Dave, the Bank Steward and the Bank Foreman to get them cleaned out properly. Dave had been a Steward on United Dairies, he had a nervous breakdown through spending too much time straightening out the books of roundsmen who took payments "on the bed" instead of in cash. At that time the Male Wages Grade Agreement had a category for <u>truckers</u>. These were not artic drivers in baseball caps, but men nearing retirement age that pushed sack trucks loaded with parcels around the bank.

Nearly everyone at Coppetts Road was a character. Jimmy Ledra, the General Foreman, was as old as God; he had worked for Major Renwick from the beginning. The Senior Shop Steward was Bill Carter, had also started with Fisher, Renwick driving the famous Scammell R8 Showboats. He was the archetypal Shop Steward; he sat on all types of Union committees. He was to attend a big BRS dinner as a Trade Union representative sitting with the BRS 'nobs' who he wanted to impress. In those days certain things could be 'obtained!' One of the checkers 'found' him a large presentation case of fifty cigars, which Bill handed round with the coffee and brandy. I've often wondered what the BRS dignitaries would have thought if they had known that their smokes came care of the GiT insurance. Bill was on night trunk and used to fly up and back to get to bed to get up early for meetings. I said to him more than once he would kill himself. He always used to say "If I kill myself driving it will be in my own car and my missus won't be able to claim". His prophecy came true; he hit a telegraph pole in Knebworth when he was going on holiday.

There was a checker, "Thomo", with a lot to say for himself, he was always the first one to speak at Union meetings, what Union men call a "bullet maker". He used to go home at midnight for his meal as he lived nearby. He asked me to run him home one night with a big package one of the others had brought in for him. When we got to the back door, his wife called out "Are you going to change your trousers and sit on a chair or are you going to sit on the box?" I then understood why he had so much to say at work.

The Yard Marshall, another Bob, had to come off the road because he developed torticolis or wryneck. Fortunately his head had twisted to the right so he could back in with ease; his problem was going forward.

Coppetts Road was the site of an experimental floor level conveyor, which is pictured in 'Ian Allan's ABC of BRS'. The Health and Safety at Work legislation would probably not allow it today; too much stooping! The driving mechanism was in a pit about 5 feet deep, which ran all around the bank and was visible between the slats of the conveyor. Guiness did a promotional offer, sending three half-pint bottles of the 'brown stuff' to every GP in Britain; each carton was a very distinctive shape. Some of the bank staff went home every morning very much the worse for wear. The carousel conveyor broke down and the maintenance man spent a long time clearing empty Guiness cartons out of the pit under the track.

With the spring I had the urge to get back on the road. Once again I called on my Union contacts that told me of holiday relief vacancies at BRS Kentish Town.

Typical eight-wheelers, the mainstays of BRS trunking until the artic. became the order of the day. Seen here in Tufnell Park Depot, which was in a British Railways' goods yard because the land all belonged to the British Transport Commission. (Photo: A. Ingram)

Great Granddad showing off a new outfit whilst working at Woolton Hill, - possibly a house called "Lilies" - outside Newbury.

"The Pantechnicon" of Belgravia gave us the generic name for all large vans. This is a classic example of a horse Pantechnicon. The shape of its roof and the folding driver's footboard and seat made it possible for it to be loaded onto a railway truck.

FORM G.H. 2/3/N   LICENCE No. **N**   19352

ROAD TRAFFIC ACTS, 1930 to 1934,
LICENCE TO DRIVE A HEAVY GOODS VEHICLE.

THIS LICENCE is issued by the LICENSING AUTHORITY for the
METROPOLITAN TRAFFIC AREA and authorises—

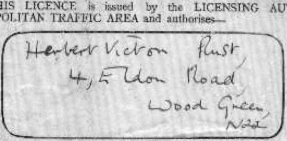

to drive heavy goods vehicles of the following class or classes :—

Strike out
those which
do not
apply.

(a) Heavy Locomotives.
(b) Light Locomotives.
(c) Motor Tractors.
(d) Heavy Motor Cars.
(e) Articulated Vehicles.

This licence shall have effect as from ....12 SEP 1936.......................and shall continue

in force for three years from that date.

Date of issue...............................11 SEP 1936..................................

Fee 3/-

Signature of licensee (see Note 1)...........*H. Rust*..................................
(in ink.)

NOTES.

(1) The licensee must sign this licence in the space provided above immediately on receiving it; but must not write anything else on it.

(2) The licensee must notify the Licensing Authority of any change of address within 7 days of such change.

(3) This licence does not absolve the licensee from the obligation to obtain a licence to drive under Part I of the Act of 1930. The latter licence has a stiff cover in which this licence when folded into six can conveniently be kept.

My Dad's first HGV Licence issued when the 1934 Road Traffic Act (which also gave us log sheets) came into force. According to Dad he had to sign a declaration that he regularly drove HGVs in the course of his work, there was no medical nor an annual renewal. This was a printed form.

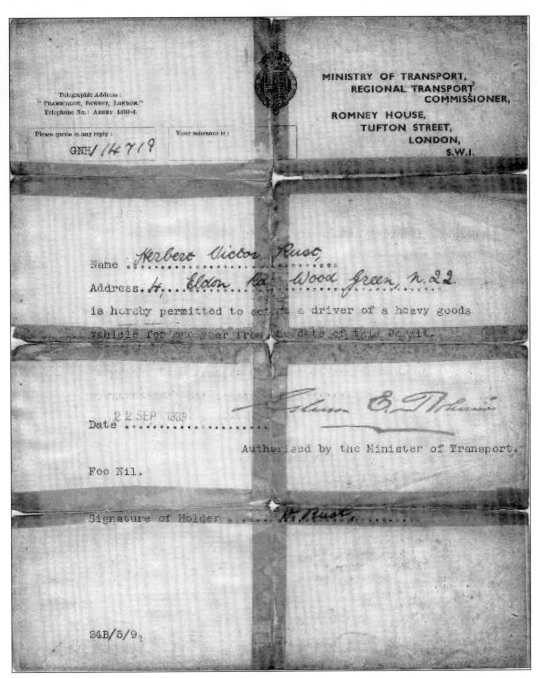

MINISTRY OF TRANSPORT,
REGIONAL TRANSPORT
COMMISSIONER,

ROMNEY HOUSE,
TUFTON STREET,
LONDON,
S.W.I.

Telegraphic Address:
" FRAMEGLOW, Sawbey, London."
Telephone No.: Abbey 1400-4.

Please quote in any reply:
GNH/ 14719

Your reference is:

Name .....Herbert Victor Rust,

Address..4,...Eldon Rd...Wood Green, N.22

is hereby permitted to act as a driver of a heavy goods
vehicle for one year from the date of this permit.

Date ....22 SEP 1939........

Authorised by the Minister of Transport.

Fee Nil.

Signature of Holder .....H. Rust,

24B/5/9.

The last HGV Licence to be issued, (for the duration), just after war broke out. It was a duplicated sheet issued by the Regional Transport Commissioners who took over from the Licensing Authority. It had to be carried at all times and produced with an ordinary driving licence and an Identity Card when requested by the police or a Ministry Inspector. Hence the repairs with Sellotape as it had to last (as it turned out) for five years. The LGV Licence scheme was not revived after the war, in fact not until the late '60s.

RUST 9 302024 R99NU

CLASSES OF HEAVY GOODS VEHICLES

1 Articulated vehicle, not fitted with automatic transmission, other than a vehicle coming within Class 4.
1A Articulated vehicle, fitted with automatic transmission, other than a vehicle coming within Class 4A.
2 Heavy goods vehicle, not fitted with automatic transmission, other than an articulated vehicle, designed and constructed to have more than four wheels in contact with the road surface.
2A Heavy goods vehicle, fitted with automatic transmission, other than an articulated vehicle, designed and constructed to have more than four wheels in contact with the road surface.
3 Heavy goods vehicle, not fitted with automatic transmission, other than an articulated vehicle, designed and constructed to have not more than four wheels in contact with the road surface.
3A Heavy goods vehicle, fitted with automatic transmission, other than an articulated vehicle, designed and constructed to have not more than four wheels in contact with the road surface.
4 Articulated vehicle, not fitted with automatic transmission, the tractive unit of which does not exceed two tons unladen weight.
4A Articulated vehicle, fitted with automatic transmission, the tractive unit of which does not exceed two tons unladen weight.

WARNING
This licence does not authorise the holder to drive heavy goods vehicles at any time when he does not also hold a current ordinary driving licence authorising the driving of vehicles in Group A (or in the case of vehicles with automatic transmission - Group B).

1

Road Traffic Act 1972
Road Traffic (Drivers' Ages and Hours of Work) Act 1976 **2/N/A 642495**

HEAVY GOODS VEHICLE DRIVER'S LICENCE

Issued by the Licensing Authority for
The Metropolitan Traffic Area

MR ROBERT RUST
37 THE SLADES
VANGE
BASILDON ESSEX
SS16 4SJ

is hereby authorised to drive heavy goods vehicles of classes 1, 1A, 2, 2A, 3 and 3A.

from 25 MAR 1987 until 24 MAR 1990 inclusive

PROVISIONAL LICENCE–This licence has effect as a provisional licence in respect of the classes of heavy goods vehicles for which it is not a full licence. Such heavy goods vehicles may be driven subject to the conditions applying to provisional licence holders and the minimum age requirements being satisfied.
IMPORTANT NOTICE– In order to drive a heavy goods vehicle on a road the holder of this licence must also hold an appropriate licence granted under Part III of the Road Traffic Act 1972.
Usual signature of licensee ....
51-5476 (6/85) FBF   DLG 2

My final Heavy Goods Licence before the issuing of separate licences was discontinued in favour of the new all-in-one licence.

This was me in Hong Kong in 1954, de-scaling a two part wheel off a MW Bedford, getting it ready for fitting new tyres. Note my moustache, the ends of which could be seen from the back!

One of the Chinese Bedford OLBDs mentioned on page 10. This fleet belonged to an ex-RASC soldier who took a local release and set up a haulage business.

An A Model Bedford "tipper", - Chinese style.

Loading a Comet tank onto an RASC transporter (hauled by a Diamond T) to be taken to the city dump for 'road testing'.

Harry Skelton, the much respected Vehicle Foreman at BRS Hampstead Depot. Wearing the 'uniform' of a pre-nationalisation 'market' driver; dark suit, collar and tie, and flat cap.

(Below) The author with his Bristol 8-wheeler chatting to Jimmy Hugget, who drove the Ford Trader on the Grey's spares contract.

Two shots of the fibreglass steeple made by Brylan Plastics for the Roman Catholic school at Tuffley, Gloucestershire.

(Top) A very unusual way of overcoming the vehicle shortage just after the war. The conversion was done by Deffries Transport of Ball's Pond Road, who were later nationalised into the New Furniture Carriage Division. Subsequently passing to General Haulage. Charlie Dormer, who had been Deffries' foreman on de-nationalisation set up C.E. Dormer Transport, changing from vans to tankers because the 'S' Licence specified "Goods in Bulk". He also won £75,000 on the pools when that was the top prize. (Photo: A. Ingram)

(Bottom) The Bedford OB that featured in the story on page 16. (Photo: A. Ingram)

CHAPTER 8
KENTISH TOWN

So the start of the next holiday season saw me transfer back to night trunking, at Kentish Town depot. This had once been the Spring Place depot of General Roadways. When it was nationalised, General Roadways was unique in being the only company to be run by a woman, Amy Alexander. She had started as a secretary with C.D. & T.

The Superintendent, Bill Campbell, (an ex-driver) interviewed me and I discovered that the Branch Manager was Abe' Allman who soon after left to become a journalist with *'Motor Transport'*, a trade paper for which I also wrote the odd article. Doug Smith my old Superintendent from Hampstead replaced him. The Vehicle Foreman was George Pentecost; he had worked from H & G Dutfield Ltd prior to nationalisation. His old guvnor was Henry Dutfield who was Chairman of the Road Haulage Association. He was leading the anti-nationalisation campaign and urging small hauliers to fight it in every way possible. His name became a dirty word when it was discovered that while he was spearheading the campaign, he was negotiating the buy out of his firm on very favourable terms. He finished up on the first Road Haulage Executive. Small hauliers who had restarted in 1954 would still refer to him as 'Judas' Dutfield in the mid-1960s, in fact I heard it used as an epithet in 1997.

Here the fleet was mostly A.E.C. Mercury artics, this being the main light artic in the Southeast Division. I am sorry to see that it is not included in the 'Pictorial History of BRS'. This Mercury had the cab like the Mk IV Mandator. There were some slightly later ones with what we called the 'high cab' (like the Mk V1 Mandator). These came with a piece of hardboard slotted in under each seat that could be fitted into slots on the front of the radiator (not the grille) to provide winter warmth. An alternative to the tatty bits of cardboard often used by drivers, but objected to by Head Office. There were some Leyland Beavers for the Max. Cap. trunks and some rigid eight A.E.C.s and Bristols based at the Dagenham detachment in Fords, plus Mercury, Seddon and Albion four-wheelers for the fruit and veg. service to Derby.

The major job was pig iron to Leamington for Fords, apparently this link with Leamington survived from the days of McNamara. There was a tea job to Birmingham that had come to Kentish Town from Royal Mint Street when that depot closed. As well as Birmingham (Cheapside), Leamington and Derby we also changed over with Wellington, Walsall, Wolverhampton, Oldbury and Coventry.

This was back to the old roads to the Midlands. Seeing many of the faces I knew well, while getting to know people who I only knew as faces in a different crowd. There were the Downing brothers, one of who was the Union Branch Chairman; the other was the night Shop Steward. Ben Pickford, Steve (whose surname I can't remember) but he had a terrible habit of creeping up behind you as you sat in a café and chewing your ear with his toothless gums. Ronnie Bunts, who was probably one of the first victims of "road rage". Way back in '63 he remonstrated with a car driver about his bad driving and was beaten unconscious for so doing.

Sid Brooks an extremely fit man who did isometric exercises as he drove. He was a fanatical rose grower. He came to work every night at Kentish Town from Brockley in south London. He was nationalised at Galleywall Road depot (which returned to Atlas Express on denationalisation) working his way through various re-organisations via Royal Mint Street to finish up at Kentish Town. I heard much later that he had been killed in a road accident.

Charlie Wilson was a character, one of those people who could find something wrong with the most perfect set up. His claim to fame was that he twice visited a bank without getting out of his lorry. Once at the traffic lights in the centre of St.Albans, the other time at the foot of Archway Road. On both occasions sliding on a wet road, doing considerable damage to the buildings, but fortunately not to himself.

There was another Max. Cap. driver, George Angel who along with BRS made it into the national press. He smoked flake tobacco in a pipe. He had an old tobacco tin bolted to the top of the bonnet, into which he dropped a flake then rubbed it and filled his pipe with his left hand.

Doing this one morning he drifted across the road and clipped a car coming the other way. The car went out of control and crashed killing the driver. His widow sued BRS and it came out of the trial that he was what we would today call a 'Whizz Kid' with high future earnings potential. Because of this the Judge made (what was then) a phenomenal damages award of £75,000 that could at that time have been invested to provide the widow and her children with a good income.

There was a very old four-wheeler driver, Teddy Rice who had had an illeostemy or a colostomy. (People used to say he had tubes in his body). He would frequently be seen asleep in a lay-by. There were two Max. Cap. (24 tons GVW.) artic drivers who did the Leamington pig iron trunk, I had met them in the Busy Bee while on Hampstead, they were Les Smith and Bob Petty. Les had a trailer uncouple while he was doing a 'U' turn on the Busy Bee car park. I came across Bob Petty many years after when he came off the road and became a steward in a Basildon club.

The final person to mention by name is George "Crasher" Haywood who was the TGWU Branch Secretary. He and I became good friends, our paths crossing many times over the years with our various Union commitments. When the time came for me to leave Kentish Town he was instrumental in finding me another BRS job to go to.

For a time I did a double changeover with Banbury depot, at the Brickhill Cafe. I could never see the sense of that one. The same result could have been achieved by each of us going straight to the other depot. It would have been possible to use the A41, instead of the Banbury man having to go four times over the very bad road from Brickhill to Banbury.

The Brickhill Cafe was a meeting point for Kentish Town drivers; it was exactly 1hr 10min from the depot. Les Smith was so precise on his running time that Joan would pour a cup of tea and put a 'Wagon Wheel' on the counter at precisely 4.35am. Within a minute Les would be pulling on to the car park. Trunkers from Robert Heaton & Sons of St Helens also used Brickhill Café. At that time well known for its fleet of dark blue Leyland Super Comets pulling BTC four-in-line trailers

For readers of the '00's, these had single-wheels carried on short oscillating axles on either side of a single spring on each side of the trailer. Although in a single line across the trailer, the wheels were far enough apart to count separately so it was classed as a tandem trailer for 24-ton gross operation. It was sometimes known as the Aberdeen or Jewish eight-wheeler. If a tyre burst or punctured the pair of wheels tended to fall over. Changing an inner wheel meant working under the trailer in a narrow space. It also involved pulling the flat tyre up onto a block so that the jack would go between the wheels. Tyre Services were very loath to attend these and knew it was a four-in-line by the tyre size, so quoted with a very long response time or were "out of stock" of that size of tyre or tube. Thus Heaton's men usually did their own trailer punctures.

All Heaton's vehicles were fitted with a Servis Recorder (the original "what, when and why? clock). Some old drivers reckon that these could be beaten on wagons with Gardner engines. A piece of 2" x 2" wood cut to an exact length to wedge between the back rocker box and the bottom of the clock. Setting the tickover to about 850 rpm produced a trace, which at a quick glance looked like travelling. There was also a desperate measure of getting a number 6-shovel red-hot and holding it close to the clock.

This melted all the wax off the disc, although you could not do it too often!

Heaton's drivers were allowed 11 hours from St Helens to London, but to get 11 hours pay the clock had to show that the vehicle was moving for that time. While those of us on changeover with a 10 hour 'job and finish' guarantee were dashing into London at 36mph (or 45 down hill out of stick!). Round about 'Mickey's Mile' or Hockliffe we would come across a Heaton's motor plodding along at 25mph making his time last out (time spent stationary in cafe's or lay-bys did not count).

Talking of Brickhill brought to mind an event dating back to my early days of driving. At that time Brickhill was formidable, a narrow steep hill with bad bends through the village. Travelling south, at the start of the village were three huge oak trees growing right at the edge of the road, their roots made a solid bank at the edge of the tarmac making the road even narrower, and casting a deep shadow. After passing the 'Pullman Cafe' you used the straight stretch to build up as much speed as possible to climb the hill. A BRS driver (depot unknown) was doing just that with an old Leyland Octopus eight- wheeler. What he did not know was that a van belonging to "Judge" Hollowware (the saucepan firm) had broken down with a total electrical failure and was thus without lights, right by the oak tree roots. He saw it too late and smashed open the van with his nearside. The sight that greeted us was an eight-wheeler festooned from end to end with saucepans of all shapes, sizes and colours!

There was another bad accident at the foot of Brickhill going north. It happened before I started to drive, but the marks were still there when I did. A BRS eight-wheeler from Bishopsgate Group was going to Birmingham with a load of Litharge (liquid white lead). At the bottom of the hill another BRS eight-wheeler from Blackwall Tunnel Group, had broken down. It was loaded with earthenware flasks of mercury, which only stand about 9 inches high but loaded all over the platform make a full 14-ton load. Making the wagon a 22-ton lump.

The Bishopsgate driver had "knocked the stick out" (it was possible to coast all the way to Fenny Stratford) when he came across the broken down vehicle, he could not go round it because of approaching traffic and hit it full tilt. The containers of Litharge were thrown right over the stationary vehicle bursting in the road beyond. When I started to drive it was still possible to see the outline of the two vehicles on the road. I only learned the full story in the sixties when I worked with an ex-Bishopsgate driver.

From the Brickhill changeover I went on to a change over with Wolverhampton Branch. The 'Wolves' service, which changed over at Bromford Lane, was raw rubber ex-Tilbury Docks up and Goodyear Tyres down, both terrible commodities to keep on a flat trailer. We shared the Goodyear work with a 'private enterprise' firm, P. & A. Carter of Wolverhampton, often running with them. In one night alone we re-stacked one of their loads of 'Mini tyres six times between Stonebridge and Barnet! On the same job I was going up with a load of rubber and it 'shot' on the tight little right hand bend behind Barnet Church. The lads all stopped and helped pick it up. However, one bale had bounced through the front window of Woolworth's shop in Barnet High Street and the police would not let us remove it until someone from 'Woolies' came to say it was not theirs!

P. & A. Carter was another old firm that existed both sides of nationalisation. It ran a nicely kept fleet of dark green E.R.Fs, and had a London depot in Greenwich. Arthur Ingram's book *'London Lorries'* has a nice picture on page 40 of one of Carter's ex-BRS Seddons, taken in 1954.

Shortly after this my Dad died (too many Players' Weights). We had been made homeless by the Rent Act, and had bought a caravan on a site near Basildon. So I got a transfer to Kentish Town's Dagenham detachment, as it was less travelling. At Dagenham I did a Banbury changeover with Wellington (Ford body panels ex-GKN Sankey). One night I broke down in Buckingham right outside the old Jail, which is now a public toilet. Jimmy Campbell, the West Indian fitter from Enfield, came out and diagnosed a faulty lift pump and found that the spare on the breakdown would not fit. This gave Jimmy a challenge, not one to be beaten he unshipped the fuel tank and placed it on the sheet rack above the cab. A brake pipe and two Cee-Green couplings later and I had the only gravity fed Mercury in Britain. Filling the tank to the brim at Banbury and Dunstable got the wagon back to Enfield where Jimmy put it back to normal. I was a bit late getting back to Dagenham but it was worth it to see the look of amazement on the faces at Dunstable when I asked for a ladder so that I could refuel!

I often wonder about Jimmy. That night he came out to me it was cold, with that cross between drizzle and fog in fact a typical autumn morning. I asked him why he had left his sunny homeland, for weather like this. He said it was all down to money. He had already got his fare home and was saving up to have the finest garage in the West Indies when he went back home. I wonder if he ever made it?

That was the job from hell! From where we lived I had to walk about a mile and a half to Laindon station for a train to Dagenham, then walk again from the Heathway to the pig-iron field at the back of Ford's. The incoming trailer had to be taken to the Cunis warehouse on the edge of the Thames behind Rainham Marshes (about two miles down a dirt road) and then unloaded. This involved what were known as plus payments, extra hours worked (with permission) beyond the guaranteed ten hours. The money was welcome, but I was only getting home to sleep. Good job I could sleep through a world war living in a caravan with two small children.

We used to get an eight-wheeler from Cheapside which was loaded with miscellaneous parts from small suppliers all over Birmingham and which took one of the internal shunters from Tuesday morning to Friday night to get unloaded! I went on that job for a bit as the night shunter but it was nearly as bad. I was so knackered that the Ford people were always waking me up to move! This is where my Union contact and good friend 'Crasher' Haywood found me a vacancy at Grays depot and I transferred there to the lowly post of fuel-issuer-cum-yard man.

A typical lightweight furniture van on a mass produced Ford chassis. Hamilton's bought a similar one for £1.00 a cubic foot, i.e. £1,500 in the late '50s. They were built in the back garden of a house in Brixton Road. (Photo: A. Ingram)

CHAPTER 9
THE GRAYS DAYS

The fleet at Grays was very mixed. A.E.C. Mandator Mk.IV's and a prototype Mk.V straight from the Commercial Motor Show, Bristol artics and rigids (of various designs), three A.E.C. Mammoth Major Mk. IIIs, three vacuum braked Leyland Octopus eight-wheelers, lots of A.E.C. Mercury's, two Seddon and two Dodge four-wheelers, an Albion with a Homalloy cab, a Mercury tipping pressure tanker and four Ford Trader's with Scammell couplings on a shipping contract for the Ford Motor Company.

BRS Grays was a merger of BRS Stanford-le-Hope and BRS West Thurrock. It was located in what had been the CWS milk depot in London Road. BRS West Thurrock came from the nationalisation of Harris Transport along with T. Mileham's from Purfleet. Harris Transport restarted in 1954 and was back in its old office right next door to BRS Grays.

BRS Stanford le Hope came from the nationalisation of Burroughs Transport. Burroughs had a long transport history going back to horses and market vans taking produce to Spitalfields and the 'Garden'. On nationalisation the Old Man had retired and his son Len had taken a post with BRS. He was now Grays' Branch Manager. There was also a satellite at Rochford, which had been Cottis Transport, who merged with Grimwade's and Puddifants, and had Stan Cottis as Clerk-in-Charge. We had a body maker, Les "Bungay" Alston, he got his nickname because his family originated in Bungay. He reckoned his family had connections to the Duke of Somerset and spent all his spare time scouring East Anglian parish registers to prove the connection, apparently there is an unclaimed fortune. But to return to the point, he always referred to the Guvnor as "Mr. Len" in the old country style. I am told that Firmin's men still refer to their boss and his sons in the same way.

Len 'Tug' Wilson was the Shop Steward and Branch Secretary at that time, he had arranged the job for me. He was a shunter, when he was on the road as a long distance driver he had received a bad back injury. He was delivering scrap railway lines to strengthen the East Anglian flood defences at the time of the bad floods in February '53. He went into a hidden ditch whilst wading through floodwater; the load went through the back of the cab.

The Superintendent was Percy Mitchell, he had been nationalised with Harris Transport and stayed with BRS. He was notorious for his filing system. His desk was always heaped with papers. Like all nationalised industries, BRS generated lots of paper. At five-o-clock he would say to the office in general, "Any of you got a claim on any of this? I was going to file it under 'R'". He would then go out into the warehouse and get the dustbin labelled 'Rubbish', put it at the end of his desk and push the lot in. Weeks later someone would ask about a certain form or letter. The standard response was "Percy had it last" or "I put it on Percy's desk".

The main customers were Van Den Burgh & Jurgens (Stork margarine) and Proctor & Gamble (soap powder). As a member of the yard staff, this is where I really learned how to rope and sheet. A full load of soap needed four sheets, all carefully overlapped to keep the water out. Shunters brought in the margarine covered with a flysheet this then had to be properly sheeted. Both types of load had to be roped using corner boards, for the trunk.

We did changeovers with Cardiff, Newport, Swansea and Ebbw Vale at 'The Windrush' at Northleach. We also did a changeover with Bromford Lane at the 'Ace' at Weedon. This last was a long and short trunk with the Birmingham man doing two short 'legs' while our two drivers started at different times to give him chance to go to Birmingham and back after his first changeover. We also changed over with Lincoln and Sheffield at 'The Afton' Godmanchester, and with Scunthorpe at the 'Compass Cafe' at Colsterworth.

Both 'The Windrush' and 'The Compass' were heavily used as BRS changeover points. They had BRS offices, really large garden sheds, equipped with telephones. These were manned at night so that depots could contact their drivers about breakdowns or delays. The key was kept in the cafe so that BRS drivers could use the phone during the day.

'The Afton' was sidelined by improvements to the A604 (now the A14); the owner had great plans to turn this into a super truck stop but was eclipsed by the opening of the B.P Truckstop at Alconbury. The Compass is now under a motel. Colsterworth was by-passed twice. The old Great North Road was diverted to pass east of the village, then the dualling and improvement to the A1 by-passed that by-pass!

On the A1 near Peterborough is a village called Water Newton (now by-passed). It had a level crossing (which was worked then and is being worked again as part of preserved railway) and the smallest BRS haulage depot, only Perranporth (Cornwall), which was under BRS Parcels, was smaller. Water Newton depot was an essential link in the trunking chain, with facilities for fuel, assistance and parking. When the accountants took over BRS from the transport men, they shut it. In those days the A14 ran from Royston, through the middle of Godmanchester (pronounced Gumster) over the old packhorse bridge and joined the A1 at Alconbury at a 'Halt' sign. At that point stood one of the famous Leyland Clocks (the one which, it was alleged, adorned a contractor's patio for some time!). Travelling south the Great North Road swung off to the right by the Alconbury Hotel, through Alconbury Weston, down through Alconbury to Brampton Hut. In Alconbury it is possible to find the end of Rust Lane, which comes out by the Alconbury Truck Stop. Back to Grays...

The Scunthorpe service produced coils of wire bound for Murex at Chatham, which prior to the opening of the Dartford Tunnel involved the shunters travelling up to the Blackwall Tunnel, although they could return empty via the BR Tilbury vehicle ferry. One of the shunters was Teddy Hawkridge, who found out he had had diabetes all his life when HGV licences and medicals came in. The other was Freddy Revel; he was born in Kings Lynn and came to London at the time of the Cable Street riots. He was knocked out by a mounted policeman's baton and was dragged into Joseph Eva's yard for safety. When he came round and the guvnor found out he was looking for work, he gave him a job. Fred worked for Eva until nationalisation, delivering flour when it was all carried up a ladder to the baker's loft. He and his old trailer mate on Eva's both died of enlarged hearts resulting from their work as young men.

The night trunk driver on that service was the luckiest man alive, he had two spectacular accidents. Ernie Thurlow was an old style trunker, suit, collar and tie and a pipe. Going up one night between Ongar and the 'Silver Wings' cafe (now the site of a huge roundabout) he left the road on a right hand bend (no one knows why) by going straight on. He jumped a bank and a ditch, demolished a hedge and finished up some 60ft into a ploughed field. We had to hire a tractor and trailer from the farmer to tranship the load to a wagon parked in the gateway to the field. Then not long before he retired he was coming down the A130 driving a late type Bristol with an all fibreglass cab. As he went over the railway bridge in Great Shelford he found a six-wheeler sideways across the road. It was that way because the road was a sheet of ice, which Ernie found out when he braked; he hit the six-wheeler amidships. The following driver, who stopped in time, found Ernie sitting on a bare chassis, still clutching the steering wheel, pipe still in his mouth. The cab had totally disintegrated, most of it lying on top of and on the other side of the six-wheeler. Ernie was unscathed and went on to have a splendid retirement party.

Teddy Hawkridge the shunter with diabetes weighed about 18 stones. He was far outweighed by Teddy Hoy the trunker who worked opposite him, who weighed in at 24 stones. He was so big he had to have all his clothes specially made; he was paying £25 for shirts in the '60s. The depot was due some new vehicles; eventually three of the last model Bristols arrived, the one with the big fibreglass box for a cab. Teddy the shunter took out the one allocated to the Scunthorpe trunk and loaded it. Duly at 19.00

the other Teddy arrived to take his new motor up the road for the first time. After a quick look round he put his foot on the step, got hold of the grab handle and went to swing himself up into the cab.

There was a thump and an agonised shout; Teddy was lying flat on his back. His hand was firmly clutching the grab handle, which was firmly bolted to the quarter panel. The problem lay in the quarter panel being no longer fixed to the cab. The other Teddy's 24-stone had finished off a day of the first Teddy's 18-stone climbing up. Examination revealed that the grab handle had been bolted through a single thickness of fibreglass. The next day the body maker was busily fitting reinforcing plates to the three new Bristols. While 'Tubby Ted' as he was known, had to wait another twenty-four hours to get his hands on his new motor.

The two-leg Bromford Lane service had two totally different characters as its drivers. Albert Rice was a 'Jack the lad' who came to work in his carpet slippers in the summer. The other was Tommy Gray. His wife had died very young, leaving him with four young children in the mid-'40s. There were no social workers in those days; it was 'The Welfare' which was treated with the same distrust and suspicion. Tom would often tell of his two abiding memories of the time his wife died of breast cancer. One was a very fond memory of her sitting up in bed making pastry for a steak and kidney pie. The other was the look on the face of the 'Woman from the Welfare' when he said, "Not today thank you" and shut the door on her. Tom went on to regular nights and brought up his four children single-handed. Two of them went on to University. He had a penchant for the 'young ladies of the road'; he did not just pick them up and use their services. He would take them home and install them in his flat for a few weeks.

He had a good mate, 'Sailor' from BRS Parcels Waterden Road. 'Sailor' had us in stitches one night. He had gone round to see Tom; when he knocked a totally naked young woman had opened the front door. Tom was expecting him and had put her up to it. There had been a slight hitch; the Council rent collector had called before Sailor to be was greeted by the same sight! Another Waterden Road driver, Georgie Wright, was the mate of all of us. I came on him one night in the lay-by on the Markyate by-pass, his engine's governor had broken and the engine was running away. We solved that by bashing the fuel pipe flat with a trailer handle as none of us had a spanner to fit.

Talking of carpet slippers reminded me of another 'Tubby' Ted, this one from Stratford Parcels. He suffered from severe gout and often wore a carpet slipper on his right foot. Someone 'pulled a stroke' on Ted approaching the traffic lights at West Ham, as the traffic stopped Ted leapt out to 'have a go' at the other driver. Unfortunately he caught his slippered foot in the handbrake and finished hanging upside down from the doorway with a broken thigh.

One of our Western District changeovers produced a Bristol rigid eight with a prototype cab. This was made of beaten sheet aluminium instead of fibreglass and was held together with pop rivets. Many miles had produced movement between the panels and enlarged rivet holes; any bit of rough road (such as Ripple Road in Barking in those days) would fill the cab with flying pop rivets. The last job of the day was to run it round to the body builder and have it riveted together again for the night run!

One of our drivers on the Cardiff changeover was Ernie Hawes. A 'day and nighter' who had dozed off ran into him. Both vehicles caught fire and Ernie received a News of the World 'Knights of the Road' award for rescuing the other driver from his burning cab. He also received a considerable sum in compensation for what is known today as whiplash injury; this was still giving him trouble up to twenty-five years later. The trailer load of 'Tide' also caught fire and burned so fiercely that it damaged several trees, a lot of hedge and the road surface. This was on the A40 at Postcombe and it was still possible to see the after effects some eighteen years later! The last time I was through there. The vehicle involved in the incident was 1A120 (217 ALB) is featured in Ian Allan's *'ABC of British Road Services'*.

How the vehicles (both diesels) caught fire and burned so quickly was a source of controversy and were subject to a lot of examination and experiment. It was finally discovered that Ernie's Bristol had been hit on the fuel tank, and as the tank crumpled a tiny split developed, the continuing compression of the tank produced a fine spray of DERV like an injector. This went on to the Bristol's batteries, which were behind the cab and had been damaged and were arcing.

In addition to the trunks, we had a large tramp operation, mostly loading from the same customers plus corrugated asbestos sheet from Turner's Asbestos, Tunnel Cement, Shell Fertiliser and Ford Tractors.

We had one very unusual customer who made fibreglass spires and church steeples that were usually very wide or very long. We also carried pre-cast concrete for a civil engineering firm at Thundersley. These were usually very long columns or half-trusses for portal framed buildings. For this we used 32-ft. or 45-ft. trailers and an eight-wheeler and four-in-line steering bogie. When I got back on the road it was with an old type A.E.C. Mercury (1A654) working on this job. I soon learned how to handle a single-axle 45-ft. trailer with a long overhang. In those days the longest normal trailer was 26-ft. as maximum overall length was 32ft 6in, so much of the concrete work was done under the abnormal indivisible load regulations.

In that period, I and another driver delivered the entire building, and all the pre-cast units for the potato bins at the Bird's Eye frozen chip factory at Great Yarmouth. (This closed and was immediately demolished in 1984). The frame for a new kiln building at Westbury (Wilts) in the days when the M4 only went as far as Maidenhead Thicket. Also all the columns and lintels for a new factory estate at High Wycombe which were made at Tyler's of Tonbridge. We also delivered all the bridge beams for the Doddinghurst Road bridge on the A12 Brentwood by-pass (I've driven over those loads many times since!).

One of the craziest jobs I did was to take 12 tons of 1¼-inch reinforcing rods in 50-ft. lengths to Skewen with instructions to return empty. Coming back along the top of the Cotswolds I was stopped by the police and told to return immediately to Newport depot where they urgently needed a 45-ft. trailer. I did an about turn and had a police escort to the other side of Gloucester, (BRS got a lot of police co-operation in those days). Into Newport, pick up the Ops 4s for the 'load and leave', round to Whitehead's to load – – 12 tons of 1¼ inch reinforcing rods in 50-ft. lengths for delivery to Hendon, north London.

The eight-wheeler being used with the bogie at that time was a Bristol. I was therefore amused to see a caption in the *'Pictorial History of B.R.S.'* which read "they were intended as solo machines but could just about cope with a trailer"! Our Bristol operated quite regularly at gross train weights of up to 41 tons, as did Brentford depot's 1A2, which is shown in its re-cabbed guise in the same book.

Grays had a working agreement of 20.5mph outside the North and South Circular Roads and 16mph within. This meant a maximum mileage for a pure driving run of 9.5 hours (plus ¼ hour book on, ¼ hour book off to make 10 hours) of 195 miles. Thus we carefully worked out our running time for various deliveries, and where we <u>should</u> be when our time ran out. It was often possible, without exceeding the maximum legal driving day of 11 hours, to be in a totally different place. There was also a rule that if you loaded during the day and had more than one hour's running time left, you had to leave. So long as the customer was satisfied and the vehicle was parked safely and out of sight, a 'blind eye' was turned as to where the vehicle actually was.

When my mate and I were doing the Bird's Eye, Yarmouth job we worked between the customer's moulding yard and the site. After the first run we found out that 'digs' in Yarmouth (in fact anywhere past Ipswich) were non-existent. So I made a couple of collapsible bunks, which fitted on the bars that went across the Mercury's doors. These bars were actually to protect the drop glasses, which did not go right inside the doors.

The moulding yard foreman wanted the finished units out of his yard; the erectors wanted them on site as they were on piecework. So Charlie Gravelly and I sat down and worked out a schedule so that we would know exactly where we should be for the purposes of filling in Ops 12s (log sheets) and claiming night-out money. In fact, we were either at home or using our erstwhile 'sleeper cabs' under the high level bridge at Haddiscoe.

One lunchtime we were going round the Ipswich by-pass, on one of the very small roundabouts (for which it was well known) the floorboards broke and my load fell over. Great consternation! We would have to inform Ipswich depot, as we would need a mobile crane to sort it out. With much trepidation we consulted our 'schedule' and found to our surprise and relief that we were where we should be to within five minutes! Ipswich was very quick in finding a crane and supplying us with sleepers to put the load on. We arrived at Haddiscoe in time for a meal and a pint in the riverside pub before it shut. After that we always loaded on sleepers.

Anyone, who knew the road between Scole and Beccles at that time, will remember that it was narrow, winding and lined with high hedges. It was the height of the pea season and we spent a lot of time dodging wagons loaded to about 9ft wide with pea vines going to the processing plant. Coming home empty, we would pull off into a wide spot (no lay-bys) and collect the vines that festooned the hedges. Our families and neighbours were sick of peas by the time that job finished.

During the course of that job we used to eat in a small cafe in Harleston (a pretty place now by-passed). It was there that we came across Fridged Freight, which was running refrigerated trailers when they were a novelty; most meat was carried in insulated boxes. The trailer were home made and massively built. I was told that the first one was two butcher's shop cold rooms grafted end to end, with the electric motor driving the compressor replaced with a motor bike engine. The weight was enormous, it was rumoured that loaded vehicles only moved by night when there was no risk of being weighed! Train weights of 30 tons were whispered about (the maximum GTW was 24 tons at the time). The six-wheel units were A.E.C. Mk III double-drive tipper chassis with a fifth wheel on a homemade sub-frame.

The job we went on next was as good. Fords had hired a lot of 8ft x 8ft x 8ft containers from CTI. These were being transferred from Dagenham to Genk, at the time there was a coaster bringing Volkswagen engines into Britain and Fords arranged for it to take the containers as a return load. It docked at Ramsgate, in what is now the Marina on the landward side of the current ferry terminal. BRS Grays and thus Charlie and I got the job. The plan was that we would load on Monday morning at 08.00 run to Ramsgate, tip, back to Dagenham, pick up pre-loaded trailers, back to Ramsgate and tip, then night out at Ramsgate. After tipping the second load we realised we had legal time to get back, so back we came and parked up at Meads Corner (now the Circus Tavern). We got the bus down to the depot to get our cars. As we were pulling out the Vehicle Foreman, Dick Nicholas appeared.

He said "I laid a bet with George (the Traffic Operator) that I would see you tonight, I suppose the motors are at Meads. Get in early and you will find them loaded. I've already worked it out that you should do eight loads each. If you do it the way you're doing it, you will do ten and still be back here late Friday. Park up right over the back of the Ford shipping job and you will find them loaded Monday. Keep your mouths shut and you can book ten hours Saturday and four hours running in Sunday plus an extra night out. Fords will be delighted because 60 boxes fills the ship and it must sail Friday night".

Dick was an ex-driver ex-shop steward and as fly as they come, that job lasted three weeks it was a nice little earner but I was sick of the sight of the M2, Thanet Way and Manston Aerodrome. This time everyone was sick of cauliflowers, I was buying them by the box (20 heads) for what my wife was paying for two or three heads at our local shop. At Ramsgate the port facilities consisted of a Coles 5-ton crane and a forklift truck. When there was no ship the "Dockers?" ran shellfish stalls, paper stalls or worked in cafes.

From time to time the Mercury drivers were sent to work on the Ford shipping job. Usually when there was a big single consignment, which involved a lot of lorries; those were the days when there could be over a hundred wagons in a queue for a ship that had just opened. No.6 Shed Tilbury Dock regularly did these, George Rounce or Rounds was a maestro with a 'cube stick', and three quick measurements and he could give the volume and shipping tonnage of a case as fast as you could write it down. The leader of the regular dockers gang was a chap I only ever knew as 'Blondie', he and the gang always regarded BRS motors as 'theirs' (they were all very pro-nationalisation).

I have been sitting well back in the rank, the gang would come back down the road from 'mugo!' or dinner, Blondie would come over and say 'We don't want our motors sitting about, go up 5 shed ramp and down the quay. We'll do you overside or in the back door". You could go down with a couple of cases for Ford's well after the closing day and say to George "You still striking for such and such ship?" His standard comment was "We're striking BRS motors 'til the covers go on. On the quay and see Blondie". That was a gang I would always help, any of our regular drivers would 'back up' other people's notes so they could work two sets of chains on the crane. 'Backing up' consisted of writing brief details of the consignment and shipping marks on the back of the notes. Then the tally clerk could read them easily without wading through all the other printed information

I was clearing up after unloading, and as I picked up a sheet my back locked (the result of an old injury), I was stuck like Quasimodo, not able to either bend further or stand up. Blondie came out of the shed and saw me and asked what was wrong. After I told him, he said, "You need Albert" and shot into the office.

A couple of the gang lifted me on to a pallet and Blondie came on the forklift. "George has had a ring round, Albert is at 21". He picked up the pallet and with the two dockers for support off we went. Blondie explained to Albert (who was the crane driver) who prodded my back asking where it hurt. He then put a large strop round me under the arms. After he carefully positioned the knot, one of his gang hooked the strop on the crane. Albert 'took the weight' until my feet were just off the pallet, and then he proceeded to pull and twist my pelvis. Next he took me up about three feet and "jiggled" the crane from side-to-side while Blondie held my legs. Suddenly, there was a click in my back, all the pain went and I dropped straight. When he put me down I felt fine; I had no more trouble with my back for about eight years after that!

Just before I finished with the Mercury I made another monster mistake. On BRS there was a rule that you were warned overnight of a 'night out'. When I booked off George called out "Night out tomorrow Bob". Next day I booked in and Reg (the other operator) handed me a note envelope and said, "Stratford pre-loaded out of the yard, trailer number on the envelope". I hooked up and away I went. Had lunch at the big cafe just south of Banbury (now a Little Chef) and wended my way down Sunrising Hill to the "A.A." lay-by on the outskirts of Stratford on Avon, opened up the envelope to discover that the delivery address was indeed Stratford, but Carpenters Road, London E.15. The only comment from the depot when I rang in was "Have a night out anyway and deliver it on your way in".

After a time I was promoted to an eight-wheeler, a Bristol 1A613 (RGC 217). This was on general tramp work here, there and everywhere. On this I did a lot of work to the Southampton area, reloading with PX stores for the American Air Force at Lakenheath and Weathersfield. Or plastic pellets for the London Docks out of the Esso Refinery at Fawley where 'Fat Harold' used to lurk in the 'mobile office' (it was a brick building!).

I delivered asbestos sheet to Calshot Spit when they were refurbishing the old seaplane base to house the refugees from Tristan da Cunah. Anyone who has been to Calshot will know why the refugees all wanted to go back home once the volcano had subsided!

While on the eight-wheeler I did one of the previously mentioned fibreglass steeples. Laying down it was 28-ft. long and 14-ft. wide, it only weighed about 7 cwt so it had to be well roped to stop it blowing off the wagon! This was to go to a Roman Catholic boy's school at Tuffley on the outskirts of Gloucester. Getting it off of the lorry and into position was an all day job. I have a very nice Alan Spillett painting of this load parked up at the 'Windrush' for breakfast en-route.

I was doing a load of PX for delivery to USAF Woodbridge and had a night out in Ipswich the day Kennedy was shot. When I got to Woodbridge the base was in uproar, everybody seemed drunk. When I finally found the stores Master Sergeant his knees were almost liquid and he offered me a drink from his bottle of scotch. I asked him why the celebration, I expected mourning, instead he replied, "That bastard Kennedy is dead, shot in Texas, and it was a good old Texas boy that did it". Woodbridge was the base of a Texas fighter squadron.

Mrs Mayhew, the wife of Steve one of the Ipswich yardmen, ran the 'digs' we used. If you got in after 6 she would ask "Seen Mayhew?" or "Any chance Mayhew will be home?" I asked her if she ever called him Steve. "Oh no" she said "Its a Suffolk thing, I never heard my Mum use my Dad's first name, I never knew it 'til I saw it on the coffin plate after he died". A style used by Charles Dickens in "*David Copperfield*" in the line "Barkis is willing" signifying that he would marry Peggoty.

'Tug' Wilson was promoted to Warehouse Foreman, the way of many BRS stewards. The night steward finished up as Manager of Containerway's. I took over the job of Branch Secretary and Deputy Steward Johnny Ponder, who became a lifelong family friend, was elected Shop Steward, I've only ever had one beef with John, he started me smoking at the age of 32.

At the Manager's request I went from the eight-wheeler to a 'high cab' Mercury (no loss of earnings if the management moved you onto a smaller vehicle). My new workhorse was AC46 (462 EYO) fitted with a burglar alarm-cum-immobiliser to do a special job with retail cigarettes to Bristol, £250,000 a load. As a consequence I became very familiar with Spring Street and Day's Road (Bristol) and Melksham depots, doing a lot of return loads out of Purnell's of Paulton, St. Ann's Board Mills and the Avon Rubber Co. - tyres were a whole lot easier in a van.

While I was driving AC46, I did a load of margarine for Ipswich. The first drop was Danish Bacon at Claydon. When I pulled in the manager came out of the office and asked if I would do him a favour for a five-pound note and his men unloading part of the load. I got in his car and off we went up the A140. He explained that he had started a new driver that morning. The driver had phoned in and told him the motor wasn't safe, he had left it at the Stonham 'Magpie' and he didn't want the job. I asked why the motor wasn't safe and he told me the driver had said it felt as though it was falling over. When we got there it was an 18ft insulated box trailer, what the unit was I can't remember. I set off very gently; as soon as I got to the first bend I knew what was wrong. It was a load of sides of bacon "on the hook", it was certainly a funny feeling, a bit like driving a tanker as they swayed from side to side and surged front to back.

About this time we got the 32-ton gross A.E.C. Mandators, which we called the Mk.VI's. They were terrible machines, obviously a hasty uprate to take advantage of recent legislation. They were underpowered, had an uncomfortable driving position, heavy steering and the most unpredictable wet weather braking. About the same time we also got the 24-ton GVW Mercury, which we called the multi-use as it could pull air- or vacuum-braked trailers enabling us to finish out the life of all our old Max.

Cap. and 12-ton trailers. This was as good a machine as the Mandator was bad. With the Mercurys came those peculiar 33-ft. trailers with the wheels only just in front of the tail lamps. What pigs in London traffic and delivering round the docks! The later 40-ft. version was even worse to handle than my old 45 footer.

Macmillan Bloedel and Mayer opened up 42 Berth in the enlarged Tilbury Dock. This berth did packaged timber, beautiful solid packs with every board in the pack the same length. No random lengths all flapping, no more loose boards as you did in the Surrey Docks. Their other commodity was huge reels of kraft liner for making corrugated board for cartons. One of Bloedel's ancestors provided the tallest flagpole on the Tower of London. It was decided that the transport would be organised by a dedicated BRS operation based on site, this would be a sub-depot of Grays.

Len Burroughs, who was nearing retirement, was put in charge and some drivers, (one made up to Vehicle Foreman) were transferred from Grays. This provided the general haulage operation with extra traffic, some of which I did with the Bristol rigid and the Bristol Max. Cap. artic. We had done some linerboard in the past for George White's Transport out of Purfleet Deep Wharf, so we knew many of the customers already.

At Grays we got a new Branch Manager, Larry Coles. He was ex-Indian Army, ex-Southampton District. He was a bowler, black jacket and pinstripe man. More an accountant than a transport man. He was a man who knew less about industrial relations than Maggie Thatcher. Harry Osborne, the South Eastern District Staff Officer became a regular visitor to the depot, as did Bill Webster who had been his predecessor and was now Staff Officer at BRS HQ. With both I established a good working relationship. In Harry's case a long-term friendship.

In the past when we had a dispute we always had use of the canteen for meetings and waiting while negotiations took place. The first dispute we had with Larry Coles, he stormed into the canteen and ordered the staff to shut it. In fact it was an independent operation open to all, although on BRS premises. When that failed he ordered all the BRS personnel to leave as they were trespassing. He was told in no uncertain terms that everyone was 'sitting in' and would have to be carried out. As is usual, the Steward had informed the 'Nick' (the gate was a traffic hazard) and as usual the local beat bobby had arrived on his bike. Coles grabbed him and insisted he evict us forcibly. The copper told him he was not carrying anyone out not even the light ones! At that moment Harry Osborne arrived and told him (Coles) not to be a prat and that the idea was to solve things not make them much worse.

By this time I had become deeply involved with the Union and the Labour party, sitting on various committees and giving up most of my spare time. Through having too much on my mind I had six minor accidents in quick succession, all silly little things due to inattention. In accordance with the procedure of the day I was 'grounded' and went to work in the Ford shipping section, unloading, sorting and assembling loads of export spares which came into the depot from three different Ford locations and were stored until called forward for shipping. This actually did me a favour, as not only did I get home every night, but was also a piecework job and my earnings went up about 20%; some punishment!

While I was on this job the Ergomatic cabbed A.E.C. Mandators arrived and the fleet quickly came to consist of these and the multi-use Mercurys, although we kept three of the very late Bristol artic units, the ones with the very square Bristol cabs. We also had an A.E.C. Mammoth Major for use with the long-load bogie, and we also got a special fifth-wheel bolsters so that one of the new units could be used on the long-load jobs

The Ford Traders had to be kept for the Ford job, as it was a condition of the contract. However, these were changed for 7-tonners and increased in number to six to eliminate the four-wheelers. We did try a big Ford D-series when they first came out. It was fitted with a thirteen-speed gearbox and Ford sent a demonstration driver to teach our driver how to use it. They picked up a loaded trailer and set off. Outside our depot was a peculiar double-camber where the run-in met the road and as the vehicle left the yard, both rear wings flew off, someone had miscalculated the under-wing clearance. Thus the vehicle started on one of its many trips back to Ford's when it went wrong, as it was on 'user trial'. When the turbocharger blew up we towed it back to Langley and never collected it again!

We had a driver who had a jack-knife accident at Hammersmith, receiving a very serious head injury. He had been driving one of the new multi-use Mercurys pulling an old vacuum-braked 32ft trailer. For a time I became heavily involved in the phenomenon of jack-knifing, attending a demonstration of the Hope anti-jack-knife device at Hendon Police College. As a result I was interviewed for the 'Tomorrow's World' television programme, at the Blue Boar at Watford Gap. When this was broadcast the girl from our canteen was having a bath, her husband called out "Bob's on the telly" and she dashed into the lounge to watch. It was not until the item finished that she realised that the curtains were still open and she was naked in full view of the street!

The father of the driver concerned was also a driver in the depot. He was a diabetic and shortly after his son's accident he went totally blind. He was a very self-reliant man and adapted well to his blindness. He went on to become very well known in the area raising money for Guide Dogs for the Blind. He used to go round with his dog giving demonstrations of its abilities. He gave a talk to my wife's W.I., when we spoke to him afterwards he immediately identified both of us by our voices.

One day the Depot Manager wrote off the company car by driving into the back of a stationary vehicle. At the time he was mentally composing a difficult letter he had to write, this made him realise how easy it was to have an accident if your mind was distracted. He told me this when he put me back on the road, and said he would keep me on locals so that I could keep up my other commitments without worrying about them at work.

I went back to one of the multi-use Mercurys and back on to the long concrete with the old 45-foot trailer. We did a job to Kings Lynn, a mill building, part of a timber merchant's expansion. The entrance was from the Tuesday Market Place in the old part of the town and the only approach was the 'wrong way' up a lengthy one-way system. After a couple of 'assists' from the local police, the Sergeant said, "You old boys seem to know what you're about, be careful and don't bother us no more." The locals soon took it for granted that they would find 55ft loads of concrete ignoring 'No Entry' signs and 'Keep Left' bollards and going the wrong way up one-way streets.

One Saturday, Scunthorpe wanted to borrow the trailer so they arranged to send an Essex load to meet me at Lynn and we would changeover after I had unloaded. I arrived at 7am as usual and in the middle of the Market Place was the Scunthorpe man already unhooked and sound asleep on the bonnet. I backed in, which involved about half-a-mile down an alley and along the quay and was unloaded by about ten-past eight. When I got back to the Market Place the Scunthorpe man was still there, so were about 200 cars! The Tuesday Market Place was the car-park for the Saturday market which was held in the next square, we not only bothered the Sergeant, but every copper in Lynn from the Super downwards, it was half-past eleven before we got away!

Then the Guvnor sent for me, he said, "I've got a job for you young Bob, right up your street. We've got a full ship of bag work, it's lying at the end of 16-17 Tilbury it's coming over the side on the ship's gear. I want you to take charge, we'll load as many of ours as possible and the office will send some Foreign Base. Dick will send a couple of shunters so you can organise some pre-loaded trailers. Off you go it's ready to start". When I arrived, the dockers had put in a 'false bank' and one of our motors was backed up to it. The winch drivers were dropping the first sett which, landed in a cloud of dust, bursting a couple of sacks. Out tumbled a lot of knobbly lumps, white, pink and yellow; I found a couple of bits, which I recognised as bone.

I hailed the deck and asked the stevedore who was 'working' the ship? He told me Ernie Appleford, he wasn't there yet, he was signing off his last ship, and they had only just got the covers off and made a start. I told them not to work anymore until I'd seen Ernie. When he finally arrived from the General Office with the loading plans and the Bills of Lading, I asked him what the Bill called for and where it was from.

He told me India and we found the bill said "Hessian sacks containing crushed bone". So I said "That's animal products Ernie, where's the Anthrax certificate?" We had a look through all the paperwork, nothing. So I said to Ernie "I'm going to pull my men back and stop any more motors, up by 14, then I'll go over to Port Health". To which he replied "You do that quick as you can, I'll get a loose cover put on and get my lot off the ship".

In the Port Health office I said to the PHO "We've got a ship on 16 discharging crushed bone from India, we can't find an Anthrax Certificate". There could not have been more action if I'd thrown in a bomb. The PMO went out of the office like a rocket. I walked back and by the time I got to the ship it was flying the yellow quarantine flag. The lads were all rounded up and we went back to the depot. When I got to the office the Guvnor was having a fit. "What have you done? I sent you down there to get things running smoothly, now its going to cost us a fortune" so I said "Why do you think we got such a good price for the job and why do you think it was specified 'over the side'? Someone knew it was uncertified bone, full of dust, so long as none of us has contracted Anthrax the only people it will cost is the shippers".

The PHO contacted the consignors in India and found the bone had been boiled clean, he sent some of his men in protective clothing to take air and cargo samples from all the hold spaces. After a week he got the all clear from the laboratories and issued the necessary certificates. We then started work. I got a big thank you from the Dock Convenor for spotting it. The Master and the shipping line got a big fine for docking the ship uncertified and unquarantined.

Once again I changed vehicles, this time to a late type Bristol unit as we were starting a new job, involving heavy cast concrete system building units. A special factory had been built at Basildon to make the units for a big estate at Deptford. The units were to be loaded on special 'A' frames. Those were the days when the Dartford Tunnel toll was 2/6d cash. As it was a night job and the roads were quiet, we used to go south through the Blackwall Tunnel, change trailers and dash back to catch the last Woolwich Ferry (the trailers were 15ft high). Thus we only needed to use the Dartford Tunnel for the last trip north so we were pocketing 7/6d per night. My mate on this job was a 'Jack the Lad' called Vic, more of him later

The housing estate job at Deptford had two night 'Security' guards. They were both part-time members of the Richardson's firm (the South London version of the Kray's). Paradoxically, that was probably the best-protected site in London.

We were also involved with a big job at Battersea, (opposite the park) which we shared with Samuel Williams Ltd. Sammy Williams was a Thames barge master, who made his fortune bringing London's rubbish down river for dumping on the Essex marshes. Ford's plant and Dagenham Dock stand on the contents of Victorian London's dustbins, as did the tank farm of the associate tanker operation, John Hudson. Sammy Williams operated one of the first Scania-Vabis units in the country. It also had (at the time) a trailer-building arm, which produced a couple of innovative designs. One had the chassis rails on the outside doubling up as raves (it made a good coil carrier), the other had a steering bogie coupled to the fifth wheel by crossover steel cables.

Sammy's was very early in landing and delivering coiled steel from the continent. It also transported long concrete pilings for Stent, whose works were next door in Chequers Lane. I delivered several loads of these to the A33 improvement near Winchester; this has now been redeveloped yet again into the M3. At that time it was bypassing the existing Winchester by-pass. I delivered 5 x 50-ft. piles at a time; the ground was so soft, that by the time I had put the gear away all five had been driven into the ground one on top of the other (250 feet).

At the time of the Battersea job, Sammy's had a depot at Andover handling the panels that were made there. The collapse of Ronan Point turned this into a vast financial disaster.

Up until that point, the units were held in place by their own weight and friction. When Ronan Point fell down the units had to be bolted together, all the units already erected had to be modified and the ensuing back log resulted in trailers standing under load for months on end and extra transport being hired in. Despite the move into containers the firm never really seemed to fully recover.

From this we moved into lightweight aerated concrete, this had been trunked down from Motherwell via Tunstall to a site in Basildon for some time. It suffered so much transit damage that Costain's opened a plant near the depot. I got on this job from the start and became expert not only on unloading the stuff (which came in reinforced slabs 2-ft. wide and up to 12-ft. in length and between 4-in. and 8-in. thick) but in its design, application and erection. It was very new and usually the first words on a new site were "What do you know about this stuff, driver?" I delivered all the internal partition walls for St. Alphages Hospital (that's the one that faces you at the top of Blackwall Lane). I also delivered the roof for the skyscraper stores building at Ford's, Dagenham and the office block at the Purfleet MoT Test Station.

The shunter on this job was Rodney Thomas, another workmate who became a life long friend of the family. He had served on the North West Frontier as a young man but had been in transport all his adult life. He had worked for the London depot of Western Transport and finished up being nationalised into Bishopsgate Group eventually ending at Grays. When I first knew him he was on journeywork with a Leyland Octopus. He was approaching retirement and was given a 'light corner', shunting.

The job at Basildon was a problem from the start its echoes were still rumbling on in 1997. Everyone is familiar with Thermalite blocks; the slabs were material like that but reinforced with wire.

The horizontal slabs that were for both floor and ceiling were designed to go one way up but were not marked. They were intended to be lifted off of the lorry with a special grab, so that they could be put straight into place. Unfortunately, the site was a mud bath and the job so far behind that the slabs were unloaded and stacked anyhow. Many "horizontals" were installed upside down and cracked. Problems appeared as soon as the first phase was occupied. As the system originated in Sweden, two experts were flown over and as I knew the site I got the job of running them up, in the company's car. As we got out into a sea of yellow clay like pudding, the expert dug his heel in the ground and said, "At home we would not build the houses on this. This system is for building on rock". They got straight back into the car. By August 1997 the entire estate was being demolished!

The St. Alphages job turned out to be very lucrative. The site was a Taylor Woodrow job. When I took the first load I introduced myself to the Site Agent, he asked if I was to be the regular delivery driver. I told him yes. He took me to the gate office, got a brand new hard hat and wrote my name on the front. He said "Every time you come on the site, you put that on and wear it at all times. This is the company's policy". This was long before compulsory hard hats.

The loads were all walling, installed at delivery, once in place and the next floor built on top they were only going to be coated with a plastic skin so all the edges and corners had to be perfect. I got 15 back off the first load and the Agent came over and said that he would pay me £3 a load to check all the slabs before I sent them up. This would save a lot of time and trouble for his erectors inspecting them, putting the damages to one side and then sending them back down. As there were about 20 loads to a floor and 3 floors, a very lucrative job.

The MoT station at Purfleet was an 'arranged' delivery, which meant the erector's crane would only be on site to do the job. It was a two-span roof, i.e. from an outer wall to a dividing wall, then to the other outer wall. When I arrived the erectors were on the roof working out of the crane's swing. The foreman explained what they intended to do. When I had had a look I said to him "What's the bearing (the ledge the slab would sit on) on that outside wall? It looks narrow from here". He looked up his drawings "Two inches," I said, "No good, Siporex specify four inches minimum, this stuff is so brittle the arrises can crumble and the slab drop, the bearing has to be under the first cross-wire, which is two inches in".

We all climbed down and into the Site Manager's office where I got the third degree. "Was I sure, was I qualified, why was I worried?" So I told him I knew the spec., I had delivered the material from day one and often advised installers on using this new material. As the roof spanned the waiting area, one-day I might be sitting there! When he got the master drawings, the bearings had been altered in ink from 4" to 2"; they had a measure up and found the outer walls were 4" too far apart. Thus the opening of the station was delayed; an extra one course wall had to be built inside the outer walls. That earned a £10 note from the Siporex plant manager.

I did a load of ordinary 6" x 9" x 12" blocks to a block of flats at Leigh, a small site, as it was a refurbishment job. When I asked where they were going to put 3,000 blocks, I was told in small lots around the site where they were needed. I must have looked dubious so the Agent asked if a tenner would make a difference.

It would, and I spent three hours going round the site. When I'd finished I went to the office and the Agent said "Sorry driver we are out of petty cash". As I was delivering to Southend in two days time I told him I would call back. When I went back, I saw the Agent disappear into the building as I walked in. When I went to the office I was told "Only the Agent can out pay petty cash and we don't know when he will be back". The Site Manager's Portakabin was next door so I went in and told him the story and asked for the money. I pointed out that the site was due another 3,000 blocks shortly and that delivery could be indefinitely delayed. He gave me the ten quid saying "I'll take that out on his arse with my boot". When I made the next delivery, the Agent met me with a tenner in his hand. Without batting an eyelid, he gave it to me and said "Same arrangement as last time driver?"

There was an incident concerning the Mk.V Mandator, which I mentioned earlier. The shunter was a little fellow Dicky Bird (he really was christened Richard) he moaned about the steering for months. Mind you, Dick could ''moan for England.' He went to A.E.C. Southall to collect a load of exports. A 'suit' came out and asked him what he thought of the wagon. Dick, in his usual diplomatic fashion, told him that the man who designed it "should be f--d with the rough end of a pineapple". "Oh dear" said the 'suit', "I designed that!" The depot was asked to send another unit while they kept the Mk.V for examination. When Dick was sent to collect it about ten days later it turned out that they had had to rebuild the front axle. They had used some revolutionary non-lubricating, kingpin bearings, which had gone rusty. It had taken three days to get the kingpins out!

We had an old shunter, Billy Webber. Known as 'Coal Sacks' because in the days of steam wagons he often slept on the back of his empty wagon under a pile of coal sacks. He was a real character, an East End cockney, ex-prizefighter. Very proud of being nationalised with Kneller and Chandler. He was out tipping cased cars at K.G. V., when the depot got a phone call, our driver had fallen off of his load, landed on his head and been taken to hospital. Percy, (the Superintendent) took me up to the Docks to finish the load. When we arrived, there was Billy with a huge plaster on his head slinging the last case. I can still see his huge beaming grin and hear his words when Percy asked him if he was all right. "Lor' bless you sir. I'm a cockney and I landed on me 'ead, anywhere else and I'd 'ave 'urt me self."

Two days later I was coming into the depot, by the gate was one of our Bristol artics. partly embedded in the depot fence, with the driver's windscreen glass (intact) leaning against the wire. When I got into the yard, George (the traffic clerk) said "Take the company car and pick up 'Coal Sacks' from Orsett Hospital, he's playing merry hell about getting back." When I picked him up he said, "Did you see that wagon? Somebody dropped diesel coming out of the yard and I found it! Knocked that 'screen out wiv me 'ead". He had a second huge plaster mirroring the other one. When he retired he moved to Clacton and got a job as road sweeper. At the age of 83 he re-married, much to the disgust of his sixty years plus children.

Vic, my mate on the Deptford job came to BRS because of a rather humorous event. He had been driving a high volume tipper on coke. He did a late delivery to a large boiler house. It was a winter's night and some of the coke had frozen right up the front of the body, the boilerman said to Vic "Don't worry about it, get rid of it on the way home when its shaken loose." On the way back to his depot, Vic saw an old mate, he said to him "I've got some coke left on, any good to you?" His mate said yes but he was on his way to work, would Vic tip it on the drive and he would barrow it round the back in the morning. Vic wangled his trailer into the driveway and tipped. What had appeared to be a little bit of coke, right up the front of the body, actually filled the small drive and garden and piled up the front of the bungalow to the eaves! Vic quickly dropped the body and disappeared into the night, but not before a neighbour had got his number. Thus he was working with me.

There were many jobs I did as a Branch Secretary, filling in accident reports, writing letters, dealing with Disciplinary Procedures, taking statements and getting information for solicitors and sick visiting.

There was a young Scottish driver who had moved down from Glasgow. He had only been with us a short while when his wife started to complain about being lonely, as she knew no one. He decided he had had enough of driving and got himself a job in the local boot and shoe factory. His first job was to stick the heels on rubber boots, the next man put the soles on then they went under the vulcaniser. At tea break they were marched into the canteen with martial music, he never got time to drink his tea before they had to march back. As a protest he put the heels on the toes, which upset the sole man. The foreman came, doing his nut so Jock told him where to put his job and walked out. When he got to the gate (which was a turnstile) the uniformed Security told him the exits were locked and he could not leave. Jock floored him and climbed out.

He came straight back to Grays and restarted driving on Tuesday. On Wednesday we had the Police in, waiting for him to run-in, the boot firm had made a complaint of assault.

On his behalf I wrote to the firm saying that the TGWU would assist him in bringing a case for 'wrongful imprisonment' which as the gate was locked would succeed with no difficulty. I also pointed out that we delivered all their raw rubber from Tilbury Dock and that all the members of the Union Committee there were personal friends and supporters of BRS. The complaint was promptly withdrawn.

I had a driver come to me for help. His wife had left him; she had also left him with an unpaid mortgage, milkman, paper-shop and grocers. He was likely to be evicted, I spent a day 'phoning various creditors and finally with the help of my Bank Manager got an immediate appointment to see the Manager at its Grays branch. In the '60's this was harder than getting to see God! With the help of Harry Osborne's office I arranged to have his wages paid straight into a bank account. The bank would work out a payment schedule for his creditors and allocate money for him to live on. Wages being paid directly into the bank was another first in the '60's. I also arranged for him to be 'up the road' as much as possible so that he could live on his 'night out money'. In those days 17/6d, (87 ½p) ,easily covered bed, breakfast, evening and mid-day meals.

There was a time when we had several young drivers who came with stories. One who shall be nameless lived high on the hog and was always short of cash. One afternoon the local council's men were cleaning street lamp lanterns. At the foot of one post they noticed a narrow newly asphalted strip leading away under a hedge. When they investigated they found that our driver had tapped-in to the street light feed and was running his electrical appliances at the ratepayers expense.

Fred one of the yardmen on the Ford job was seriously injured in an accident with a crane, suffering a broken thigh. I visited him in hospital for many weeks. BRS's insurers flatly denied liability. The Union's solicitor arranged a meeting with the Barrister at Fred's home. As I had not long before done the Union's residential course on law, I wrote up a brief for the Barrister.

After a couple of days there was a message left for me at the depot, by the Barrister, saying that my brief was better than many he got from his juniors! Fred got a considerable sum in compensation. Unfortunately Fred had not been back at work long when his other leg was badly injured by the same crane. I immediately wrote to the Union's solicitor drawing his attention to a 'Stated Case', which exactly fitted the circumstances. He passed a copy to the BRS's insurers who settled at once, again for a large sum!

I had another member, Bill Blisett; he was climbing a ladder carrying a sheet up onto a load of soap powder when he fell. Once again the insurers forced us into Court. In his opening address to the Court, the insurer's barrister said "It is the contention of my clients that they have no responsibility in this matter. Mr Blisett should not have been up a ladder. He is employed as a lorry driver, not a window cleaner".

The Judge stopped the case at that point. He said "Mr X, your clients are the insurers for a road haulage company. They, more than us should be aware of the diverse nature of a lorry driver's job. I shall direct the Jury to find for the plaintiff and ask it to retire to evaluate damages".

The same driver went to load at the Shell Haven Refinery. As he was going into a 'Volatile Area' he had to have a 'spark arrester' fitted to his exhaust. While the security man was doing this, someone, it was never ascertained who, banged on the nearside of the cab. Bill took this as the signal to proceed and drove off, right over the security man, killing him outright! I had to arrange for the Union's solicitor to represent him at the inquest.

I had a rather odd case of attempted fraud involving but not perpetrated by one of our young drivers. He was a boy for the young ladies and had something going with a girl in a café, in Kelvedon, which he used regularly. He was given a Disciplinary Notice for not reporting an accident. When we got in front of the Branch Manager it transpired that he was supposed to have badly damaged a car belonging to the man who lived next door to the café. He denied all knowledge, so I asked for time to investigate. When we got out the Ops 6s covering that period it showed that for three weeks around the date the accident was supposed to have happened he had been running to the Northwest. On the actual date his Bristol had been in Manchester workshops with the diff. removed (broken pinion). The Claims Investigator went to the address to see the claimant to check on the date. The claimant was positive, he had the garage invoice for towing the car away and yes, he had written down both the fleet and registration numbers when he heard his car being struck. When George told him that it was a physical impossibility for a vehicle that was broken down in Manchester to have hit his car he immediately owned up. He had done the damage himself; a friend had told him to write down the number of a BRS lorry that regularly used the café and claim it had hit his car. His friend reckoned BRS was such a big organisation it paid out without investigating.

I can't leave my time at Grays without mentioning some of the characters that I met along the way, that have not been mentioned already.

There was a black driver from Oxford, always known as 'Black Jack' or 'Treacle'. He could not go roaming because in the '60's a lot of 'digs' would not take him in. The 'Professor' who could speak several languages and did the 'Times' crossword in about 15 minutes often accompanied him. They were regular visitors.

Tiny Ross from Tunstall was the biggest man I have ever met. He could only drive an underfloor-engined Sentinel; Tunstall's was kept for years after it became life expired so that Tiny had a job. We had a very small driver, Johnny Donald, who always gave Tiny a load of verbal. One day Tiny picked him up complete with the chair he was sitting on, turned it upside down and stacked it on another chair with John sandwiched in between. Unfortunately Tiny was killed when his wagon ran into the gable end of a house.

I had only been at Grays about a week when I met Bonny from King's Lynn depot. After he had signed for his fuel, he said, "When did you move away from Lynn, boy?" I told I was born and bred a cockney. He told me accents were his hobby and he could hear Lynn in my voice. I told him that the nearest I had ever been to Lynn was by having a Granddad who was born there, but had moved away as a boy. If he could hear Lynn in my pronunciation it had been passed down from Dad who had also been born in London so must have got it from his Dad and Granddad.

Bonny was himself a cockney who had been a trunker for Eastern Roadways in the straight through days; he had married a Lynn girl and moved. I always called him the "King's Lynn cockney" after that. I was asked the same question over twenty years later when I did a regular timber delivery to Wisbech. The side loader driver who asked me, said he knew I had East Anglian connections when I pronounced the name of the town as *Wisbeck* (the proper way) and over a couple of visits had pinned me down to Lynn.

Little Arthur from Melton Mowbray Branch came every week for a couple of days while he delivered Pet Food products round the Essex kennels and dog breeders in his 5-ton Austin FG dropside. He was a proper lorry driver of the old school.

These were all "foreign based" characters. We had a few "home based" ones.

My children (the youngest is now 38) still speak fondly of Eddie Defont. He became Union Chairman when Fred Revel retired; he became a good family friend. For twelve years after I left BRS Grays, Eddie would call in for a cup of tea on the way home. His health deteriorated and he had to take quantities of pills, he had one of those pillboxes with compartments for different times. He would be drinking his tea and would say "Time for my pills" and open his little box.

All of a sudden there would be no input from Eddie, he was sound asleep. At half-past six my wife would wake him up saying, "Come on Eddie, Ivy will wonder where you are". He would get up, stretch and go home. Ivy told me that Eddie liked to come to our house because we took no notice if he went to sleep.

George Richardson, the Traffic Operator who I have mentioned several times, was a Japanese PoW, it had affected his health and he always had an air of suppressed urgency about him. He always smoked Black Beauty roll-ups, the strongest tobacco on the market.

Reggie Cox, the other Operator I met by chance in Sainsbury's in 1997. Still going strong at 85 or 86.

The last I heard of Len Boroughs he was Captain of the Stanford-le-Hope Bowls team.

In the summer of '69 a big 'Time & Motion' study scheme started ready for the Productivity Bonus. I became deeply involved in this and started to do a bit of journey work again, as it was agreed that the work study team would only go out with Union lay officers to start with. Before the scheme was finalised I back loaded out of Corby for the London Docks and ran out of time at Woodford. Lifts were hard to get that night so I dropped the trailer and took the unit home to Basildon. It was spotted there by the police, parked on waste ground and duly reported to the management. After a disciplinary enquiry, BRS and I parted company.

This is the end of 'Red BRS' as we called it. But before I leave BRS completely, two more stories which are sagas in their own right.

A double drive Leyland Octopus with a Crane four-in-line steering bogie with a full load of long girders. (Photo: Source Unknown)

CHAPTER 10
TOO HIGH, TOO WIDE, and TOO HEAVY

Early one morning, the Guvnor called me up to his office. He said, "You're the boy for the odd shaped loads. I want you to take Billy, Dave and Charlie down to the old Wouldham works. It's being demolished and some sections of the kiln have got to go to Stoke. There are two 15-ton lumps, a 12-ton and a 9-ton. They are all 11feet in diameter and they've got to go on sleepers so you will be about 16 feet 3 high. Here's the paperwork and the movement order. I will be down later on to see how you are getting on, so that I can give the 'Met' a pick-up time for the escort. Peter, the bodymaker, is coming down to saw the sleepers to length and help with the scotching up".

Off we went, two Bristol eight-wheelers, a Dodge four-wheeler and my A.E.C. Mercury 12-ton artic with a 32-ft. single-axle trailer (a specialist long load unit in those days!). When we got to the site the demolition men were just burning off the first piece of the kiln - like a very long steel tube. Each piece was measured, burnt off and dropped onto the lorry by a large crawler crane. This was a long drawn out business what with cutting sleepers, scotching and chaining down, as there were no ratchet straps then. About half-two the Guvnor arrived a bit excited. The 'Met' had been on saying that if we could not move before 4.00 o'clock we could not move until 10.00 next morning.

We were just chaining down the last load so I said "Tell 'em we'll be at Rainham just after 3.00 and get Dunstable to book us four beds at the 'Three Sisters' in Markyate". I had a quick check round and off we went. In those days the route was Rainham Road, Whalebone Lane, A406, Hedge Lane, Stag Hill, Mutton Lane, South Mimms, Ridge Hill, London Colney, St Albans and the A5 to Markyate. We finally parked up at about 7.00 pm. The final instruction on the 'Met's' movement order was 'Proceed North via M1 Motorway (unescorted) - time at drivers discretion'.

In those days the morning hold-ups at Junction 6 was northbound (all those FG Fodens and Leyland Octopuses [or should it be Octopii] struggling up the long drag heading for Birmingham), so we decided to get on the road at 8.00am. I've just realised that in those days the motorway junctions were not numbered, the A5 turn-off was called Friars Wash.

The next morning at 8.00am we set off, past the Watling Street Cafe up onto the M1. Just dropping down towards Toddington (which had not long opened) 'Ole Bill came alongside and directed us onto the hard-shoulder right outside the Services. "Right" said the Sergeant "Who's in charge of this little convoy?" I said, "I am the senior driver, I've got all the paperwork". "Come with me into the Police post, because this has got to be sorted out. You should have a MoT authority for 'out of gauge' loads on the motorway and we should have been notified. How high are you? The last bridge knocked a load of twigs off one of those loads". I said that the eight-wheelers were 16ft 4in. He said "It's a good job we spotted you, the three bridges past Newport Pagnell Services are only a bare 16ft on the nearside lane.

When we got to the Police post I was shown into a small room, when I heard the lock click and saw the spy-hole I realised it was a cell! Through the door I could hear a lot of phone calls being made, finishing with a very raised voice saying "You blokes in the Met don't know your arse from your elbow, you could have caused a very serious pile up". Finally, he let me out of the cell and told me to take my merry men for a cuppa. His control was sending a car and a couple of bikes.

We were to leave the motorway at the Newport Pagnell turn off and proceed through Wolverton and rejoin the A5 at Stony Stratford, then wend our way northwards along the old well-accepted routes to Stoke. When the escort arrived, off we went again. At each bridge they took us into the middle lane 'just in case'.

At the start of Wolverton, by the carriage works, we stopped again, and told to go very slowly as there were so many parked cars that the escort had to go well ahead to stop the oncoming traffic and get some moved. I said to the 'copper "What about the phone wires? Some look a bit low" he replied "They ought to be l6ft 6, if they are not they will have to take their chance". They certainly did, I could hear them falling on the cab roof hoping all the time that none of them were high voltage wires for the street lamps! Halfway down there were some strings of bunting - these added to our wide load markings! It took a long while to get to Stony Stratford. When we reached the lay-by at Potterspury we were sent off on our own with instructions to wait at Towcester Racecourse for a Northampton team.

On their arrival the Sergeant in charge said that they had found a way to avoid the 14ft railway bridge (it's gone now) beyond the police station. Left at the lights on the A43 towards Brackley for about six miles then right up a lane which went over the railway, then right again back on to the A5. This brought us out by the Wool Packers just beyond the bridge, twelve or thirteen miles to make about 800 yards. We pulled into The Towers for a late dinner. I phoned the Guvnor who said he had heard via City Road (the South East District HQ) that we had had some trouble with the Bedfordshire Police. I said that one day I would put the story of this trip in my memoirs (little did I know!). I asked him to arrange parking and book beds at Rugby, and said that Charlie was moaning about the way the four-wheeler was laying over. He said, "You've been in the game long enough, scrounge some timber at Rugby and block the axle!"

Strangely enough I had never been to Rugby from the A5 side, so I had a look at the map. The first route involved the sharp left turn at the bottom of Kilsby by 'The George'. With the way the four-wheeler was rolling I opted for the next one - the A428. We had gone down that about a mile when without warning up came a sign '12ft 6in bridge 200 yards ahead'. Reverse gear for about half-a-mile to a nice hard farm yard to turn round, back on to the A5 and left onto the A427 through Clifton on Dunsmore where I spotted the Police House. Mrs Village Bobby said, "I've never dealt with wide loads before. I'll have to speak to the Sergeant in Rugby. Anyway, my husband has only got an L.E Velocette". Eventually a car arrived and we finally got backed into Rugby depot just at knocking off time.

As we had left from the site when we loaded, we had not drawn a cash advance and were getting a bit short. A request for money caused chaos and finished up with all the office staff turning out their pockets and handbags to produce four lots of night-out money. I managed to borrow a spanner and pliers and found some timber and wire. I took the bump stops off of the four-wheeler and wired some timbers to the chassis to allow about an inch of travel on the springs. The Manager made arrangements with the Police for us to leave at 8.30 next morning. A fitter took us to the digs in the workshop van with an arrangement to collect us at 8.00 the next morning. The digs was called the Silver Grill a café with some bedrooms above.

I woke up at 8.30 and dashed downstairs. The landlady said "The depot's been on, there's no rush, look out of the window". Outside were three or four inches of snow. The fitter finally turned up and took us to the depot. The Manager told us there had been an overnight blizzard and the Police would not let us move. We were to go home on the train and come back when the roads were passable. We got our railway warrants (we were all part of the BTC in those days) and a lift to the station. The announcer said that the train was due in twenty minutes. When we got onto the platform there were tea trolleys all along it. Dave, 'the gannet' fancied a tea and a cake. When we tried to pay, the lady said it was all on B.R. When we got on the train we found out that it was the overnight express from Scotland, which had been caught in a blizzard and stuck in a snowdrift. The refreshments were for the benefit of the hungry passengers.

It was late on Friday afternoon by the time we got back to the depot. We were told to book four hours for the Saturday morning and ring in at mid-day for instructions. When we did, we were told to make our way back to Rugby on Sunday morning to arrive about 11 am. Then to go as far north as possible, so I told George the traffic operator to book us beds in Lichfield.

The lorry park there was big enough and the St Michael's Café right next door. When we got to Rugby there was no answer from the depot and nobody to meet us so we took a taxi. The depot was locked up, but there was a note on the gate saying that the key was with the lady next door. There would be no escort as traffic was light but we were to contact the Police when approaching Lichfield.

The run up the A5 was uneventful. I decided not to use the cut-off beyond Tamworth, to go into Lichfield past the Whittington Barracks, as the roads were narrow. Instead we carried on up the A446. Just outside Lichfield was a long, sweeping left-hand bend. Because so many cars had gone through the hedge the Ministry of Transport had decided to include it in the then experimental super-cambering scheme. This meant that the corner was slightly banked. As the hedge and some bungalows made it a blind bend for traffic coming towards us, I sent Dave round on foot to stop the traffic. Charlie set off with the four-wheeler but as soon as he got onto the bend the whole lot leant over at an alarming angle. Charlie stopped and jumped out - getting a nasty surprise as the cab step was now about 2ft 6 from the ground.

I backed it onto the level bit of road and it came upright with a rush and then stood swaying gently from side to side until it settled. At this moment a very young, very inexperienced WPC arrived in a Mini panda car, she was all they could spare to escort us into the lorry-park. "Could we go a different way?" she asked. "Not really, it would mean reversing back to the A5 as we had not passed any likely turning places and in any case the sun was setting and the loads were unlit, we were only supposed to travel in daylight".

Fortunately, part of the road improvement had been to widen it. I proposed putting one of the eight-wheelers on the nearside as close as the lamp posts would allow, then drawing the four-wheeler alongside it and take them round the bend side-by-side. We put a couple of extra chains over the eight-wheeler's load and off we went.

As soon as they got onto the camber, the four-wheeler lay over and the loads came together with a resounding clang. With Dave and me guiding, they crawled round the bend back onto the level, where the four-wheeler stood up again. The WPC then set off to escort us to the lorry-park. This she did by going up the wrong side of the road with all her lights on and forcing all the oncoming traffic on to the pavement. As we approached the turn into the park she leapt out and regally waved us in. She then came into the cafe for a cup of tea and said that Traffic would send some men at 10.00 next morning.

Duly at 10.00 two motorcyclists arrived. We were going to go north on the A38 then left on the B5016, then right on the A515, left on the A50 and in to Blythebridge where we were to deliver. They said that we could not go via Kings Bromley because we would never be able to make the right turns in the middle of the village. It was a beautifully sunny day as we set off up the A38. Progress was slow, as in those days most of the roads were contra-flow. As soon as we got to a wide bit or lay-by we were pulled in to let the tailback clear. The A515 is very hilly and pretty through the Needwood Forest and there was time to admire the view with long stretches in crawler gear.

Climbing out of Draycott-in-the-Clay there was an almighty bang quickly followed by another. The way my ear was ringing I knew I had a double burst on the offside. We had a roadside conference and decided that by the time the tyre fitter got out to me we would be too late to deliver that day. A decision was made for the escort to take the other three to Barry Brash's place at Checkley and book beds. At the first 'phone (no radios on police bikes in those days) they would arrange for a tyre fitter. Because the trailer did so many overhanging loads it was on 36 x 8 12-ply 'new' tyres. To get new tyres (as opposed to remoulds) on a trailer needed an engineer's authorisation. Thus it would have to be done through

Derby Repair Centre so I sat back and waited, and waited and waited.

Eventually, Kennings arrived. Because the message had been through several hands (or mouths) he had been sent to Draycott on the other side of Derby. Then he was redirected to Draycott-in-the-Moor on the Stoke side of Checkley. Then the police control contacted the escort at home (he had finished his shift) and he was finally directed to the right place. We had to use two jacks in tandem to lift the axle. The promised escort never arrived, and as it was getting near knocking off time for the sun, it was a case of off we go and hope that everyone was looking where they were going! A patrolling police car picked me up and took me past Uttoxeter then I was on my own to the Checkley Rest & Station. I arrived to find the others with tea dripping from their ears, while I hadn't eaten since breakfast.

The escort arrived bright and early giving us an easy ride to Blythebridge where, thanks to their local knowledge, we arrived at the right quarry gate. There was then a cross-country trek along a narrow haul-road to a new part of the quarry. A new spoil heap was being started and the old kiln was going to form a tunnel through it for the internal railway.

The crane was already in position and they wanted the eight-wheelers first. The crane driver asked the weight and I told him - two 15's, a 12 and a 9. His was a very new machine and, after consulting his tables he said he could lift off with us on the haul-road and slew 180 degrees and drop the pieces right in place.

We slung the first load and he took the weight. Immediately klaxons blew, lights flashed and buzzers sounded. The crane driver swore loud and long. It would have to be 'plan B'. He picked up his outriggers and came up close to the lorry. He would have to lift, slew and drop the load on the other side of the crane, then drive round it, lift again and then slew it through 180 degrees and drop it in position. He lifted again slewed to the other side of the crane, and then he luffed out until the buzzer went.

He jumped down and said, "I reckon you're a bit overloaded lads! My crane says that the 15-ton piece weighs **22 ½ tons!** He did the same with each piece and came up with figures of **22 ¼ tons, 15 ½ tons and 12 ¼ tons**. No wonder the four-wheeler had rolled and my tyres burst. It was certainly a tribute to the Bristol's that they never batted an eyelid at 30-plus tons gross. With all the re-positioning of the crane it took a long while to unload. With only one hard road in and out it was a case of waiting until the last one was unloaded before we could get out. I phoned in empty and was told we were all booked into Tunstall, our beds were booked in Stoke and the late fitter would run us to the digs. It was coming on for 7.00pm when we parked up. I'm sure old drivers will remember the digs in Stoke, the Capesthorne Hotel. It was a row of terraced houses. You ate and washed in one house, went into the street and into the house next door to go to bed. The TV room (an innovation in those days) was in another house next door but one.

In the morning, the two eight-wheelers were sent to Richardson's Metallic Tile Works at Silverdale to load for London. The four-wheeler went to 'the Michelin' to load for their Chelsea depot and I loaded crockery in barrels for export via Tilbury Docks. Thus we split up and made our separate ways home. I delivered my load next day and ran into the depot in the late afternoon.

As I passed the workshop I saw the four-wheeler over the pit so I took the bump stops round to be re-fitted. Len, the depot engineer, was just emerging from the pit looking very cross! When he saw me he said, "What the hell have you done to this bloody motor? Charlie says you're responsible. Come and have a look". On the offside, the bottom flange of the chassis was bent up about 45 degrees. On the nearside the flange was folded up almost up to the web and there were two big gouges where it had ridden on the spring bolts! The blocks were still firmly wired on but were lying at peculiar angles. The main leaves of the springs were bent down at the ends where they overhung the second leaf.

Len said, "This is going to have to go to Enfield to be straightened. When Charlie Luckin sees it he will know what's been done, even if we remove the evidence. He's going to make out a misuse report to Mr. Sharpe (the District Engineer) then there will be a court of enquiry and someone will finish up on a disciplinary procedure".

I said, "When a depot manager is on a DP who does he appear in front of? Because the Guvnor authorised me to block the chassis". At this his eyebrows disappeared into his hair. Then he asked what load was on it, I told him, "An A.I (abnormal indivisible) 16 feet high and 11 feet wide weighing 12¼ tons." His eyebrows went up further, he said "Jesus H Christ" and lit up a fag despite already having a lighted one between his fingers! The chassis got straightened and new spring fitted and not another word was said!

That Dodge was an unlucky motor! About three months later Charlie was going to Jurgens for a load of margarine. As he was passing the old Tunnel Cement works a locomotive came on to the ungated crossing and hit it square amidships and bent it like a banana. The crossing keeper had recently been replaced by flashing lights. Charlie said they weren't flashing, and the engine driver swore he had a green light. Nobody made a fuss because Tunnel Cement was a good customer. The Dodge got a new chassis and Charlie got promoted onto a Bristol.

When I next saw the Guvnor I asked how we had done financially on that job as it had taken six days all told, cost two new tyres and repairs to the Dodge. He told me he had gone back to the demolition firm who had arranged the movement and threatened them with a fraud charge for mis-declaring the weight. They said "How much?" and he had said twice the original quote plus the cost of two tyres and the repair. They said "Done, that still comes to half of what Pickfords quoted and they quoted eight days site to site."

So ends the saga of the redundant cement kilns.

An A.E.C. Mercury of the type mentioned in the above chapter, although this load looks to be much lighter. (Photo: DNM Photos)

CHAPTER 11
IN THE PINK

This little story contains some information which I have since been told could be a scam by one of the people involved. Therefore I have left out anything which could identify the place.

I was walking down the yard, when the Guvnor stepped out from between two trailers and fell in beside me. I was the deputy Shop Steward and this meant he wanted an 'off the record' chat. He opened the conversation with "Where the hell is *******?" I told him that it was a village that I knew well. He then asked if I had heard of anyone having a 'greenacre' around there, something that management was being kept in the dark about. I said "Not a whisper. No canteen gossip, nothing in the 'digs'. We finished our stroll in his office, where he showed me a letter. "This was forwarded by City Road, luckily unopened, have a read".

The letter was from an insurance company that had received a claim for replacing four sets of net curtains and the lime washing of a cottage at an address in this particular village. It went on to say that the damage resulted 'from an incident involving one of your vehicles.' and that re-imbursement would be expected from our insurers. In fact BRS insured itself. I promised to see what I could find out and went on my way.

Next day I brought in a load and put the notes into the office. The traffic clerk said "message from the 'old man', see him a.s.a.p." When I went in, he waved two letters, saying, "These came via City Road. It's getting worse". One was from the NFU insurers claiming for 1,000 gallons of contaminated milk 'arising from an incident involving one of your vehicles'. The other was from a river Catchment Board saying that 'contamination of the river had occurred which had been traced to an incident involving one of your vehicles'. Going on to say that 'if on analysis the contaminant proved harmful a prosecution would result'.

The Guvnor said he would have to involve City Road, but, "We would look a lot of idiots if we knew nothing about it". Then he said, "Will you do me a favour? Ask George for a load up that way and have a nose around. We need more information". I said "A load into the area, back empty will do and I'll have a go". I finished up with a load of cartons to a major customer and ran back to the village.

I parked up near the white cottage at the end of the village on the right going south which was now gleaming. I knocked on the door and said to the lady who answered "I'm from British Road Services. You had a problem with one of our lorries and we need some more details to satisfy our insurers. She invited me in, made a pot of tea and got out the home made cakes.

She told me this story. "I was watching the lorries go by out of the window. This BRS lorry came round the bend and a big drum fell off the back. As it hit the road the top popped off and a big plastic bag shot out, slid across the road and hit the bank outside. There was a big cloud of dust that quickly blew away. Anyway, the lorry stopped and the driver got out and came back to have a look. Another lorry stopped and the two drivers dragged the bag, which seemed very full, up the verge and dumped it. They put the drum back on the B.R.S lorry and the driver borrowed a broom off of a tipper driver and swept all the powder that was on the road into the hedge. Then they all went on their way."

"We had some rain that night and when I looked out in the morning, the road was red and so was my grass. Then the postman knocked on my door and said ""What's happened to your cottage?"". When I went outside to look it started red at the bottom, going lighter up to the thatch. When I went into the front room and the front bedroom, I found the curtains were all pink. So I thought that was that powder off the lorry, it blew everywhere and the damp had made it change colour."

"When I went down to the shop I was telling the other women about it and one said, ""You should claim for that. Your cottage will need lime washing and your curtains will need washing or cleaning if it will come out"". I said I know it was a BRS lorry and it came from Grays as I had seen the name on the side. It stuck in my mind, as there are always town names on BRS lorries but I had never heard of Grays. One of the other women said, ""I walked by as the driver was sweeping up. There was an address on the side, City Road, London. It reminded me of Pop goes the weasel"". I got on to my insurance company and made a claim, telling them that the lorry belonged to British Road Services, Grays, City Road, London."

"Two days later a chap knocked on the door and said he had heard about my pink cottage and now his cows were giving pink milk and the M.M.B. wouldn't take it. I showed him where the bag had been dumped, it was empty by this time, but the bank and the water in the ditch were still a bit pink. He worked out that the ditch ran into the stream that went through two of his pastures on its way to the river. He dashed off to move his cows as they drank from the stream! I gave him the address, which I had given to my insurance company. Then the river man came, saying the farmer had sent them so I gave him the address. My heavy curtains cleaned alright, but the nylon nets stayed pink".

So I told her "That's cleared up a lot of the mystery, but what was the driver like? We don't know which vehicle it was". She said "A little fellow, skinny, glasses, dashed about a lot, reminded me of a ferret!" Immediately I thought of Charlie, he of 'Too High, Too Wide and Too Heavy' fame. She confirmed my thoughts; "It was only a small lorry, not one of those in two parts or one with a lot of wheels".

When I got back to the yard I went straight to the Guvnor's office. As I walked in we simultaneously said "Charlie!" I asked how he had found out, as he hadn't got a clue the day before yesterday, he replied "Reggie (the other traffic clerk) was off sick when the letters arrived. He came back yesterday while you were away and I asked him. He said he had had a funny phone call from Charlie. He (Charlie) had loaded smalls and phoned Reg to say he had had a drum fall off. Reg had asked him if it was empty, he replied yes, so Reg told him to get it back on and we would sort it out when he got back. Reg could not make out why he had rung about an empty drum. By the time Charlie got back, Reg was off sick so it wasn't followed up".

At that moment, Charlie was in Bodmin so we had to wait for him to return. When he appeared for his disciplinary hearing, (failing to complete an incident report) the conversation went like this: -
"Did you have a drum fall off?"
"Yes guvnor"
"Did you phone and report it?" "Yes guvnor"
"Did you tell Reg it was empty?" "Yes, guvnor"
"Why?"
"Because when Reg asked me, it was empty"
"Why didn't you tell him that it had been full?" "He never asked, guvnor"
"Do you know how much trouble you have caused?"
"No, guvnor"
"Well I'll tell you. You've ruined a woman's curtains. She's had to have her cottage lime washed. A farmer reckons he had to throw away 1,000 gallons of milk, and, I've had a threatening letter from the River Board. Bob's been off playing 'Sherlock Holmes'"
"Sorry, guvnor"
"Now I've got to explain to City Road why I am employing a prat who can't load a cardboard drum so that it stays on the lorry. What have you got to say for yourself?"
"Sorry guvnor, I do my best"
"Right then. Four days suspension for insecure load, three days suspension for failing to report an accident and damage in transit"

"Thank you guvnor, very reasonable under the circumstances"

"One other thing. When you get downstairs Bob will show you how to tie a barrel strangler. Practice it while you're suspended and say a little prayer that the drum wasn't full of cyanide crystals".

Fortunately, the drum was full of a water-soluble pigment for making coloured ink. This incident occurred before the epic journey to Stoke and was the reason that Charlie was only driving a four-wheeler.

How it used to be in the '50s. All kinds of loads were carried on all types of lorries. Traffic levels were relatively light on the main trunk roads. This was the A1 at Stangate Hill. (Photo: The Ratcliffe Collection)

CHAPTER 12
LIFE AFTER BRS

Then came six months on the dole; the only firms that would take on a driver sacked by BRS were the sorts of firms that I would not want to work for. Then, by a stroke of luck, just as my earnings related benefit was running out, a night job came up with Neale's of Dagenham, which had a detachment at the Ford Tractor Plant at Basildon. This was with a very small Ford D-series four-wheeler collecting and delivering urgent parts to Heathrow Airport and the main line railway stations.

I was sent for this job by the Labour Exchange, but found out on going for the interview that I had known the Manager for many years when he was a driver.

R. J. B. Neale of Dagenham was founded as a result of an accident. Reg Neale was employed by Ford and was badly injured in an accident, which left him with a crippled leg. He bought a lorry with his compensation money and Ford gave an undertaking to always find work for it. From this he built up his fleet, mainly working for Ford's. At one time he had a couple of eight-wheelers although the bulk of his fleet was always Fords, mostly bought second-hand from the Ford and Briggs Bodies' fleets.

When Ford's tractor operation came to Basildon, Neale's quickly set up a detachment, bringing many of the ex-Briggs Thames Traders. These were the world's worst starters. In the winter everybody concentrated on getting one going, then using this to tow all the others! The Lorry Park was shrouded in an eye watering blue fog.

Neale's stewards negotiated one of the 'Sick Pay' for drivers' schemes. Not long afterwards Frank Godier went into hospital to have a lung removed due to cancer. Reg was adamant that the insurers should not pay out. The insurance policy carried a clause excluding "accidents and illness existing at or before the start of the policy". Reg argued that cancer did not come on overnight and that Frank must have had it before the policy started. A real old-time haulier!

Reg had three sons, none of who were interested in transport, so when he decided to retire he sold up. The fleet Transport Manager, the Basildon manager and the traffic clerk pooled their redundancy money and bought up part of the fleet to form Ross Roadways (named after Barry Ross the fleet manager). This is still doing some of the work previously done by Neale's. When I drive past the plant, now owned by New Holland, I often see my old mate Mick Connolly sitting in the queue waiting to load tractors; he is now literally a greybeard.

Reg Neale made the national press and received a Royal Humane Society Award for saving a drowning man in Ramsgate Marina despite the handicap of his crippled leg and advancing years.

Incidentally, Neale's had some special semi-low loading four-in-line trailers built and was the first company to be able to deliver tractors 'to the ground' under their own power. A vital adjunct at Felixstowe, which had no banks and where an old 40ft trailer minus wheels had been used as a makeshift unloading ramp.

This brought me into contact with Mortons (BRS) Limited which also had a detachment in the Tractor Plant. The Manager there was my old Superintendent from Grays. Morton's had recently established a depot at nearby Pitsea and when it won a contract to deliver spares for the Rootes Group on a nation-wide basis, the southern centre was established at Pitsea. When the staff was being recruited, my old friend offered me a night trunk job. First this had to be approved by BRS headquarters as I had previously been 'removed from service'. With BRS this was a kind of second-class sacking and meant that you were not out forever. Fortunately the BRS Group Staff Officer, Harry Osborne, was a friend and sometime adversary with whom I had been dealing over the past eight years, so I was in again. Dick had left BRS with some acrimony.

As he said to me "If Len had still been in charge instead of Coles, you would have got a slapped wrist and still been at Grays and I wouldn't have felt compelled to leave".

Morton's was a very old company, 1866 according to my friend John Mollett. Horse drawn coal merchants in the beginning. The Managing Director, Eric Shortland, used to tell of how they made up and sold John Innes potting compost in the summer when the coal trade was slack, this continued right up to the acquisition by the Transport Holding Company (T.H.C.) in 1966. Its acquisition was a voluntary one, like that of George Read's from the Forest of Dean. At the time we in 'Red BRS used to say, "They have seen the light and surrendered".

Once back in the BRS fold, I quickly got re-involved in Union activities. The Shop Steward at the time was Billy Rogers, who wrote the most beautiful Gothic script. Even a quick note from Bill was a work of art. His successor, John Morris, eventually became General Foreman and then left Morton's to become Manager at the newly opened Basildon depot of White Arrow (the home delivery arm of G.U.S.) whose workers I also organised.

During my time representing Morton's men I experienced an unprecedented event. We had all been called to the H.Q. at Rowley Road (Coventry) for a management report on the progress and future of the company. The General Manager was in the middle of his talk on the company's finances when in came two old friends; Bill Webster and Harry Osborne. They called Mr. Mousley into his office and we never saw him again. After a while, Bill Webster (BRS Staff Officer) came out and went to the blackboard and announced "Mr. Mousley is no longer with the Company, I will be taking the chair for the rest of the meeting". Apparently, so it was alleged, some of his other business activities resulted in a conflict of interest with his BRS duties. A very senior manager being more or less publicly sacked in the middle of a meeting was unique.

The job, which brought Morton's to Basildon, was a contract with the Ford Motor Company to move material between Basildon and Harwich for shipment to the Antwerp plant. Tractor gearboxes and back axles were machined and assembled in Antwerp from castings, forgings and brake assemblies supplied from the UK, while all the engines (and later, cabs) were built at Basildon. The Antwerp plant took other miscellaneous material from British suppliers while the Basildon plant took such items as seats, front axle beams and certain specialised castings from Continental vendors.

All the material was carried in standard stillages called ZE35s and Ford's had worked out that a full load of these in a standard trailer left too much space down the sides and an unused bit at the back. As the shipper charged by the square foot, Morton's had to supply 95 tilt trailers 7' 4½" wide and 31' 4" long in unwritten Ford blue. Anyone who has used the A12 between Chelmsford and Colchester must have followed or been passed by one (nobody ever passed them!). When Morton's took over the job in 1968 it was being done by Spurling's with Leyland Super Comets and van trailers and Morton's recruited most of the ex-Spurling drivers, who after four years knew every inch of the road. Given the superior power and handling of the Ergomatic Mandator which Morton's supplied there was no holding them! The Mandators were delivered to Basildon direct from Southall, and carried fleet numbers W490 to W494 (KKV 15-19F) the last being scrapped in late 1979 after extensive use as a slave tractor. These units were double-manned and did two round trips to Harwich on each shift covering 472 miles each day and had done about 600,000 miles when they were withdrawn from service, nearly all "flat out" miles at that! The engine out of W493 was fitted in the BRS Rescue A.E.C. Mammoth Major recovery which featured in Rescue ads.

Rootes built and re-conditioned all the TS3 engines at Maidstone and my job was to take a load of these to the Spares Centre (the old Singer works) in Coventry Road, Birmingham and bring back a load of worn out ones to go back to Maidstone. My day shunter was another former Grays driver who had been 'caught' in the same way as I had been. The wagon was a Commer two-stroke artic. (SRW 12H) and I was back on the Ml in the inevitable cloud of sparks. This job went nicely for a year, in which time I renewed a lot of old friendships with trunk drivers from my early BRS days.

However, Rootes became Chrysler (UK) and because of problems over the German licence to manufacture the TS3 its production was discontinued, as was the trunk. While on the Rootes trunk I had two disasters. The gearbox went on the two-stroke and the fitters replaced it with one out of a 'scrapper'. When I got on the Ml I found out it was a 5-speed with no overdrive. I thought no more about it until I was half way up Kings Head Hill at Chingford coming home, when the engine stopped. It had run out of diesel, the increase in fuel consumption meant a full tank would no longer do a round trip. I was passing a parked car and with no vacuum in the brake I couldn't properly get it into the kerb. When the rush hour started the traffic jam stretched back to Enfield Town and caused a problem where Southbury Road crossed the A10. Eventually, a Met. Traffic Land Rover came to investigate having followed the jam. The crew put their towrope on me and towed me to a wide bit, - fourteen tons up a 1-in-12.

Not long after, the old unit went and we got a brand new one with a Perkins 6.354 engine, which had only about two-thirds the power of the two-stroke. On the second night I picked up an Arlington's plate driver at Ponders End. He was on his way to Leyland and was hoping to pick up a Sutton's changeover wagon at the Malt Shovel. I was only carrying empty spares cages weighing about 2 tons, but when I got on the M1 there was a head wind. I soon realised they should have been sheeted (a load of holes creates a lot of drag), I was only making about 35mph. Approaching the Blue Boar I was an hour late and the 'plater' said he would get off and catch the Ribble coach as the Sutton's would be all gone.

When I reached Knightlow Hill there was a lot of debris on the road. There was the stump of a telegraph pole about 4' high, sticking out of the verge and about 10' above, it the last 6' of the pole hanging on the wires. No sign of wreckage so I carried on. As I got to the Newsome's roundabout on the Coventry by-pass I was catching up on a London Carriers 32-tonner, I thought that odd as I was over an hour late, but that was the place I usually caught him. We both stopped at the Warwick Road lights. The lights changed and he immediately started to pull away from me, just then I noticed a running figure on the pavement. When I looked back to the road, London Carriers had stopped; I pulled out much too late and hit the offside corner of his trailer with the nearside of my cab. The debris stopped flying and I looked at the nearside of my cab, the dashboard was pushed back to the back of the passenger seat with the cushion folded in between. That 'plater' was a very lucky man. I finally found my glasses, undamaged behind the driver's seat. The dripping blood signalled a 2" cut in my forehead. I was hauled off to the Coventry Hospital for a bit of embroidery.

In the casualty department were a man and a woman both in a right mess lying on trolleys. When the nurse was sewing my head, she told me they were from an RTA at Ryton and were so full of alcohol they could not be treated. This explained the debris I had seen.

Once I was done, the hospital phoned the Coventry depot and Johnny Gibbs, the night foreman collected me. He told me that my nice new unit, which had done just 1,012 miles was a write off, the chassis behind the cab was bent down and nearly touched the ground. He had arranged for a London man from BRS Parcels (next door) to wait for me. He dropped me at Scratchwood where I found a driver from Lewco's who was going to Walthamstow. He dropped me at Ferry Lane and before I could stick my thumb out a bakers van pulled up, he was going to Southend. When I told him my story he said he would go via the A13 instead of the A127 and drop me by my home. By 06.30 I was in bed. When I got up at 14.00 my wife told me that Arthur Bond (the day foreman) had called round about 09.30 (no 'phone in those days) to tell her I had been in an accident and no one knew when I would be home. She had said to him "I hope he's home now, otherwise I've been sleeping with a stranger!" which rather confused poor old Arthur. I got a night off, as they hadn't got another motor.

Back at work the night after, I stopped on the Ml Blue Boar and saw the London Carriers driver. He said to me "You were lucky mate, I was held up for an hour by an accident at Knightlow. Did you see that telegraph pole? A Jag did that, he hit it about 8ft from the ground". I told him I had seen the couple at the hospital. He told me they were both dead and he would have to go to the inquest.

I asked why he had stopped and he told me he had seen what he thought was a girl walking down from the lights. After I had hit him he found out it was a longhaired youth (my running figure). His trailer was 'written off', it had lozenged about 3'. We both went to court in Coventry. I got fined £5 for having the accident. He got fined £10 for causing it! The depot got another old two-stroke as a replacement; it pulled even better than 12H! Not long afterwards the trunk was withdrawn.

There were no driving jobs vacant, but Morton's had just won a contract for moving tyres from Goodyear at Wolverhampton to the tractor plant. These came down in racks, standing on edge while Ford's were geared up to handle wheels and tyres laying flat. I got the job of unloading them from the trailer, taking them out of the rack and stacking them in piles of six and running them into the plant on a slave trailer. The tyre job for Goodyear had been started with an A.E.C. Mandator (W644) but the peculiar airflow around the load caused a partial vacuum in front of the Mandator's radiator, and with it, severe overheating problems. It was decided to experiment with a Volvo F88 on lease hire. This experiment was so successful (604,000 miles in three years without a single breakdown) and the price so reasonable that these replaced the Mandators, as they became life expired. The company tried some Guy Big J's but the rear suspension could not cope with the roll propensity of the narrow trailers. These were often loaded to the roof. The job also involved solo running when shipments got out of balance, the Guy's bounced so badly that two drivers developed back trouble in a very short time.

Eventually a vacancy arose on the general haulage side and I was back up the road with an A.E.C. Mandator with a small engine (AV760). This was a financially good time as Morton's had maintained its pre-acquisition revenue sharing scheme. Most of the work was Ford orientated, tractors outward and materials from Ford's suppliers' back.

We did a job taking cylinder block castings to Lye for heat treatment, which was done in 100-ton lots involving five wagons. Now most of the 'General' drivers were youngsters with Scammell 'Crusaders' and Cummins-engined Guy's, flying machines as they thought. I was called all kinds of devious old sods as, although I left before them, they always passed me when I was having breakfast in the Blue Boar (I always tried to park the wagon where they could see it!). Lo and behold, when they arrived at Lye there I was, quite often unloaded, while their tongues were hanging out for the want of a cup of tea. Even this never quite convinced them that the A45, Five Ways and Mucklow was a better route than the Ml, M6 and M5 route. Although one did have the good grace to admit that once he got past 'Chrysler Spares' he would not have a clue as to which way to go! This head start enabled me to get into Garrington's at Bromsgrove and collect the load which had been standing ready overnight, and get back to Basildon the same day. This not only earned bonus on two lots of revenue, but also a 'bonus night out' for 300 miles and back to base, much better than all the hassle of a dodgy one!

When I left the plant in 1981 all the six-cylinder blocks and heads were coming from West Germany. These had already been stress relieved, sand-blasted; red leaded and were of better quality than those from the Dagenham foundry. The reject rate was about 2% and the vendor paid the cost of machining up to the point where the flaw was discovered. The four-cylinder blocks came from Dagenham often warm from the mould, in the black and only roughly fettled. They had to go to Lye for stress relief and suffered a rejection rate of about 35%, faults coming to light at the cylinder boring stage, which was among the last of one hundred and forty-two operations. Dagenham only credited initial supply cost so it was no surprise to me that the closure of the Dagenham Foundry was at that time imminent.

During the '70's the pace was hotting up and drivers no longer had time for the skylarks, which produced the characters of the old days. There was one driver who had a 'girl-friend' who lived just outside Coventry. No matter where he went in the British Isles it was always via Coventry. Another would give you his delivery notes and say; "Do you know that one?" You would pick a landmark and give him directions and off he went. It was a long time before I realised he could not read or write, but had a phenomenal memory for directions.

One of the Ford FLT drivers was a Cork man, who came to Dagenham as a very young man with his parents. His Granddad was a member of De Valera's IRA pre-partition, he was a very interesting man to talk to, your typical Irish philosopher. While I was on 'days' I met Wally Wharmsby who came every day from Kentish Town BRS with a load of smalls. Wally had started with Carter, Paterson as a 'monkey' boy on a horse van (he swung on the rope on the back!) and eventually drove his own horse van before converting to motors. He had also worked for Bouts, Tillotson at Waterden Road before it became Stratford Parcels.

There was one real nut, a prodigious drinker, Peter. He would go into a busy pub with three mates and crouch under the bar. His mate would order four pints, as the barmaid got the glass for the fourth one, his mate would give him a nudge and he would pop up, grab a pint, crouch down again and drink it. The barmaid would put down the pint she was pulling, which only made three so she would go for another glass and the process would be repeated. It had been known for him to have four empty glasses on the floor! His mate has only paid for four, which were still on the bar and the barmaid none the wiser! He had a saying "Terrible night in the digs, belching, spitting and farting--- and that was only me".

Morton's also had a depot in the old military transit camp on the outskirts of Harwich. This had its own manager and a small staff of drivers. One of the Harwich men was on his way into London with what some called the 'jinx' motor. Its fleet number was W643 and the registration number was 436, both of which add up to 13. Going up onto the Barking Flyover, he was hit head on by a tipper. The eastbound traffic had stopped; the tipper driver could not, so pulled out right into Doody's path. Not only was the front of the cab stove-in, but also the turntable became detached from the chassis and the trailer came into the back of the cab.

Anyone familiar with the Ergomatic cab will know that behind the driver's seat in the offside corner is a space. It was into that space that Doody was packed. It took so long to cut him out that the Harwich manager, Jim Saunders had time to drive from Harwich to the scene before he was released. He was badly injured, the worst being his left leg, which was broken in several places. The last time I saw him he had a stiff leg and a bad limp and was working as a trailer checker.

Examination of the vehicle revealed that there was a major manufacturing fault in the fifth wheel sub-frame. On each side of the frame there are two plates that stick up, the tops are radiused out to accept the sleeves for the turntable trunnions. The points of the plates had been tack welded to the sleeves, but the run of weld to secure the sleeves to the plates had been omitted. The unit had run tens of thousands of miles with the fifth wheel held on by eight ¼" tacks, but they could not sustain the force of the unit being stopped dead.

Eventually a vacancy occurred for a driver on the Ford contract. I joined the job at about the same time as the Volvos and soon learnt the road and developed the knack of getting the trailer up on two wheels in the appropriate places. I learnt some time later that I had disappointed the old hands; they ran a book when a new driver came on the job on how long it would be before he tipped one over trying to keep up with them! My feel for high loads from my furniture van days and the high loads of soap powder at Grays certainly stood me in good stead.

This job was fairly uneventful, although I did find time to fight a campaign to keep the all-night cafe at Marks Tey open. The Bungalow had been there since 1938, but the newly moved in neighbours found it too noisy. I am sorry to admit that I lost that one and a valuable facility went from the A12.

I was involved in a spectacular accident outside The Bungalow. The lorry-park was full and I had to back in. About three quarters of a mile away I could see some headlights. I pulled across the road and backed in. I was in all but the unit, when the headlights resolved into a car coming towards me at about 60mph. I could reverse no faster and I watched it drive unchecked into my side.

It was like one of these TRRL slow motion films. I watched the air tanks fly off the Volvo, then the bonnet of the car folded and the front collapsed. As the windscreen broke I saw the head and shoulders of the driver come out through the windscreen opening. He was taken away semi-conscious, one of the other drivers who helped get him out said he smelled like a distillery! Morton's eventually got a letter from the police saying that I was not to blame, but no action was being taken against the other driver. The owner of The Bungalow, who was a good friend, later found out that there had been a big do at the hotel in Marks Tey, which had been attended, by most of the county's dignitaries.

In mid-1975 Essex got a new Chief Constable, he was a speed fanatic. You could have bald tyres and a candle in a jam jar for a tail light so long as you kept below 40. I collected two endorsements in quick succession, one at two in the morning on the motorway standard bit of the A12. I had never heard of a trunk driver getting "done" for speeding in the middle of the night! But the local police were hot on speeding and the Volvo F88 was the motor to encourage it! With a third endorsement looming up, I took advantage of a row between one of the night shunters and a Ford foreman, to get off the road.

My mate on this job was one of the ex-Spurling men, who had been taken off the road on disciplinary grounds. Between us we knew more about building tractors than the Ford foreman did! We knew which bit went where and if spares were short, where on our trailers they could be found. We had a first class working relationship with the Ford staff and were often treated as Ford employees.

We arrived for work one night to find, the Ford Materials Handling Manager waiting for us. They had a batch of gearboxes rejected, Antwerp had managed to get a trailer on a ship bound for Felixstowe, and the load had to be available for the start of the next day's shift. My mate and I tossed up and I lost so off I went. When I got to Felixstowe the trailer had just been landed, when I got to the gate I could not get out, as HM Customs had not released it. I found the HMC duty officer, to be told that he could not release it because the necessary documents had not been lodged. The only way he could let it go was for the owners (Ford) to lodge a cheque with him covering the retail value of the load plus VAT. He got on to his oppo. at Harwich who looked up a similar load and said, "about £150,000 should cover it". I 'phoned Ford's Manager and got him out of bed, he got the bank manager out of bed to issue a certified cheque drawn on his own account. It was collected by motorbike courier and run up to me. The courier duly arrived in about an hour, smelling of hot engine and hot Ferodo the cheque was given to HMC and I got the gate pass.

There was a regular driver, Albert, who drove for Worton's of West Bromwich. He got an industrial injury pension for deafness caused by the noise in the cab of Guy Big J's. He came into our office one night and said, "There's a bird doing the CAV-Lucas pump delivery. You want to get round to Receiving early tomorrow morning and watch her perform. Crafty cow tried to get me to back her motor into Bay 5 (a very tricky 'well' bay). I told her to piss off, she was probably paid more than me". The next morning we parked our unit and sat and watched. She eventually pulled up, put the cab light on, did her lipstick, fluffed up her hair and undid the top button on her blouse. She then went onto the bank. The forklift drivers were all round her like dogs with two cocks. There was no one waiting so she had to back it in herself, what a dog's breakfast. After a week of " knock backs " from other drivers she never came again.

That Bay 5 also figures in the next incident. As I said it was a "well bay" which means that the bank went all around it at trailer floor level. It had a 12' doorway immediately narrowing to 9' 3". As you backed down the slope into it, on your left was a retaining wall with a rail on top. To your right was a stretch of wall about 15' long then the doorway to Bay 4. One night my mate and I were out on the lorry-park getting trailers.

Jimmy Phillips the Receiving Foreman came hurtling up on the bank bike. "Can one of you come and put a trailer on the bank? The Foundry has sent a load of blocks down on one of Reader's. Everybody's there waiting and he's been trying for half-an-hour to get in Bay 5. He's in such a state Alfie Kench (the Night Manager) is afraid he will have a heart attack".

My mate Jack said to me "You go, you're better at Bay 5 than me" so we put Jim's bike on the unit and off we went. When we got to the Receiving, there was this artic, the unit was completely hidden in a haze of blue smoke. It was perfectly backed onto the wall between 4 and 5. Jim said "He's had it there three or four times, he's even had it best part into 4, but we can't do it over the back, the floor is too weak".

I got into the old 'D' series, it was red hot, and the clutch had had such a hammering it only just made it up the slope. Once I'd lined it up right, it went straight into the bay in one go. When I got out everyone was still there, Night Manager, Night Superintendent, General Foreman, and QC Foreman. The four forklift drivers were on to it in a flash, getting the load off. As I walked round to my unit the Reader's driver came over, his exact words to me were "Flash bastard, you did that to show me up".

Eventually Ford had a new receiving building and warehouse. It had the latest high-speed doors, which were just gigantic roller blinds; they opened or closed in three seconds. The procedure was to stop at the pedestrian door, press the button, back in, then walk over and press the button again. One night, I had opened the door and was backing in. This involved putting the trailer wheels about 3" from the guard post. I was concentrating on this, when the light went, by the time I realised that some one had shut the door I had backed right through it. No one ever owned up to pressing the button.

In early 1979 Ford was anticipating an increase in gross vehicle weights and wanted a new fleet of 40' trailers, which could be of standard size as the whole Ford Empire, was changing over to a standard metric size stillage, which would not fit the old narrow trailers. Morton's could not get a renewal of the original long-term contract. Hessenatie, a Belgian company, provided a fleet of new trailers. When the Harwich run was lost, the Plant Manager insisted that Morton's continued to provide the shunters.

In September '81 Ford were seriously hit by the recession and in looking to cut costs wanted to employ shunters on an 'as required' basis. Our expertise was therefore no longer required as the pressure was so much reduced that there was time to trace obscure parts through the paperwork. A local one man band was prepared to accept the new terms and undercut our price by about 50% and so ended Morton's long association with Ford. Strangely enough, this was just at the time when Midlands BRS were negotiating its centralised vendor movements operation.

I spent from September 1975 to September 1981 shunting inside the tractor plant. We were a happy little band. Jack and I worked with two regular night shunters from Neale's, Eric and Tony who were banger racing fanatics. For a time they were supplemented with two extra drivers. One was a convicted armed-robber, and the other had done a long stretch for attempted murder. There were two regular FLT drivers (Ford always called them Hi-Lo drivers) and two checkers, who worked rotating shifts. Thus we all knew one another very well and co-operated in getting and keeping each other out of trouble. When my mate and I left, we got a personal letter of appreciation from the General Foreman - the only one in my working life.

The motor spares operation was still running at Pitsea, now for Talbot. Some astute observation by the local police had just created three vacancies. The most senior day shunter and my mate were offered jobs driving delivery rounds with Mk.1 Dodge 'Commando's while I was offered the job of Night Supervisor. I was a little unwilling to take this at first, but a visit from the General Manager from Coventry headquarters considerably improved the financial terms offered so I had a go.

The two loaders got in at 7pm and loaded bulk loads from the yard or which came on the early trailer from Birmingham. I got in at 10pm as the urgent spares trailer arrived from Birmingham. The first job was to sort out some 1,200 notes into rounds and then into dealers and tally these up onto waybills. Then we had to count all the individual items on to the four-wheelers and I had to supervise the loading of heavy items such as engines, gearboxes, pallets of oil or batteries or maybe a 5cwt case of sparking plugs.

There were a few bits of excitement on that job. One of the delivery drivers had come to us from being an HGV Class 1 driving instructor with a local HGV driving school. When my loaders went home, their last job was to put the bulk load artic up the middle of the shed, thus blocking in all the four-wheelers. When this driver was in first, he always came into the office and asked me to back out the artic, to quote him "When I back it out I always get in a mess!" This same driver was doing the Kent run. As he was going down the A2 he heard a bang and his engine started to die. As he was pulling off the road he looked in his mirror and saw an enormous pile-up happening behind him. When he looked round his motor he found that he had run over and thrown up half of a mono-leaf spring. This had gone through the bottom of his diesel tank, dropping 40 gallons of fuel on the road.

In the early hours of one morning, I was chatting on the CB when there was an enormous flash and a bang. I had a look outside and could see nothing. When I got back inside, a security guard on a building site a mile away called me (he and I talked regularly) to ask what was happening down my way. He had also seen the flash; the police car crew to whom he was giving a 'cuppa' had been called to a suspected plane crash on the marshes. Then the police car arrived, "Had I had a vehicle in, in the last half-an-hour? It dawned on me that the recovery artic. had come in while I was talking and I hadn't seen the fitter (we were part of BRS Rescue). When we went to look, it was pulling a low loader trailer on which sat a Volvo F88.

This had a CB aerial on a mag. mount fitted to the cab roof. From the base of this there were burn marks running right down the side of the cab and front wheel to the trailer. The constable told me that it had hit the overhead cable at the level crossing and put the railway out of action.

We had a similar incident when Ford started fitting radios to its tractors. The first one to be brought in for storage (by Neale's) had the cab top aerial touch the overhead. The flashover burned out all the electrics, burst the tyres and welded the front wheel rims to the locating pockets on the trailer.

Early one Tuesday morning I heard a wagon pull-up at the gate, it was from Midlands BRS. The driver asked if I could get him out of trouble, he had done a "jack-knife turn" in the tractor plant and torn an airline off on a rope hook. I fixed him up with one from a unit under repair, and sent him on his way rejoicing. Funny thing was, I had watched him win the Lorry Driver of the Year on the preceding

Sunday!

On the way into work one night I was stopped by a Coventry driver. He had put a load into our yard and picked up an empty and now he could not get over the level crossing and up the slope to the main road. Beyond our yard was the infamous Pitsea Tip, someone coming from there had covered the road with some kind of soapy slurry. I crept down very carefully and phoned the police from the yard. The police called the fire brigade, who spent half an hour with a high-pressure jet washing the road clean.

Sometimes in the early hours people turned up with odd requests. A Siddle Cook's wagon pulled in and the driver asked if he could back his trailer into our shed so that he could look round it. When we had a look, the back twenty feet of the chassis, the springs, axles and under run were all bare gleaming metal as though they had been sandblasted. There was liquid dripping through his floorboards. We hosed down our floor, which left patches of bone white concrete.

I got out our steam cleaner and left him to it. He later told me he had picked up a load of 45-gallon drums from Middlesborough. These had been imported from Holland for disposal in the Pitsea Toxic Tip. He had noticed the 'leakers' when he unloaded. His was the first of several loads, and we got the regular midnight visits from other drivers with trailers in the same state to wash down. I always wondered about the motors that had followed these loads on the way down.

It reminded me of an incident in '61. A tanker from Graesser Chemicals with a load of phenol had a foot valve creep open just a fraction. The A45 from the 'Malt Shovel' to the 'Ace' at Weedon smelt of carbolic for three nights. Writing this brought to mind another incident when a Newport BRS driver had a leaking sack of nails at the back of his load. All the tyre firms in the Chepstow and Gloucester areas were completely sold out of tyres and tubes. It cost BRS a small fortune.

Once the loaders went at 1.00am I was alone until the day shift arrived at 5.30am. Once a week I did the throughput figures and last week's tacho charts and that was it. As I said earlier at the time I was a CB fan and had permission to erect an aerial which gave me a link with the outside world - just as well for the depot was in the middle of Pitsea marshes over a mile from the main road. I also knit Arran style jumpers and found time to make two jumpers and a cardigan and a full-length ladies coat for my daughter (for which an American woman offered her £200 in the middle of Oxford Street!).

One day we all had an instruction to attend a very special meeting at the depot, no details could be given. The traffic office was fitted out with a TV set and a video recorder. Stan explained that the senior management had made an offer to the Government, for them and all employees to buy the National Freight Corporation. We were then shown a video explaining what was going on and asking us to buy shares in the new concept. The company was even prepared to make a short-term interest free loan. Despite opposition from the TGWU, I thought this is a chance too good to miss. I borrowed the £200 off the firm, another £500 from my son and managed to rake up enough to put in £1,350. This was the best move I ever made, with the phenomenal successes in those early days there were scrip issues and share splits, enabling me to give shares to my children and grandchildren and eventually to pay cash for my house. I still have enough shares to provide an income to supplement my pension.

The people running the show were the same ones I had known for many years. It proved something, which I had said for years. The alleged failings of nationalised industries lay entirely at the feet of the Treasury and its conservative attitudes. Once the transport men were allowed to do their job without tripping over Civil Servants, the people who had been presiding over a large loss became able to turn it into an organisation capable of making vast profits. The City eventually fell over itself to buy shares in it.

On page 87 is a copy of a Telex which those at Pitsea who were wise enough to buy shares asked me to send to Peter Thompson.

In September 1982 the company sent me to Aston University in Birmingham for two weeks to get my CPC (which I did). In June 1983 the Peugeot management insisted that Talbot put the job out to tender. Swift's of Birmingham undercut Morton's by about £120,000 and so, on 19th November 1983 Mortons severed a thirteen-year relationship with Rootes/Chrysler/Talbot. The following week I severed a thirteen-year relationship with Mortons (BRS) Ltd. and twenty-two years six months with BRS (less six months in the middle).

With Basildon's unemployment running at about 22% following closure of the Carrera's factory things were not looking too good. One of the ex-Morton's drivers answered an advert for a 'mature very experienced long distance driver able to sheet and rope'. At the interview, the Manager complained about the 'heavy footed young drivers who blew engines up and shot loads', the next day he got a letter saying he was 'too old' - he was just 44.

A Morton's Commer artic. with a load of components. Rootes of course owned the Commer marque, so Morton's used vehicles made by its customer. (Photo: Peter J. Davies)

```
XXXXXXXXXXXXXXXXXXXXXXXXXXXXXXXXXXXXXXXXXXXXXXXXXXXXXXXXXXXXXXXXX
XXXXXXXXXXXXXXXXXXXXXXXXXXXXXXXXXXXXXXXXXXXXXXXXXXXXXXXXXXXXXXXXX

XXXXX   XXXXX   XXXXX  XXXXXX      XX      XX    XX  XXXXX  XX      XX
XXXXX   XXXXX   XXXXX  XXXXXX      XX      XX    XX  XXXXX  XX      XX
XX  XX XX   XX XX  XX   XX  XX     XX      XX    XX XX   XX XX XX XX XX
XX    CC    XX XX  XX   XX  XX     XX      XX    XX XX XX     XX XXX
XX     XX   XX XX  XX   XX  XX     XX      XX    XX XX XX      XXXXX
XX  XXX XX  XX XX  XX   XX  XX     XX      XX    XX XX XX       XXXX
XX  XXX XX  XX XX  XX   XX  XX     XX      XX    XX XX XX    XX XX XX
XX   XX XX  XX XX  XX   XX  XX     XX      XX    XX XX XX    XX XX   XX
XXXXX   XXXXX   XXXXX  XXXXXX      XXXXXXX XXXXX     XXXXX   XX      XX
XXXXX   XXXXX   XXXXX  XXXXXX      XXXXXXX XXXXX     XXXXX   XX      XX

XX      XX XXXXXXX XX      XX      XXXXXX   XXXXX  XX   XX XXXXXXX
XX      XX XXXXXXX XX      XX      XXXXXX   XXXXX  XX   XX XXXXXXX
XX      XX XX  XX  XX      XX      XX  XX XX    XX XXX  XX XX  XX
XX      XX XX  X   XX      XX      XX  XX XX    XX XXXX XX XX  XX
XX      XX  XXXXXX XX      XX      XX  XX XX    XX XX XX XX XXXXXXX
XX  XX  XX XXXXXXX XX      XX      XX  XX XX    XX XX XX XXX XX  XX
XX  XX  XX XX      XX      XX      XX  XX XX    XX XX  XXXX  XX  XX
XX XX XX XX XX      XX      XX      XX  XX XX    XX XX   XXX  XX  XX
XXXXX   XXXXXXX XXXXXXX XXXXXXX    XXXXX   XXXXX  XX      XX XX XXXXXXX
XXXXXX  XXXXXXX XXXXXXX XXXXXXX    XXXXX   XXXXX  XX      XX XX XXXXXXX

XXXXXXXXXXXXXXXXXXXXXXXXXXXXXXXXXXXXXXXXXXXXXXXXXXXXXXXXXXXXXXXXXX
XXXXXXXXXXXXXXXXXXXXXXXXXXXXXXXXXXXXXXXXXXXXXXXXXXXXXXXXXXXXXXXXXX
```

WE' VE SHOT THE SHOP STEWARD, TOPPED UP THE TANKS, CHECKED THE TYRES
OIL AND WATER, AND CLEANED THE WINDOWS. SO KEEP TO THE NEAR-SIDE AND
KEEP YOUR ELBOWS IN. WE' RE GOING OUT TO EARN SOME DIVI.

BEST WISHES TO PETER THOMPSON, THE DIRECTORS AND ALL OUR FELLOW
SHARE HOLDERS.

THE SHAREHOLDERS AT MORTON'S (BRS) LTD., PITSEA, ESSEX.

ATTN:

THE SHAREHOLDERS
99242 MORTON G
826803 NFCBED G

25.2.82   10.55AM   6126

ATTN:

THE SHAREHOLDERS AT MORTONS (BRS) LTD - PITSEA

FROM:

PETER THOMPSON

MANY THANKS TO YOU ALL AT PITSEA FOR YOUR IMAGINATIVE TELEX
WE HAVE PUT AWAY THE CHAMPAGNE, SENT FRATERNAL GREETINGS TO
THE TGWU, ARRANGED FOR INTEREST RATES TO DROP, AND ARE WELL ON
THE WAY TO THE FIRST INTERIM DIVIDEND

REGARDS
PETER THOMPSON
826803 NFCBED G
99242 MORTON G

CHAPTER 13
THE FIRST AGENCY

I had heard about agencies and at the time I was paid off there was one in Basildon advertising for drivers so I went along. Most of its work was in East London so I was put on the books of its Stratford office, right next door to the old fruit and veg. market. I went along to see the manager, Rodney. In the course of our conversation it turned out that he had worked for Tibbett & Britten. I mentioned that I knew that firm when Mr Tibbett and Mr Britten were in charge, I had run on nights with Les Anderson (while I was on Kentish Town) who had pulled one of the very first hanging garment trailers. It transpired that Rodney had been Les's mate when he (Les) was on days.

The first job I did was for Bar Distribution Services, which was a joint operation between BRS and Whitbread's. The depot was in Waterden Road, part of the old Bouts Tillotson depot. The major part had been re-developed from the old Stratford Parcels depot into T&B's high-tech distribution centre. Just across the road had been the depot of R. J. Weeks, one of the pre-nationalisation meat hauliers. I was supposed to drive a six-wheeler but the driver turned up so I was found a day's work as a trouncer. After that I did odd days here and there, nothing memorable.

Then I was sent to Bejam Frozen Foods working out of the Frigoscandia cold store at Chobham Farm, Stratford. This was a bit of a pain as it meant travelling up from Basildon every morning. This was an easy enough job, put a 20' fridge on the bank, wait for the loaders (all agency men) to load it, take it to the lorry park, fill the donkey engine tank with red diesel, and plug the fridge unit into the mains. The last job of the day was to go round and log all the box temperatures and make sure all the units were running. Rodney phoned me one evening and told me that Bejam's had asked for me by name and I was to report there every day. After about a fortnight the manager asked me if I would like a full time temporary job. It was early December and the Christmas rush was in full swing. I was able to negotiate a good pay deal and flexible hours to suit my domestic situation. It was a frantic operation, but finally it slackened off and I was the last casual to be paid off at the end of March.

Bejam's (now part of Iceland) was a weird outfit. An Indian family owned it; the name was the initials of the family members. It had started off supplying freezers retail. Then the shops started to stock some frozen food to put in them. It went rather spectacularly skint. Then it was restarted the other way round. It sold frozen food and would sell you a freezer to put it in. The head office was at Milton Keynes. At the Stratford end it did not seem to own anything and the only full-time employees were the manager, four drivers and two shunters. Everything else seemed to be hired, leased in or self-employed sub-contractors. The manager lived in a caravan parked by the hired Portakabin office.

Bejam hired two cold 'pots' from Frigoscandia. Once the rush was over one was completely emptied and taken off hire. Immediately (late January) the empty 'pot' started to be filled with chocolate Easter eggs. While I was working there I learned something which reinforced my belief in the total inadequacy of warning signs. Outside each store was a huge sign "Absolutely no smoking inside this cold room". I said to the fridge engineer "Why the huge signs? There can't be a hygiene problem, it's minus 22C in there and we are in and out with fork and pallet trucks". He explained that the air being so cold made it denser, thus increasing the oxygen content. When you drew on a fag it burned at a very high temperature and the superheated gas stream could damage your throat and lungs. He demonstrated by taking my fag and walking into the 'pot'. Immediately the end started to glow as though it was being drawn. The notice should have said "Don't smoke in the pot, you could burn your lungs".

As I said, I was paid off so I phoned Rodney to tell him I was available again. He told me he had immediate work, one of the firms I had done a couple of days for had asked for me by name. He went on to say "You won't be on the books long, when people ask for a name, that bloke soon finds regular work".

An impressive heavyweight Luton van body on a Bean 6-wheel chassis operated by a North London company.

At least they had electric lights in those days! (Well some of them did).

CHAPTER 14
HERONFREIGHT

Rodney was proved right. I got a phone call from Stan Newton, we had worked together as drivers and for a period he had been Branch Manager at Morton's. He was now manager for Bailey's of Westbury at its West Thurrock depot. He had a vacancy for a night driver on a parcels operation that was being started, would I like a job?

There is a story against Stan, which I don't think he will mind me telling; it is a warning. He was travelling north on Purley Way driving a Ford D-series. He stopped in the big lay-by near the old aerodrome to use the toilets. When he went to pull away he could not get the handbrake off. They were well known for it. There was an umbrella handle sticking out of the dash, you had to pull it and twist it at the same time to release the ratchet. After several tries it would get wound up so tight you could not move it. Stan adopted the standard procedure and got underneath with a screwdriver to prise the pawl out of the ratchet. He succeeded all too well; the wagon rolled down the slope and ran over him, he'd forgotten to drop the red airline. He has a permanent dent in his head as a reminder.

Bailey's of Westbury Ltd., was set up by Bill (Piggy) Bailey an ex-United Dairies driver. Just after the war there was another Bailey's of Westbury, hay, straw and fodder on muddy mauve eight-wheelers with a huge hayrack over the cab. All the time I worked there I tried to find a connection, the nearest I got was a suggestion that it might have been Bill's Dad. The modern Bailey's became involved with the Heron organisation through the carriage of imported Suzuki motorbikes, which actually came complete in a huge carton. Heron bought out Bailey's to give it an 'in' to road haulage and distribution.

My first contact with Heron goes back to 1949. In those days I serviced an 'O' model Bedford owned by H. E. (Henry) Ronson who traded as Heron Furniture. Henry was a typically small East London furniture maker. He supervised the mill, did a bit of repping and drove the van. As I write I can picture the van, milk chocolate colour with a dark brown heron in flight on the side, the tip of the beak in the top front corner of the Luton, the feet trailing back to the bottom rear corner of the drop well. I first knew Gerald Ronson as a small boy with no seat to his trousers and a runny nose.

Another of Bailey's drivers, Lenny Tappin had the same memory (he had also been a furniture bumper). He mentioned it at the inaugural meeting after the take-over and was persona non grata for the rest of his service. By that time Gerald Ronson was well known. Not only for his petrol stations, Suzuki motorbikes and property empire, (which I was told was founded on the sale of Henry's redundant furniture factory). But for stopping thirty bob (£1.50) from the fiver wages of a filling station girl who had had a fill up and drive away. Later he became even more famous for being a stock market player and guest of HMG!

Bailey's with Heron money bought Greenwood's Transport and the city pages at the time said, "The Sprat buys the Mackerel". Greenwood's was the successor to St. Ives Sand & Gravel and thus was a subsidiary of ARC. It had quite a militant Union organisation in the land of the forelock touchers. Part of the Greenwood's show was a magazine distribution operation at Hoddesdon, with a Union organisation very much in the restrictive (and pricey) style of Fleet Street pre-Murdoch. This did not sit easy with Heron and did not last long.

In this operation was another link with the past. Part of the job was Radio Times. This was originally done by vehicles in Radio Times livery operated by Hellmuth's of Lambeth. In its time it was innovative in using lightweight artics on distribution work. Its WSS Bedfords were very rare animals. According to Ron Copp, an ex-Hellmuth's driver, their Flexion semi-trailers were referred to as 'attachments'. I do love a bit of history.

My invitation to join Bailey's came with the start up of Quick Link. This was a parcels operation with Mercedes 308Ds. Its major traffic was Suzuki motorbike spares, but took on third party work to make it viable. My job was to sort the days' collections, load all those not for our area into one of the vans and run it up to Warboys (near St Ives), unload the lot, reload for our area then do another sort when I got back. A Warboys driver did the same run in reverse. One thing I learnt, is that it is two miles further from West Thurrock to Warboys than it is from Warboys to West Thurrock, largely due to the layouts of the M25/M11 and A604 (A14)/A1096 road junctions. Also that 308's will do 28mpg fully loaded and driven flat out. Another silly little thing, in the eighties there were fourteen pairs of Kestrels between Cambridge and the A127.

After an abortive attempt to set up a hub system at a warehouse near the Saltley Gasworks, made infamous by the miner's strike; the Quick Link operation was wound up in June 1984. Heron worked a 'no-notice' policy. The drivers ran into the depot and were given an envelope containing their P45, two weeks wages and money in lieu of notice and that was it. Gerald Ronson was alleged to have said, "People working notice are never loyal. Pay 'em off and get rid of them". The next morning a contractor came and took the sign down. A minibus full of drivers came and took all the vans away and Quick Link was a memory.

At that time Bailey's was doing a certain amount of general haulage and as I had an HGV licence I was able to transfer on to that side, driving a Leyland Clydesdale (wasn't it nice when motors had names instead of strings of numbers?).

After the buyout at Greenwood's its many large depot sites were transferred to Heron's property division and sold off. Eventually the Bailey, Greenwood and Heron operations were merged to become Heronfreight in September 1985. We were out of haulage and into distribution. Suzuki motorbikes, Zanussi white goods, General Foods, CPC, Lyons Tetley, Alcan Foils and polythene goods, and Tredaire carpet underlay.

West Thurrock became a distribution point for Tredaire. This was brought in 20-ton lots by Curries and Graham Bell of Carlisle to be unloaded into the warehouse by the remaining yardman. By this time the staff was Stan, Jill and Denise (office girls) Richard (yardman) John who drove the T45 with Hiab on the motorbikes, my son Ian and me on the Tredaire. The Tredaire job was generally a very happy job. Most of the carpet people were like the old furniture men, people who got on with people. We took orders, did out of sequence deliveries to get carpet layers out of trouble. Even hid rolls of underlay early in the morning before the shop was open so they could have it first thing. We knew South London, Kent and East Sussex intimately. My son and I were always trying to find obscure routes to get to jobs.

Harris Carpets and Queensway both had large deliveries to warehouses across the road from one another. Mike at Harris's was really pleasant. But John, who was the senior warehouseman for the Queensway Group (he did all the training) was the nastiest, obnoxious and awkward man you could ever imagine. Every furniture, bedding and carpet driver in the country talked about him. Many swore that it was John who had trained the SS and the Gestapo.

Warboys became the break-bulk centre for General Foods, CPC and Lyons-Tetley and sometimes I was sent there on loan to do one of the East Anglian rounds. My furniture days and BRS roaming became useful again; it made me quite unpopular because I would do many of their rounds better than they could do them themselves! The idea was to do the round and then reload for our area for the following day, suddenly my reload wasn't ready until late and the whole operation getting more and more chaotic. There was another change of plan. Stan was made redundant and Jill made Clerk-in-Charge. Richard went and John left to become an insurance man.

The old Clydesdale was scrapped and we got two pre-loaded curtain siders from Warboys overnight. Harris and Queensway had been merged to become Harris-Queensway with its distribution being done from central warehouses by BRS Contract vehicles. We were left with the small carpet shops and various specialist items to supermarkets and the small grocery chains.

Three days into the new set up I had a load for Kent. There was a delivery for ASDA Swanley marked '8.30 am booking' along with twelve other drops down as far as Ramsgate. As we started at 07.00 I was there by about 07.20. When I booked in I was told to park-up round the public car park, they would get to me about 14.00. So I went and did the rest of the load and sent the ½ pallet of ally foil plates and dishes back as undeliverable. The next week on the same day, back came the same pallet by now made up to a full one. I didn't bother with ASDA and went to Ramsgate and worked back in the normal way. I got to ASDA about 16.30. The Receiving Manager went loopy "Where were you at 8.30? I've got no stock on the shelves; I've had people waiting for you all day. You're barred, I don't want you ever delivering to my store again." Then he wouldn't take the pallet so back it went to Warboys.

A couple of days later I was passing the store so I went in to see the Manager and told him I was the envy of every grocery delivery driver in the south of England. Getting barred from ASDA Swanley was equivalent to winning the pools! The pallets came down again on my son's load; he did the drop where it fitted in with the run. He asked why his Dad was privileged in being barred when he wasn't? After that one of the Warboys' subbies always got that drop.

While I was on this job I met the most stubborn man ever. It was Friday afternoon and I went to a grocer's in East Ham with a full pallet of Maxwell House coffee. As I walked in the shopkeeper said, "We don't take in on a Friday, bring it back Monday! Anyway what is it?" So I told him "Maxwell House". He said, "I've been waiting for that, there's none on the shelves, I'm desperate". So I offered to wheel the board up to the door (we had tail lifts and pump tracks) and stack it in for him. "Oh no!! Can't do that we don't take in on Fridays". Back it went to Warboys.

Almost as bad was the Co-op in Gamlingay. I went through to the stock room and said to the woman there "Where's the back door man?" she said "I am the back door person the Co-op is an equal opportunities employer". She told me that there was no goods entrance it all came through the shop, she reappeared with a sack barrow saying "You'll have to bring it through and stack it - women are not allowed to lift and carry".

Tesco's were good deliveries. At that time it had a rule that so long as the store was open it was possible to deliver. Many of the small grocer's were operated by one of the many branches of the Patel family. I had a pallet of Instant Whip and Angel Delight for one at Tilbury. I was very late (about 18.15) having been right over to the Clacton and Walton area. I thought I'd give him a try on the way to the depot. "Would he take a pallet at this time of night?" His exact words to me were "Driver, if you don't deliver it I can't sell it, so I don't get my profit. You're welcome to deliver to me any time the light is on upstairs". This was pretty much the attitude of most small shops.

One Friday afternoon I was having a cuppa with one of my regulars in Sevenoaks; he had a query about a future delivery so I said I would ring Jill and find out. The phone was answered by a male voice, which informed me that Jill had gone home. I knew she was 'expecting' and thought she was ill. I went back to the depot to be met by the Warboys manager. He gave me an envelope and said, "Get your gear out of the motor and take any personal stuff out of the office, this depot is closed". Ian got the same when he ran in. The envelopes contained pay to date, redundancy pay, money in lieu of notice and P45. The 10th October 1986 out of work again.

The South East distribution was done from Warboys for a while, then that was closed, I believe that was taken over by Premier Brands delivery service. Heronfreight then concentrated on Zanussi work from Rownhams (Southampton) and a dedicated Gateway RDC at Bristol. The Suzuki spares had long gone to Securicor. Much later Heronfreight took over from R. J. Simms on the Sainsbury's job at Hoddesdon.

I went back to my old agency, which at that moment were recruiting. I filled in all the forms and was waiting to be interviewed when the Southern Area manager walked through the office. He looked at me and said, "No need for all that rubbish, I'll dig out your old file. Same phone number?" When I had last worked for them he had been a newly appointed operator, what a memory?

A Hellmuth Bedford artic. on the Radio Times delivery contract, mentioned in this chapter.

Underneath the Arches". Hellmuth's haulage yard at Lambeth was typical of premises used by scores of firms in the '40s and '50s, totally unsuitable for today's requirements to comply with Operator Licence conditions.

CHAPTER 15
PARKER MORRIS

Ian had got a job with a paper haulier, Parker-Morris Ltd.; I had only done a couple of weeks with the agency when Ian got me a job with his employer.

Parker Morris was an unusual firm. It was divided into two sections. The blue fleet, which operated in the livery of Finland Transport and exclusively carried the products of a group of Finnish paper mills. The white fleet, so called because of its white painted units, provided additional vehicles for the Finland job and also did some general haulage.

The operation was based in an old chalk quarry at Purfleet, once part of Tunnel Cement. The yard varied between 3" of slurry and more dust than the Sahara Desert depending on the time of year. Working boots had to be removed on the doorstep. Most of the vehicles were elderly to say the least. The policy seemed to be 'run 'em 'til they drop', then cannibalise the scrappers. The replacements were second hand. When I joined the blue fleet consisted of seven ERF B's, two ERF C's and two Seddon Atkinson 400's. The white fleet was four SA 400, about half a dozen ERF Bs. There were also a couple of Bedford four wheelers. I was put on the white fleet and soon got a Seddon Atkinson 400 (Gardner 8LXB), registered VDG 117S. It was old but a good reliable motor, which I tinkered into being quite comfortable. There were some curtain-siders on the blue side, but the biggest majority of trailers were tandem axle flats, with a few tri-axles.

I very quickly learned that once you got two decent sheets, half a dozen good ropes and a set of scotches and a back scotch; you guarded them like the crown jewels. If you had not got a load on wheels over the weekend you carefully hid all your gear or took it home! Some of the flat trailers were sent abroad unaccompanied, hence all the rear lamp lenses, bulbs and airline couplings were removed. Thus the other essential was a stock of bulbs, lenses and couplings. The firm spent a small fortune on these items, which were always going missing. Drivers on the white fleet came and went so quickly, you often did not learn their names.

This turnover of drivers and removal of couplings produced one memorable incident. A driver was instructed to pick up a trailer and deliver it to Edenbridge. Eventually he phoned from Crockham Hill to say that his "brakes had gone". He had managed to stop but there was 'oil' pouring out of the front drums. When the fitter arrived, the 'oil' proved to be the grease from the hub bearings. Further examination showed the airlines still stowed on the A frame. When he was questioned about it back at the yard he said that he knew nothing about putting on couplings, that was a fitter's job. If they weren't there he thought he didn't need them. Needless to say he did not last long!

The majority of the work in my early days with the firm was paper. It came from Purfleet Deep Wharf, Erith Deep Wharf and Convoy's at Deptford. The National Dock Labour Scheme covered the labour on all three. It was no different from the dockers of old with long tea and lunch breaks. Very many hours were spent queuing to get loaded. Nearly as many, queuing to get the paperwork to get loaded.

At Purfleet, the procedure was to park up in the top compound, and then get in the queue of drivers waiting to get to the window. There could be between twenty and thirty waiting. When you finally got into the lobby (most of the queue was in the open). You would find that most of the activity in the traffic office consisted of discussions among the clerks about how their team did last Saturday or how they were going to do next (the change usually came on Thursday morning!). Once of the football was over, the subject became anticipation or post mortem of summer holidays.

George White Ltd. ran this office, which was the haulage arm of Purfleet Deep Wharf. Purfleet and

Erith Deep Wharves along with Convoy's was the wharfage arm of the old Northcliffe Newspaper Empire. Not long before I started, the infamous Wapping dispute had come to an end. When this dispute had started the wharf staffs had a nasty surprise when they found they actually worked for Rupert Murdoch. They were given an ultimatum, keep the paper flowing or else! This dated back to the days of Harold Harmsworth, later Lord Northcliffe. Northcliffe ran a large newspaper empire, including such titles as *The Times* and *The Daily Mail*. He even started *The Daily Mirror* in 1903. Northcliffe was a newspaperman pure and simple. His mother, Geraldine Mary Harmsworth (the park round the Imperial War Museum is named in her memory) was the matriarch of a family of seven brothers. She ordered her second son Harold to give up his safe job with the civil service and take over the business side of his brother's papers. He saw that the way to make more money was to control the supply of newsprint. Through the Anglo-Newfoundland Development Corporation (founded in 1906) there was the ownership of forests and mills and the control of shipping and landing.

The whole of the newspaper industry was a maze of sales, buy backs and mergers. Kemsley Mill and village near Sittingbourne was named for Lord Kemsley, formerly one of the Berry Brothers, with whom Rothermere had had dealings. When Northcliffe died Lord Rothermere took over the *Daily Mail*; this was passed to his son on his death. It surprised me that no one on the wharf had made the connection. Its registered office address was 30 Bouverie Street EC4, right in the heart of newspaperdom. Not only was the crypt of the Whitefriars Monastery underneath it, but it was at the time the registered office of *The Sun* and *The Daily Express*.

Anyway, George White's!! I had seen the office manager in the background a couple of times and vaguely recognised him. Then I heard one of the clerks call him Bev and realised it was Beverley White who had been the wharf foreman back in the 60's. What a difference twenty odd years had made. I remembered him as a young man in a sharp grey pinstripe suit and sporting a big blond quiff. Like me he was now late middle aged, bald with grey round the edges and wearing a comfortable cardigan. When he came into the lobby, we had a reminisce about the old days. Bev and I had many arguments about loads of Kraft linerboard going to a job in Harlow. Their entire stock was kept in the open but Bev tried to insist that their loads be fully sheeted. I discovered that the current foreman, Derek Egan, had been a young docker in those days.

The conversation got round to the eight-wheeler and trailer days of George White's and Wally Freshwater the trailer boy of prodigious strength. Wally would unhook a drawbar trailer and wheel it into position like a barrow. For a bet he would roll out a quarter reel of newsprint (about 3 cwt.) and then stand it on end on a bit of wood. Then he would get his fingers under it and put it back on the roll. My 6' 7" son walked in and I said to Bev "I bet you don't remember telling this little boy to stay in the cab and behave himself, if you do, I bet you wouldn't tell him that now". I'm reminiscing again, back to the procedure!

Once you had the tally in your hand it was down the road to the wharf proper (which was over a level crossing on the LTS main line and shared with Esso), to get in another rank to see Derek Egan. When you got to the front, Derek would direct you to the shed and door where you were to load. Then it was wait again until the gang came. If you were keen you could have a look round in the shed and find the reels and mark them for the checker. When the gang came there would be the checker (who was a Tally Clerk), a clamp truck (like a fork truck with jaws) and a mobile crane (both driven by dockers), and a general hand. In the shed the reels were stood on end, the clamp truck would pick them up, rotate them onto the roll and drop them in the doorway. The general hand would roll them down and put the crane grab in position. The reel was then swung up into position on the lorry and the grab would disengage itself. A good crane driver made life easy, putting the reel exactly in place and nipping it on the scotch.

The clerk tallied the reels on the tally card in the traditional llll (five-bar gate) fashion. Tally Clerks were the elite of the docks. Since Victorian times they had been paid more, initially because they were literate. Some printers were taking reels on end; in that case there were two clamp trucks. The cranes had just started to be replaced with pole trucks, which was a FLT with two long round steel poles instead of the usual flat blades. All of Purfleet was rail tracked. Flat railway wagons drawn by a diesel locomotive were used to transfer reels unloaded from the ship into the sheds. In my BRS days there were ordinary line and sleeper tracks, but were being converted to tramlines flush with the concrete apron making much more parking and manoeuvring room, so long as they did not need to get the rail trucks in.

Johnny Whitbread, one of the foremen, was Fatima 'Javelin' Whitbread's Dad. While 'Donkey' Callender, a docker, was the Dad of Jill who used to be the clerk at Heronfreight. One of the crane drivers was always known as 'Weary' John. Once he had loaded a lorry, he slewed the crane to a safe position and went to sleep in about 30 seconds. When the checker got the next job, John would be woken up to move. I have even known him to drop-off while the clamp driver was getting the reels out! Once you were finally loaded it was a case of queuing once again to see "Hi-fi" John and collect the delivery notes and sign for the load.

With going back into Purfleet, I renewed an old acquaintance with Vic the Dartford Wharfage shunter. He pre-loaded trailers for his firm and at the end of the day took a load of reels to Odham's at Watford. Dartford Wharfage & Transport started back in the late 18th Century as the Dartford Canal Company. It traded coal and wood pulp along the partly canalised River Darent to Horton Kirby Paper Mills bringing back finished paper It found that operating the wharf where the canal meets the Thames was more profitable than operating a canal so it became Dartford Wharfage. In the early 80's it closed the wharf and paid off its dockers becoming Dartford Wharfage & Transport doing a lot of work from Purfleet and Erith. In '87 it moved to Slade Green and became part of TDG.

Erith was a much smaller wharf, run much on the same lines. The office was a one-man operation Brian was brilliant. Tallies issued as soon as you arrived and delivery notes handed out, as you were loaded. Bill, the foreman, was always all of a dither, and the rest of the dockers were very laid back in their attitude. There was one who was an irredeemable alcoholic. At morning tea break he was over the pub as soon as it opened. The afternoon tea break was at 3.00pm, if he was loading approaching tea break, at 2.45pm he would say "I'm going for a pint before they shut, I'll be back a quarter of an hour early".

I did a job at Erith, which brought back a memory from my BRS days. I loaded some bulk tissue reels. These are 4ft in diameter and 6ft 6in high (on end). These went two across and ten along, with six on the roll on top at the back. In the BRS days, four of us went to load these for British Tissues at Wrexham. We were loaded by tea and decided to sheet up afterwards and run back. Two loads were going on trunk and two of us would leave next morning. We had finished our tea and were wondering why John was missing. As we walked back to where the wagons were parked, there was a voice saying, "Where are you all? Get me out of here". When we got up on John's trailer we found he had slipped into the space where four reels met, his arms were pinned to his sides. He had been there for the whole tea break!

Convoy's at Deptford was a law unto itself. It was one of the last upper river wharves and access was down a narrow residential street off Evelyn Street. Delays there were legendary. Here again the procedure was to join the rank, then walk back to the wharf office to collect tallies. The office lobby held about eight drivers at a squeeze, the rest queuing outside. The window clerk, Len was an ex-docker doing a light corner job. He had the most irritating penchant for neatness. Everything was always precisely lined up even his paper clips, he would spend a lot of time tearing the tractor strips off computer printed documents, which then had to be stapled together because the four-part sets fell to bits!

Often you would get to the window only to find there was a query on your load. This meant a walk across the wharf to the offices of Varma Services, which was the agent for the Finnish mills. Once the problem was resolved, it was back on the end of the queue for the window. This office also gave out the gate passes, thus there were plenty of comings and goings. Once the paperwork was right, it was a case of moving along with the rank to see "Ted the Coat" the wharf foreman. At Convoy's all the loading was done with clamp and pole trucks, plus some funny ones called tipplers which could pick up the reel on end and tilt it over to the on the roll position, thus being able to land it vertically downwards anywhere along the trailer. Unless there were several lorries loading from one place, the gang would report back to Ted to be allocated a fresh lorry.

The ships were ro-ros and the cargo was loaded onto huge industrial trailers called Mafi's. These had solid tyred wheels at one end; a tractor fitted with a hydraulically raised gooseneck picked up the other end. These had a driving position, which could be rotated through 180 degrees. As the dockers drove those tractors and the one lot of dockers did all the work in the ship and discharging into the sheds, when a ship was in the rank it was horrendous. There was a period when there was a lot of paper coming out of the wharf and ships coming in one after another. We were getting to the wharf earlier and earlier while the gate could not be opened until 6.30am because of local planning rules.

The rank stretched right up New King Street, stopping local residents going to work. Wagons coming from the east were queuing towards Greenwich blocking one lane. Wagons from the west queued along Evelyn Street. One morning the residents complained to the police. The Panda car came and we explained to the PC that if we could not queue we would be forced to drive in a big convoy round and round Deptford until 6.30am. The copper went to the security guard and ordered him to open the gate. When the guard argued the copper told him "You've got 30 seconds to open the gate or you're in the car and down the nick for obstructing a policeman". After that we got straight in to rank up inside. At that time it was possible to spend a very long day just getting a load on wheels.

There was one compensation at Convoy's. It had an excellent canteen, run by Dot a formidable Scottish lady. She looked after everyone well, but treated the dockers like her sons. One of the staff, Ann, had driven one of the Morrison electric mobile canteen vans operated by the Port of London Authority. It was these, which added the word 'mobile' to the docker's vocabulary synonymous to tea break. Particularly those dockers who had come over the river from the Royal Group, who at five to ten would say "knock it on the head driver, mobile" even some who would shout down the shed "Muggo!!" Which dated back before the PLA and the NDLB to days when each docker had his own mug and someone brewed a bucket of tea.

Talking of old dockers, one of the tally clerks had inherited his Union card from his uncle (a usual practice at one time). His uncle, in his youth, had been one of the last clerks to use proper tallies, a stick with notches cut in it.

When I first started going to that wharf there was one docker I was sure I knew. He was loading one afternoon and the sun was striking off the river so that every time he came to drop a reel I got a clear silhouette of his profile and the penny dropped. When we had finished loading I told him we had worked together in the past. He said that from the first time he had seen me in the canteen he thought he knew me but couldn't remember where from. I said to him "1966, five the George?" "No?" "How about stainless steel bucket?" Then the light dawned, "The whisky lock up, you was on BRS, you used to bring in the export Scotch, we were young and fit then, 1,250 wooden cases all hand ball". I said, "Wasn't it funny how one case always fell on its corner and had to be drained into that stainless bucket". To which he replied "That old Customs Watcher was only interested in twelve unbroken capseals, he had his share out of the bucket, he died of cirrhosis of the liver, just before the docks shut".

For anyone interested in history Convoy's wharf was a fascinating place. It actually dated back to the days of Henry the Eighth. Queen Elizabeth the First knighted Sir Francis Drake there when she inspected the Golden Hind. In 1698 Peter the Great of Russia worked there and at Woolwich as an apprentice, while studying shipbuilding. He stayed at Sayes Court home of John Evelyn a diarist pre Samuel Pepys. This was demolished in 1729 and a workhouse built in its place. That still existed although for some reason the dockers always called it Nelson's House (which was actually at Woolwich). In 1869 it became the Foreign Cattle Market. One of the sheds is like an enormous Nissen hut this is the old slaughterhouse and is a listed building. (I have recently discovered that the listing is not for the building. It is because that underneath there is a Tudor dry dock that forms part of the extensive archaeology under the wharf. The entire site is being properly researched in 2006). Enough of the history lesson! Back to haulage and my life with Parker Morris.

Many of the deliveries were the same ones I had done many years before with BRS; others were not even built in those days! One of the first I did was to Eddie Shah's works at Colnbrook. While he might have brought printing into the 20th Century with his new technology, paper deliveries were still rooted in the days of the horse and cart. With the high-speed web-offset press, which had low roller pressure and high tension in the web (paper), paper quality was paramount. Yet loads were still carried under sheets which had to be pulled off in the road in all weathers. Reels were still held in place with a wooden scotch. The reels in the second tier were still allowed to drop onto the trailer floor. Restricted entrances and nowhere to park were still the order of the day, even in modern purpose built works.

All the presses seemed to want their paper delivered yesterday, until the wagon arrived at the door. Then it was the old story "Get on the back of the rank driver, we'll call you when we're ready". A prime example of this skimping on facilities was a brand new newspaper press at Reading for the Berkshire Chronicle. The unloading point was a yard at the end of a shared access. This involved wangling your way through everyone elses' parked cars and vans and reversing out the same way. Nowhere to turn and the wagon needed to be in headfirst. I arrived with a load, there had been rain on and off on the way down and the sky was overcast. So I asked the reelman should I unsheet? It was a company rule to ask permission as there was another rule that the sheet be taken off completely and would not be put back, there was no rolling the sheet back a bit at a time. This was on the grounds of safety as a driver had fallen off of a load and fractured his skull.

The sheets were just on the ground when the rain started, it poured, the wrappers turned black and when the clamp squeezed the water ran out. The reelman said, "Sod 'em" and carried on unloading. When we were having a cup of tea afterwards, I asked why as they had no bay, had the yard not been covered. He told me that towards the end of the building works money became tight, it became a choice between finishing the front of the building with a fancy entrance, car park and shrubbery. Or, putting a canopy over the unloading area which no one saw, "That's why I said sod 'em, clean shoes were more important than dry paper".

There were three other presses in Reading that we did regularly, all had a story. There was an old book printers, Cox and Wyman Ltd. up a narrow street with houses down one side. The loading bay had been built for 24' trailers but we still had to get in with 40's. It was a blind side back in which would not have been too bad if the residents opposite had not insisted in parking his car exactly outside his house, putting it dead centre with door. Every time a wagon backed in he would stand at his window to make sure his car wasn't hit. I delivered there in late April, the clamp truck driver had just got his pay packet, which contained his P60. He opened it and said "Bloody hell x thousand pounds!!!" I remarked that I thought print workers earned much more than that. He replied "That's not earnings, that's tax". It was about £2,000 more than my P60 showed for gross pay for the previous year!

Round the corner was another newspaper press, the Reading Evening Post. You had to be outside with the sheets off ready to back in the moment they opened. In the interests of economy! The staff had been cut to the bone. The reelman, who unloaded the lorry, had also to prepare the reels and put them on the press, which started running at 09.00 sharp. If you weren't unloaded by then you could wait until 15.00 when the run finished. If you were prepared to you could get the remaining reels ready. This involved putting the reels into the centre of the trailer, make sure they were running the right way, and then take off the end caps. Then he would fly out grab one and put it straight onto the changeover. This way you could be away by about 12.30.

The other Reading drop was a carton maker and printers. The Berkshire Printing Co. was the printing division of Brooke Bond OXO. Tea packets; fried chicken buckets; etc., using good quality fine white board. This came ready cut into sheets and banded onto pallets, for sheet-fed machines. The tiniest bit of damage on the edge of the sheets would cause two sheets to feed at once and jam the machine, so the inspection was meticulous. There would often be a queue of wagons right down the road, which ran alongside an infants' school. With the way the pallets were handled in the docks the reject rate was high. There was an added problem with this cut board. When humidity was high the edges of the board attracted moisture, when the strapping was cut and the top cover board taken off the board would wrinkle because the edges had stretched. I have taken 20 tons and got the lot back for just that reason.

Another big regular delivery was to a printer's in Norwich round behind the cathedral. I had done that one in my BRS days, at that time we used to go straight through the centre of Norwich. Now it is all round the inner ring road. Also in the intervening years a new warehouse and unloading bays were built. I soon found out that I knew one of the bank men. We had first met when I used to deliver wooden casks of lemon juice for BRS from British Waterways at Brentford to Reckett & Colman, and again later when he moved to the printer's and was involved in an incident which I witnessed.

The old goods entrance was through a pair of doors opening straight off a road. With an eight-wheeler it was necessary to pull right across the road and back in at right angles to the wall. A driver watched one side the bank man the other, which was a long left hand bend completely blind because of the high wall on the left. There were three of us waiting, we got one of the wagons unsheeted. While one of the others stopped the traffic, my mate watched round the bend for a gap in the traffic. He stepped into the road and held his hand up, then the lorry driver pulled across the road and started to back in. A car screeched to a stop right by my mate, the driver jumped out and punched him right in the face, saying "Don't you go stopping me, you'll make me late for work". My mate was off work a couple of days. The next week the same three of us were back again, my mate said "I've been watching that bloke who hit me, he comes along the same time every morning, if you don't mind a bit of hassle we can fix him. He'll be along soon". We sorted out the lightest load and put it ready to back in, while he watched round the corner. When he saw the car coming we stopped the traffic our side and as the car approached the bend he waved the eight-wheeler forward. As the car appeared the eight-wheeler was right across the road and the car ran straight into the drive wheels.

Mr. Plod arrived eventually (on a bicycle). He said to my mate "Why didn't you stop him when you knew there was a lorry across the road?" To which he replied "I was all ready to step out and put my hand up when I saw it was him. He punched me in the face last week and told me not to stop him, so I didn't. You ask these drivers, they were here. I had to have time off work". We all confirmed it to the copper, who went over to the car driver and said "Looks like you got your come uppance boy, the old boy from the printers don't want to do anything about the punch. You admit to the BRS man it was your fault, and then I won't be doing anything about it. Good Morning". Then he got on his bike and rode away. When we got back to the yard, I wrote out two statements and the Accident Report and that was that, until twenty odd years later when we had a good laugh about it.

Peterborough was another major delivery point, with a magazine printer and a newspaper press (which did *The Independent*). I got there one day and the clamp truck had broken down. Another driver and I had been sitting for about two and a half hours when a chap in a suit came out and gave each of us a fiver to go across to the cafe for a meal as the delay was likely to be another two hours.

Another time I was delivering a load to the magazine printers on the east of the town. There were road works on Stangate Hill and as I came up to Norman Cross I waved to one of the blue fleet drivers who was just joining the back of the stationary queue. They were waiting for my load and took it straight off. I decided to use my knowledge from Heronfreight days and went Whittlesey Road, Pondersbridge, Ramsey, Warboys, St Ives coming out on the A604 (now A14) at Hemmingford and back to Convoy's where I was lucky enough to get loaded straight away. I was booking out as the blue fleet driver came to book in. He looked very puzzled, saying "That was you who waved to me at Norman Cross? I never knew we operated helicopters". So I told him that there was a time when you had to know your way about and that knowledge still came in handy.

Bourne was a place I hadn't been to since the '60s, when I got a load I automatically went into Stamford and over through Toft. When I got into the job, the clamp truck driver, Frank, said "You must be a proper lorry driver, I saw you turn right into the yard, you came through Stamford". So I told him that the last time I was in Bourne was 1967-8 when there was a BRS depot; that was the way I had always come. We got to yarning and it turned out that he had courted the daughter of Mrs Sharpe who did digs for BRS men. We always had a good yarn whenever I went there and on one occasion he told me a story well worth re-telling.

He was driving an artic coal tipper and had loaded small coal for London. The shovel driver had dropped the last couple of ton to the nearside giving him a bit of a lean to the left. On the newly opened Stamford by-pass a police car stopped him. The copper said to him "Your trailer's laying over driver, you must have a broken spring" to which he replied "Can't have, there aren't any springs on this trailer, without them we get another half a ton of coal on". With that the copper shot under the trailer and came back saying, "I'm forbidding you to go any further until this trailer is examined by the MoT. It's a danger on the road without springs". It transpired that the Ministry man had to come from Lincoln. When he finally arrived he went straight under the trailer and came straight out again. He said to the copper "Have you never heard of Norde rubber suspension? Fetching me out on a wild goose chase". Then he said to Frank "He's obviously a 'Johnny know-all' but you should have told him. On your way". Frank said "Too late now, my time is up in five minutes. I'll leave it here until morning and walked across the field to Stamford and got the bus home!"

While most of the loads were done on a return empty basis, we collected baled waste paper on some of the longer distance jobs. There were also some local merchants from whom we collected as a primary job. Waste was an eye opener varying from 'state of the art' recycling to shades of Steptoe & Son.

The first load of waste I did was from Leicester Waste. I found the very small yard and the squeeze truck driver told me to see Neville in the office. Neville said something to me, which I had to ask him to repeat a couple of time. He suddenly said, "You never did understand me, did you? You don't even recognise me". It took some time to reconcile the prosperous looking businessman in the suede coat, with the slim young chap in overalls I recalled. It was the Birmingham/Leicester/Norwich accent, which gave the game away. We had been on night trunk at the same time in '61-62. He was running from Norwich to Birmingham for Pointers carrying Boulton & Paul joinery, he had married a Birmingham girl, then moved to Leicester.

One Monday morning I was sent to Bromley to load KLS (Kraft Liner Scrap) for Reed's Island Site at Aylesford. I loaded the usual load of forty bales for 20 tons on a four-axle artic. When I started to climb up past Knockholt I could feel something wasn't right, I thought the filters needed changing. Going down Polhill into Riverhead I realised I was overloaded. I went very steady from there on and finally got to the Island Site using a lot of adrenaline. There is a right angle right hand turn with an adverse camber half way down a 1 in 4 on the way in.

I pulled on to the weighbridge, but before I could get out the foreman, Clive came out of the office and told me to pull off, go back out to the trailer park and have a tea in the caravan. He came over to the caravan and took me outside, he said "We couldn't let you book-in, you weighted 39 tons, I bet that load's from Bromley". He explained that he couldn't take part of the load off to send me back, so what he proposed was, that I pulled back on the bridge and dropped the trailer, then booked-in. The trailer alone weighed in at 32 and a quarter tons. When I got the sheets off he got out the moisture probe, he said, "Look at that driver 35% to 37%. What you've got on there is 20 tons of waste and 7 tons of water, we knew that crafty old sod damped his paper, he's forgotten to turn the hose off over the week-end".

That favour was finally repaid several years later. I did an experimental load, collecting baled waste direct from a supermarket instead of it going through a merchant. It was a bad job; the supermarket had only an ordinary FLT so all the bales had to be manhandled into position. As I was moving them about I could see they contained all kinds of rubbish, there were boxes of rotten fruit, meat and fish trimmings, broken glass, even broken pallets. When I got to the Island Site I called Clive out and told him to have a look at the load before I weighed in, you could see the rubbish just by pulling the sheet up. After a long wait, I was sent to another recycling site on the other side of Maidstone. From there, after another inspection, I was redirected to a Kent County Council landfill site where the load was pushed off of the trailer into a hole. Not only did the supermarket not get paid for the load; it also had to pay all the cartage and the cost of the disposal. It also ended the experiment.

The company took on a timber carrying job for the same group of Finnish mills. This was much more to my liking. Paper, especially newsprint, was all rush and tear deadlines, timed deliveries, JIT, and everyone getting very excited. An old George White driver (back in my BRS days) had said to me "I don't know why they get so hot under the collar about newsprint, tomorrow it will be fish and chip wrappers." (That was before food hygiene and carcinogenic ink but it was a view I shared.)

Timber yards, builder's merchants and shed builders were generally glad to see you. The staff had a much more relaxed attitude to life, something, which had not changed since the '60s. We were fortunate at Convoy's in that there were some old PLA timber men who had come down river when the Surrey Docks had shut.

Most of the timber came in what were called truck packs. These were about 3' 6" square and could be up to 18' long. One end was square and solid; the other was all flapping ends what we used to call 'randoms'. There was a trick to loading these; you put two on the floor up to the rave, loose ends to the headboard. The next two went the other way round at the back leaving a 4' 6" space in the middle. Then you put two 8'–3" x 3"s across each stack and the next tier was put directly on top but pushed in to touch in the middle. The last two bridged the gap with the solid ends at the back (without bearers). The whole lot could then be secured with four ratchet straps (six if you weren't sure of your driving or inclined to take liberties). This gave a load height of around 16'. A long measuring tape was a vital tool

This method of loading made me very unpopular with some of the drivers who thought it unsafe. In fact it amounted to 6½ Baltic Standards on a 40' trailer. In the '60s we were putting five standards on a 24' eight-wheeler. I have a thick skin so it did not bother me; I liked the work and was going to do my best to keep it.

After the fancy lining was put on the northbound Dartford Tunnel (pre-bridge) loads had to be no more than 16' or it was Woolwich Ferry or Blackfriars Bridge. I regularly left trailers parked at the south side of the Tunnel if I was delivering south of the river the next day.

I had a load of 25 x 150 or 6" x 1" as they called it in the trade. It was for Watford so by using 2" bearers I got it to exactly l6'. When I arrived at the Tunnel I was stopped, the detectors had shown me overheight, and the measure showed 16' 1" at the front. I got up on top and found that one board in the top bundle had jumped up on edge, I slid it out and was allowed through. I had great respect for that detector after that.

The conflict in measurements was quite funny. Pack lengths were shown in feet (the length of the longest board or boards) but all board sizes were metric in millimetres i.e. 25 x 50, 38 x 100. If you went into a timber yard and said "I've got a load of 75 x 75 for you" the yardman would call out 'The 3" x 3" is here". Even young lads who had only learned metric at school. It is going to take a long while for Imperial Measure to die. Especially as American and Canadian paper is still measured in inches, weighed in hundredweights, quarters and pounds and graded in ounces per square foot.

There was a ten-pack load (16' 2") to a timber yard whose address was X & Co., Bicester Road, Aylesbury. Bicester Road was the main A41 so I headed out of town towards Waddesdon. On the right was a tea stall in a lay-by where I stopped to ask for the address. The stall owner knew it, but said, "You won't get there with that load, it's the other side of the railway bridge (15' 3"). Turn round, then take the lane on the left at the end of the lay-by, over the cross roads, first left, straight down over the railway, over the cross-roads and you'll come to the A41, turn left and its on your right". What he didn't tell me, was that the lane as far as the crossroads was not only a 'mirror brusher' in places, but was also gated across sheep pasture. When I finally got to the job, the FLT was 3' too low to reach the top packs. We hunted round the yard for short, thick timbers and with my short bolsters we built a 'bird cage' on the blades. Once the pack was off the wagon it had to be rested on two more stacks of timber so that we could dismantle the 'bird cage' and put it on to the ground on ordinary bolsters. I took a similar load to a furniture firm in Andover, but the FLT driver refused to use a 'bird cage' so I took it back to Convoy's, got the top two taken off and then took it back to Andover.

We did a lot of timber for Crosby Doors & Windows to its works and Farnham and Eastleigh (both sadly now shut). I was going to Eastleigh, as I turned off the M25 on to the A3 (I always went A31 to the A33) I saw in the nearside mirror that the back bottom pack was collapsing. With a lot of straps, I made it as secure as possible, and took it very steadily into Farnham. Jim the foreman came out of his office took a look and said, "I knew it wasn't for us, you obviously need some help!" Then he called his side-loader driver over and told him, "Top two off, dodgy one where the lads can put some bands round it, then reload 'em with the dodgy one on the off-side top". I was back on the way in half an hour. Such was the helpfulness of people in the timber game.

We had three deliveries in Wisbech, a timber yard, a builder's merchant and a shed-builder. I went the way I had gone for years. A10 turn left at Littleport, (A1101) across Welney Wash, and coming into Wisbech alongside the remains of the Wisbech Canal (now filled in, although it still had water in it in the sixties). Past the Tramway Farm Shop, which had been the terminus for horse and steam trams in the early 1900s. All the way from Outwell through Emneth and the edge of Walsoken it is possible to see traces of the old canal. It originally joined the Old River Nene with the New Nene at Wisbech docks. The new road, which bypasses the shopping centre to reach the Freedom Bridge, commemorates the canal with an addendum to the road sign saying it was built on the course of the Wisbech Canal.

On one occasion I had just pulled into the timber yard when a carpenter's van pulled up beside me. The driver and his mate came over, laughing. The driver told me he had seen me come out of the Wash Road at Outwell. He had said to his mate "I'll bet you that driver is only a bit younger than God, all these modern flyers come via Peterborough or Chatteris and March since the by-passes have opened". It was the same place that the side-loader driver recognised my Lynn connections. Another young driver there brought home the vagaries of English usage.

I asked, "Where's the old boy that usually drives the loader?" To which he replied "Do you mean the old 'old boy' or the young 'old boy'?" Anyone who remembers "The Dukes of Hazard" will remember people being referred to as "Good old boys". Well! North East Anglia was the place the expression originated.

One morning there were orders to go to Harcross at Fishers Manorway, Belvedere. I was to collect a load of 12" x 12"s to go to Solihull, "Must be delivered today the job is waiting!!!" When I got there, there was hardly anything left in the yard (it was closing). I had delivered there many times, but now seeing it empty I realised that I had delivered there in my BRS days, when it was Parker Timber. I found the foreman and told him what I wanted. I then remarked that I remembered the place from the past, but recalled it as running right down to the river to a barge landing. He explained that the river frontage had gone when the Thames Flood Prevention measures had caused the building of the embankment, which now backed the yard.

I went on to say that I remember timber being run up sloping planks out of the barge holds and hand stacked, as indeed was the timber off our wagons. He replied "Don't say that driver, my ear 'ole as gone sore. In my young days I was one of them deal porters, I've still got scars on my right shoulder". It finally dawned on me why I had not recognised it as soon as I went there on Parker Morris. In my BRS days the Belvedere Manorways were unmade roads bounded by dilapidated corrugated fences, with the odd gas lamp, in the winter a thoroughly dismal place. Now it was proper roads with kerbs, pavements, cast concrete fencing and electric light.

Having loaded, I went to Solihull. The only address I had was the name of a firm (which I can't remember) Solihull, Warks, quite a normal sort of delivery address. In touring the town I asked at a couple of building sites and two big garages without joy, so I found the local Nick. The WPC at the desk could not help, nor could anyone else in the station. I was asked to wait while they did some phoning and radioing to area cars. A very long wait!

There was a bit of light relief while I waited. A couple came in, obviously father and daughter. She had borrowed Dad's car, which had broken down on the M42 in the early hours. Dad had gone with a mate with a tow truck, but the car had gone. The WPC informed them, rather gleefully I thought, that it was not stolen but in the pound. A patrol had found it and as it was not logged had had it towed away. It was going to cost £169 to get it back. Apparently the girl and her boyfriend had climbed over the fence to the adjoining road and walked home without telling the police. They left the station arguing violently, with Dad threatening all kinds of mayhem.

Eventually the WPC came back with a hand-written A4 sheet of detailed instructions on how to get to my job. This I followed to the letter, arriving at an industrial unit behind Elmdon Airport. Yes the name was right and they did use timber, but not 12"x12"s. They made packing cases. There was a construction firm with a similar name working on an estate at the other side of the airport. This meant going back on to the A45 and round by The Malt Shovel and in from the back. This estate proved to be finished and deserted. A patrolling security man finally turned up to tell me "That firm is working somewhere at the front of the airport". As I went in yet again I saw a dumper with some 12" x 12"s on it, but that turned out to be a red herring.

I finally finished up outside the main entrance to the terminal. I asked a cabby, who pointed towards some tower cranes near the station. I asked him where the signs were and he pointed to a scaffold tower on top of a sound barrier mound. The name I was looking for was about 40' above the road, at that moment an old Transit pulled up; it was the men from the site. They had been going home when they saw me coming in, (for the third time). Only once before have I been unloaded so quickly!

On that occasion I was delivering sleepers to the site of Sainsbury's RDC at Buntingford. I arrived very late in the day and was directed under a crane to unrope. The crane driver told me to drop the trailer; he then put a wire rope on the kingpin and stood the trailer on end; 14 tons of sleepers off in about 4 seconds!

We delivered quite a few loads of timber to a merchant at the back of the docks in King's Lynn. First time I went, I hadn't been to Lynn for years. There was a big new roundabout on the A10 for the A17 by-pass, with signs pointing to "The Docks" so I followed them and had the grand tour. Next time I ignored the signs and went the way I knew, as I turned at the roundabout at the Saddlebow Road I was confronted by the 14' 6" ancient city gate about which I had completely forgotten. Fortunately it only spans the northbound side of the road, so I pulled into the middle of the road to go "wrong way" round the end. There was a car coming the other way, I was going to let him through, but he stopped well back and waved me through. After that I always used that route, the locals must have been used to high loads dodging the arch as they always stopped and gave you room. Very laid back and helpful these East Anglians.

The timber work began to drop-off, we had been undercut, although anyone who undercuts the rate on timber must be mad. This work was replaced with hauling cocoa and coffee beans for a broker. There was also an increase in the amount of unaccompanied trailers being pulled for Continental hauliers, containers and timber and ply out of Tilbury Dock.

The beans were in hessian sacks, which were imported, packed tight in 20' ISO boxes. The broker unloaded them onto pallets, which were then loaded onto our trailers. The cocoa beans were a bad load; the sacks spread once they were out of the container so the load could be 9' 6" wide. I have tied down a flysheet in the rain and been bone dry because I was under the overhang. We did a lot of loads to Fullers of Slough on behalf of Mars. There was another haulier taking cocoa beans to Chirk for Cadbury's. It used curtain-siders, which bulged so much that "wide load" boards had been painted on the curtains at either end. All illegal of course, a couple of drivers on another firm got done on the M25 for being overwidth.

There was a job with a reinforcing rod (rebar.) from a small wharf, Pinn's on Barking Creek, where the bar was being loaded from small European coasters. Most of this was to a firm of bar workers at Addlestone. With a bit of luck it was possible to do two loads a day.

Back in the '60's we had shipped thousands of tons of plastic pellets from Monsanto at Fawley to the Continent via the Regents Canal Dock. Now these were coming from Europe on unaccompanied trailers for delivery to many of the places, which I had done as Monsanto's domestic deliveries. More imported unemployment.

There were also containers from Tilbury Docks and occasionally from Felixstowe (a dock changed out of all recognition). We had a big order for containers of axle nose castings. These were made in Brazil, shipped to an eastern American port. Shipped across to Rotterdam, transhipped into a small vessel and landed at Tilbury. We delivered them to a warehouse in Electric Avenue, Whitton, Birmingham. Part of what was the GEC works, only twenty minutes drive from the Black Country where hundreds of thousands of tons of castings had been produced both for the British car industry and for export.

Late one day I was asked to go to Tilbury to collect an urgent box. Another driver was going to do it, but had run out of time. According to the traffic clerk, "He had checked the skeletal trailers and I could use either". (I had seen him looking round them). When the box was dropped on, the tyres on the second axle spread out to about double width, the manifest said the box weighed 15 tons. I got the trailer round under a light and found that the axle had only the outer wheels on and they were only held by two nuts, with some of the studs broken off. This resulted in a slow run back to the depot and a late night for the fitters. By the time I got back the next day, there were a lot of trailers sporting V.O.R signs something we had been asking for, for years.

The amount of stuff, which was being imported, was amazing. I have mentioned urea, rebar., plastic pellets and castings. There was also joinery, lemonade, coal and steel plate. Lemonade by its very nature in 95% water yet it used to come in 24-ton loads for small chain grocers. While it was quite common in Purfleet to see coil carriers from South Wales collecting steel strip from the continent for delivery within the shadow of one of the biggest strip mills in the British Isles.

There were orders to collect six container flats (what we used to call Lancashire Flats) from a repairer for export from Felixstowe. After a bit of difficulty loading I got to Felixstowe and into the usual queue for the window. When I finally arrived at the front I was told that I needed some paperwork from an office outside the dock. When I came to the gate I was told "You can't take them out, you need a gate pass". I found a corner to drop the trailer and then collected a lad from the office and took him back to the dock, where he took some numbers and filled in some forms. I picked up the trailer, went back to the lorry park and back into the queue for the window. At the front once again I was told all the numbers were one digit short! Back onto the trailer park, sure enough he had left off the last digit of each number. Once more to the window and finally a location to get unloaded, the sun was well in bed by the time that I got home from what should have been a simple job!

Coal and smokeless fuel was another commodity, which we carried as a return load. There was a British Fuels coal yard right by the depot gate. This had been a proper old-fashioned coal merchant. The coal was delivered in tippers and weighed out into hundredweight sacks. Then the whole job was modernised with all the coal coming in sealed plastic sacks on pallets. We loaded from a bagging plant at Ollerton. When you stood on the load to sheet up you could see the winding gear at Ollerton Colliery and yet the coal came in tippers from East Coast ports having been imported from Poland. We also collected from an NCB bagging plant attached to Kersley Colliery just outside Coventry. The pit's main customer was Hams Hall Power Station. As I write, Hams Hall has gone and the site is in the process of being made freight terminal for the Channel Tunnel. There were bagging plants at Water Orton and Kingswinford, both supplied by fleets of tippers.

When we started this job, there were many deliveries to small coal yards in obscure places. I found that the easiest way to find these was to use my 1961 road atlas and find where the railways ran pre-Beeching. All the small coal yards had bought their coal by the railway-truck load. Even the one outside our yard had been rail connected, as were the adjoining Tunnel and LaFarge Cement works.

I enjoyed the coal work. A full load of coal could be covered with a flysheet. I quickly fitted mine with long thick 'strings' which could be dollied, after that I never used rope on coal. In the same way, I had never used rope on the loads of margarine that I carried while on BRS; this avoided using corner boards. It seems strange looking back thirty years, to realise that foodstuffs, which are now carried in controlled temperature, van trailers used to be carried on flats. In the summer we used to watch for dark stains appearing on the sheets which showed the marg. was melting, we even put 3" x 3"s on the top covered by an extra sheet to make a sun shade.

Sheeting and roping was one of my fortés, when I was young it had to be. For a time I took out newly qualified drivers to show them how it was done as well as how to use a Fuller crash (CMDE) gearbox. My Dad always told me, "If you drive a wagon as though the load is not roped, then every rope you put on is a bonus". It is a fact that a roped load is mostly held on by friction between its component parts. A rope only holds the top tier. I was shown a demonstration that I have used for years. If you tie a piece of string tightly round a match box sleeve it is then possible to lozenge it until it is almost flat before the string comes loose.

I picked up a load of made up cartons from Reed's at Aylesford, these were banded up in blocks the size of pallet. The loads were so high the girders in the roof of the sheeting shed were padded in case you banged your head. Anyway, I took this load to Hoddesdon. At the delivery address I was redirected to their warehouse at the other end of the estate. The FLT driver there said to me "You took a chance 'drive', bringing that round from the number One Site with only those few ropes". I told him I had only been diverted from One Site, the load had come from Aylesford and had not been touched since it was first roped up. He took a lot of convincing assuring me that Reed's would only bring those loads in curtainsiders because they would not travel on flats. I asked him how they got their cartons before curtainsiders were invented and the M25 built? I had brought the same loads from Aylesford in the company of Reed's driver's when the estate was first built and they had managed all right then, and they had to go round a lot more sharp corners.

There were interesting and unusual jobs. There was a 40-ft. canal narrow boat that had to be collected from Reedham Ferry in Norfolk and delivered to a boat yard on the Grand Union Canal at Uxbridge. It was lifted out of the water by one of the oldest cranes imaginable, it appeared to have been converted from steam to diesel. There is one like it at Ponders End on the old British Waterways wharf on the Lee Navigation; hundreds of drivers must have passed that one without a second glance. Or, realised that the fancy pub on the other side of the road was once a canal side warehouse going back to the 19th Century. Right! The boat! The Uxbridge boat yard was behind a terrace of houses and the entrance was down a 10' alley between two gable ends. Just to add to the difficulty of having garden walls right up to the pavement, the Council had put a lamppost exactly opposite the entrance, this was a back-in with feeler gauges job.

There was a nice job at Bromley. An envelope maker had sold all its old machinery to a firm at Walsall. All the machines had to be loaded as they were removed. I learned a lot about the art of machinery removal with two jacks, skates, Jack Johnsons and timbers, an all day job. By coincidence, on the first night there was a Starr Roadways of Bilston driver delivering next door to our yard. I got a perfect set of directions from him that put me right outside the delivery point next morning well ahead of the machinery men who had toured half of the Midlands.

The second day's loading was rather spoiled by the additional driver who had been put on the job. He was not content with a crane loaded job with a good cafe on the corner, but spent the whole time moaning about having to put sheets on greasy old machinery. Despite the fact that one unit alone was worth £250,000, a moan which continued all through the unloading process. Without him the third day went as well as the first.

The reconstruction of Liverpool Street Station had been completed and the Portacabins used by the builders had to go to a new job at Broxbourne. This was a Sunday job. For a reason best known to it, the police routed us all through the City and Holloway to the A1 and South Mimms. The snag arose at once, as we could not turn right out of the site. As the City Police HQ was on the doorstep we got a prompt re-routing and a motorbike escort off City ground. That was a long day. We had to do two trips loading and unloading each time. It's a good job it was possible to come straight back down the Kingsland Road.

For a time we did deliveries to a supermarket RDC. These were timed deliveries, if you got there too early you would not be let in; five minutes too late and the load had to be re-booked. Once you were in it was anyone's guess. I had a 10.00 booking and was finally unloaded at 23.45. There was a very inefficient Tannoy and no driver's room. Most drivers congregated on the corner of the bank by the drink machine. During one of these waits, a driver put his money in and pressed the button. The cup did not drop and the little plastic door was missing, thus his boot was filled with a stream of boiling water.

While he was tearing his boot off the foreman came out of the office and said, "That bloody machine again, that's been like that for weeks". I never saw him again to find out if he made a claim, he ought to have done, he had plenty of witnesses.

One winter's day I was sent to collect an empty 20-ft. box, which the customer was going to stuff. It was then to go to Parkestone Quay for shipment. The customer turned out to be a dealer working from a shop, who made up loads to go to a colleague in Nigeria. Under CMR rules all the driver has to do is present the box, but he offered me £30 to pack it while his men brought the stuff out. It was an all-day job which brought to the fore my old van packing skills. I managed to get in everything he wanted to send, which resulted in £40 instead of £30. It was about 16:00 and the fog was coming down, but the box had to go as it was being shipped next day.

There were signs of a big accident at Kelvedon and as the fog was still thick I phoned the yard at 18:30 to let them know where I was and that I was still on the way to deliver the box. I found out when I got to Parkestone that the accident had closed the road for some time. I was also told to watch out going home, the fog was still bad and the road was again closed at Rivenhall End. As I had to pass home on the way back to the yard, I parked up there at 23.30. When I got into the yard there were orders for a pre-loaded trailer of paper for a 09.00 delivery at Uckfield, it was then 09.00 so I got to Uckfield about 11.30, which upset all concerned. It certainly proved that traffic operators don't really listen when you phone them.

About this time Purfleet and Erith wharves closed. As I write, Erith is still closed and Purfleet is a ro-ro and new car terminal. All the paper was coming out of Convoy's, Chatham and Rochester. Parker Morris bought George White's fleet, which included what, were known as system trailers. These were curtain siders equipped with special floor tracks and could be unloaded automatically and mechanically at suitably equipped printing works. *The Daily Mail* at the Surrey Docks and *The Sun* at Wapping had such banks.

At these banks there was a fifth wheel under the bank, while under the back of the trailer was a rubbing plate and kingpin. The procedure was to open the doors, then unlock and swing back the corner post. As you backed in the fifth wheel picked up the kingpin, thus lining up the tracks and locking the trailer in place. Then an airline was connected to a point on the trailer. Long chains of skates extended from the bank under the load and the bottom of the track was raised by compressed air. This enabled the entire load to be drawn off of the trailer in one go. All you had to do then was uncouple the airline and pull off and close up.

The Daily Mail loads were taken from Convoy's and parked, to be dealt with by a shunter. I did the shunting job for a bit, but up and down into the cab 168 times in a day did my arthritic knees no good at all. Hence I went back to ordinary driving. With all the work coming from Convoy's there was now an internal shunter there, pre-loading the fleet of ex-TIP curtain-siders, which PM had acquired. It became a matter of dropping an empty and picking up a nominated trailer. Although it was still necessary to load your own at Chatham and Rochester.

It was from Chatham that I put on a load of reels for Knebworth. There were still done on the roll, two across the trailer with two on top. I was unloading at Knebworth the following morning. As I dropped one of the toppers it went sideways into the curtain having caught the edge of the bottom reel. It was not possible to get to the side of the trailer; it had to go out of the back. After a lot of barring and heaving the bank man and I managed to get it safely down, but a 20-minute tip had extended to an hour and a half. By the time I was ready to pull out there was a queue so I decided to go to Hatfield where there was an accessible phone box to let the depot know.

Just my luck, as I pulled off at Hatfield the weighbridge was being used by the MoT Nuts and Bolts.

There was a long wait to be inspected and I got a delayed GV9 for a leaking axle seal. I had my break then 'phoned in to tell them I had been delayed and went on to Convoy's to load for Faversham.

After loading I 'phoned in to say there was no point in going as they shut at 16.00, to be told "I don't care what time they shut, you're going with it", so I went. When I got to the warehouse, the regular shunter from the other contractor they used was in the process of locking the barrier. He told me he had two trailers to do in the morning; mine would not get done 'til after eight. If I parked up he would give me a lift to the motorway. I got a lift in about two minutes and was dropped at the back of the yard. Over the fence, across the waste ground and I had my car. I also arranged with one of the lads to get a lift to Sittingbourne. In the morning he dropped me at the roundabout. A car stopped straight away, the driver was a traffic clerk from A. & R. J. Woods, he went out of his way to drop me right at the job. He told me people often went out of their way to drop their drivers at the depot on the old A2. He was just repaying the compliment. When I 'phoned in after unloading I was called back to the yard.

The Manager said "You never had a night out, the foreman fitter saw you as he went home. I've not been satisfied with your performance since you've been back on paper. Clear your gear out your fired". I appealed through the disciplinary procedure, such as it was, and lost. I then went to an Industrial Tribunal to no avail. Between the appeal and the Tribunal, the manager left to run a cake shop. Really they did me a favour; I wasn't happy with the paper job, just too idle to make the effort to move. Rather unusually, I still have a good relationship with Alan Parker Morris, the owner of the firm. Since leaving the firm, I have helped out from time to time with casual driving until I lost my licence.

"Lon..........g Timber"

This old picture reminds me of the time when Dad went to Surrey Dock to pick up a piece of 12" x 12". When he presented the order he found it was 40-foot long. As he only had a four-wheeler it was on the bolsters well over the front and back. When he got to the gate he could not get out as the timber hit the houses opposite well before the back end cleared the gate. He backed in again and 'phoned the firm, he was told they only wanted 33 feet. So he found the carpenter's shop, borrowed a saw, and cut 7 feet off of the end. He repositioned the long bit, put the short end in the lorry then went back to the gate. He was promptly arrested as he had a gate pass for only one piece of timber and he now had two. The Guvnor had to take a fresh 'delivery order' from the firm in North London so that the right gate pass could be raised before they would release him and the load.

CHAPTER 16
THE AGENCY YEARS

Once again it was back to the agency. The Stratford and Basildon offices had closed; I was now under the control of the Barking office where the operator was Fred Sharp an ex-Beck & Pollitzer driver.

The first job I got was with Tracto on container work. This was run of the mill CMR work. Present the box, open the doors, go to sleep, shut the doors, and take the box back to the yard. I had one odd job while there. I took a 40ft soft top to a colony of car breakers beside the M25 just outside Colnbrook. I spent the entire day reading a book and occasionally moving up and down the yard, while a Nigerian gentleman loaded the box with an assortment of second hand car parts, most of which I would have consigned to the scrap metal merchant. When he finished he laced the cover and gave me a "tenner for my trouble!"

After that I fell in for a nice job. W.J. Simms at Hoddesdon wanted a large number of agency drivers for the Christmas rush on its Sainsbury's contract. It was a 14.00hrs start but paid £5.50 an hour with a guarantee of 12 hours. After booking on you sat in the canteen until called for. There were agency men from all over Essex, some from as far away as Colchester. From the conversations it was obvious that some agencies were on the make, Simms paid one rate for the job to a main agency, which then farmed the work around. Although the bigger agencies were paying £5.50 some of the smaller ones were paying as little as £4.25.

When you were allocated a job, it was necessary to find the unit, which would have just been brought in by one of Simms own men. One of the first of these, I took over from was Chris with whom I had worked on Parker Morris. He had been very lucky; he had been found to be 6 tons overloaded on the Dagenham weighbridge. He employed his own solicitor and received an Absolute Discharge. The firm who loaded him wrote to the court and said it was its fault a load for a 38 tonner had been put on a 32 tonner in error. That's by the way.

The next job was to find the trailer; this could be on Sainsbury's bank, pre-loaded in the trailer park or even an empty to go on the bank for loading. After the usual hiccups in getting the paperwork it was off to one of the stores to deliver. I went all over the place with these. The goods were all in roll cages and there was no difficulty in getting unloaded. There are only three jobs that stand out.

One was at Eltham with a full load of wines and spirits. To get to the back door it was necessary to join the queue of cars waiting to get into the car park. As this was full and had a barrier system that only let one car in when one came out, it was a case of moving up one car at a time. When I finally got on the bank they were desperate; the shop was completely out of drink!

Then there was a load to Fareham, I was late leaving because the trailer was not loaded and the day driver had committed the ultimate sin of not filling up. Fortunately I had done a paper delivery just round the corner so was able to go straight to the store. The manager was just locking up, but quickly reopened - a load of roll cages has never come off so quickly!

The other one was Fulham, which was on the site of the old Fulham Power Station. When I got there the street was full of wagons. There had been an outbreak of food poisoning among the staff; staff from other stores had replaced all the regular staff. The canteen was shut and wagons were only being let in one at a time with the drivers not being allowed in the building.

The last and most important job of the shift was fuel, oil and water. It was the only firm I have ever worked for which exercised absolutely no control over its fuel and oil issue. It was just a case of parking the empty trailer, getting on the pump and filling to the brim. No one had a regular unit; any unit parked facing the gate was ready to go. The fleet was all Leyland DAF most in Simms' dark blue, but some of the newer ones were in Sainsbury's colours.

There was one bit of excitement. The tyre fitters came with a load of tyres to do some changes. While they were in the office getting numbers, someone nicked their truck. It was taken to the trailer park in the next street and the load transhipped. The whole event was recorded on the security video but I never knew if anyone was caught.

By the time that job finished I could get from Basildon to Hoddesdon in 25 minutes. The M25 was good for something!

After that I did odd days for Haywood's Safety Glass. A lot of the Agency men would not do this one as it involved handling glass. There was already an agency man working full time and another regular casual.

Then I went to a flue contractor for a couple of weeks while their driver was sick. They had a maximum length four wheeler with half the body as overhang. I had one job, not peculiar but daft. I went to Princes Risborough with three chimney pots. After much hunting I found the site. I arrived at the same time as the groundwork gang, it had not even been pegged out, it would be months before they got to the chimney pots.

From there I was asked it I would mind having a go with a gardening contractor. It had a contract to cut all the grass around Metropolitan Police married quarters and stations. I never realised just how big a landlord the Met. was. The motor was a very old Bedford TK. Once we arrived at a site it was part of the driver's job to push the rotary mower. The regular man operated the cylinder mower, a 30" job. He was a stickler for morning and afternoon tea breaks and a good lunch hour. It wasn't far from home and that was a very pleasant summer.

Then the grass stopped growing and it was back to Haywood's with a bit for MK Electric. I also did a couple of days for Securicor on its parcels side. One day was sixty-four drops without going more than three-quarters of a mile from the depot. There were only two absolute rules. Lock the van every time you get out and take an hour for lunch. Driving work dropped right off and I was asked to help out on the warehouse side. I did a couple of weeks for DSL, the Marks & Spencer warehouse at Thurrock. This was a brain dead job, taking clothing out of packaging and hanging it on rails or packing it on to mobile shelving for delivery to stores. It involved standing for eight hours and did my back in so I pulled out of that one sharpish. Christmas might have been coming but I didn't need the pain. The chap I took to work was an ex-continental driver and personal friend of Abba (the pop group). At the time Agnatha was staying with him on a visit to his family.

After Christmas there were more odd days for Haywood's. Then I was asked if I would mind travelling to Canning Town. This turned out to be Beck & Pollitzer's ICI Contract, delivering Dulux paint. It was all pallet work in swop bodies. Greater London, Kent, Surrey, East and West Sussex as far as Worthing. The regular drivers were on a fixed pay scheme that made the long runs unpopular for them but allowed me to clock up plenty of overtime. I also did some night work with a lorry and trailer, two trips a night to Stowmarket, shuttling pre-loaded swop bodies from the ICI works.

All the wagons had cab phones and all the delivery notes had the stores phone number. We did a lot of the DIY superstores and the regulars told me that if I get messed about at the back door just to phone the shop manager and ask him to sort it out. It worked wonders especially with the ones who shut the shutter and ignored the bell. If it was late in the day you could phone up and ask the last drop if the delivery was urgent and were they prepared to hang on. This was a full summers work and I was treated like the regular staff.

I was very surprised to be offered this job since I had done a couple of odd days earlier in the year. During one of these I was doing a big delivery at Shepherds Bush, wheeling a pallet of 5-litre cans of emulsion down the van I caught the tailboard just wrong and it ran away.

I dropped the pallet but the paint kept going resulting in a ton of emulsion in a big heap in the yard. I phoned the foreman who said hang on. Eventually two of the regular drivers arrived with all the gear to clean up the mess. When I asked the foreman why he had taken me on for the holiday relief he said everyone had the odd accident and I had gone on to clear the rest of the load.

After Becks I went to Parceline at Woodford, first on nights on its Dudley Stationary contract. Then on days with a Mercedes 16.17 delivering into the Lakeside shopping complex. That place is specifically designed to discourage deliveries. There are four unloading areas each one involving going out of the complex round the road and in at another entrance. Nearly all the deliveries were via a maze of fire escape passages. This meant that every door you came to opened against you. Some bigger drops required several trips with a loaded sack truck. Some of the units are so small they have no stockroom, the back door opens straight into the shop. It was common to find girls taking their break, sitting on the stock in a passage. They did not even have a toilet but went out onto the mall and used the public facilities.

From there I went to Atlas Express. Because I could drive a Fuller gearbox I was given a B-series E.R.F on bulk work. I soon found, that as I knew my way around it turned into 40' multi-drop. It ended up with my doing 200 rolls of cloth to the first floor in Mile End Road finishing at 17.00hrs so I made my way back to the depot. When I got back I was told that wasn't good enough, I should have gone out to Woodford to collect. So that was the end of that!

It was back to the odd days at Haywood's. There was also a nice local job with an old Transit truck delivering bits and pieces for a plumber's merchant. Then the grass started to grow and I went back to the garden contractor. The old TK had gone; there was now a new Ford Cargo. This job went along for a while until a new full time driver was recruited. I was contacted by the plumber's merchant and went to work for them direct for a bit, again the truck had changed to a brand new diesel Transit. At the same time, Haywood's had been taken over by Pilkington's and I was under pressure to go back as the regular casual as the other agency driver had been taken on full time.

This suited me nicely; I liked the work, the customers and most of the drivers so I made it my sole customer. The foreman phoned me when he wanted me and the agency paid the wages. I was treated like regular staff and was working practically full time. In February '96 Ronnie the ex-agency driver died and I was offered full time employment.

Throughout the period '93-early '95 I did odd days here and there on jobs which are well worth a mention. Northern Telecom (NT) which succeeded Standard Telephones was installing a fibre optic network for British Pipelines. It operated a couple of 4x4 Mercedes 16.17s, a Ford Cargo and a couple of specialist Ford Transit vans plus three workshop caravans. These needed to be moved between sites and occasionally brought back to Basildon. The first job I did for NT was to go by train to Chester with two other agency men.

From there we went by cab to Ellesmere Port where we picked up the Mercs., the Ford and the caravans for movement to Basildon. We got expenses in advance and everything was paid for, meals, taxi and train fares - the lot. I was allocated the Ford and a caravan with close-coupled wheels. This was coupled to a ball hitch, converted and fitted into a jaw coupling. Coming down the M6 I found that it snaked like mad at 50mph and you needed to come down to 45mph to make it settle. This was due to the fact that the converter was worn out. Just past Stoke 'ole Bill' came alongside and signalled me off down the slip road. Someone had reported I was drunk and I was duly breathalised. You could see the disappointment on their faces when the light stayed unflickering green.

It was a very sedate run home with a late finish. We worked out afterwards that with our wages and expenses and the agency fee the cost of moving those three vehicles about 230 miles came to about £1,200. Fortunately that trailer did not last long, one of NT's men was doing a short move with it when it flew off the coupling, through a hedge and was smashed to bits. In the course of squaring up the paperwork for the police in connection with the stop, I established a good relationship with Jane; NT's transport manager. As a result she 'phoned me at home and fixed up the job then told the agency.

The gang had been working at RAF Lyneham in Wiltshire. On Friday, Terry (the friend of Abba) and I were told to go to a big Ford dealer near Swindon. First train out of Paddington meant 05.00 from home (paid from the front door). When we got to the workshops one caravan was in pieces waiting for brake parts, the other was almost ready, the Mercs. were fully serviced. We had to take these to Gainsborough. Terry had horses to look after so I said I would wait, he could go home again. Eventually I got away and everything was going nicely until I came off of the A34 onto the M40. 'Fsht', 'fsht', 'fsht', 'bang!' The caravan went all ways, when I got on the hard shoulder one of the tyres was in shreds. I 'phoned the tyre firm from the cab and then set out to 'phone the police. I had picked the only place on the motorway where it was three-quarters of a mile to the SOS phone instead of the usual half-mile.

On the way back to the wagon a police car pulled up. They told me that where I had stopped was the most dangerous spot on the motorway hence no 'phone post. They gave me the number of the control and told me not to let the tyre fitter start work until a car had come and the road coned off. When I got back to the wagon, there was a 'phone call from the tyre firm. The tyre was obsolete, it was a cross-ply, the nearest replacement was a radial, and a pair would have to be fitted. I told them to go ahead, this was a money no object job.

Next problem, they had not got any but one of their other depots had. A fitter had been sent hot foot. After a long wait the fitter 'phoned. When he got to the other depot it was shut, he had collected the call out man from home. After turning the place upside down, no tyres. He had traced another pair but they were over near Solihull. I told him to go ASAP as I was starving. Eventually, he arrived and while I waited for the police we ate chocolate, which was all the food he could get. He had had no lunch either. A very late lunch was finally taken at Leicester Forest East on the M1.

I arrived at the pub-cum-restaurant, which was being used as a base at 19.30hrs. Carol, the landlady, told me that if I got a cab into Doncaster I would get the last London train. When I got to Doncaster the last train had gone! Fortunately, Carol had a bed so it was back to Gainsborough. I looked up the timetable for the Saturday train, which left at 09.10hrs. I found out that if I had gone to Retford (which was nearer) I could have caught the night train. Arriving at Retford the following morning at 9am, I, along with several others, found that although the train was due at 09.10hrs, the booking office did not open until 09.15. Fortunately the Senior Conductors on Inter-City can take credit card payments. That was a very lucrative two days!

On another occasion there was a call from Jane. She had a Transit to go to Bournemouth next day. Could I collect it now as it was in the works and I would not be able to get it out until 9am. When she showed me the van the battery was dead, she called out ATS who fitted a new battery. I set off for home, at the first roundabout the engine died and would not restart. Jane sent the AA; the AA man diagnosed a flat battery that would not even open the shut off solenoid. After a jump-start the engine would run on the alternator. Back to the ATS depot, keeping the revs up and driving on the handbrake to get the last battery in stock fitted by a fitter who had stayed late to do his own car. Northern Telecom closed its Basildon factory (the site now contains a huge Argos RDC), and moved to Harlow.

Jane called me one Friday afternoon; she had an instrument van to be at Gainsborough at 8am Monday. I could collect it Sunday and take it home for an early start Monday morning. Anyone, who knows what was British Rail, will know that to go from Basildon to Harlow involves going into Fenchurch Street across to Liverpool Street and back out to Harlow. The van was duly delivered. I was just getting out of the taxi at home when my wife called from the front door "Hurry up, Jane is on the phone". Would I get the first train in the morning to go back to Gainsborough? One of the instruments had failed; it needed to be repaired at Harlow! By the time I got home from Harlow there was another message from Jane, "Keep the rest of the week free!"

Late on Wednesday she called, asking me to be at Harlow about mid-day Thursday when the van would be ready. To save hassle with the train she had already booked me a bed at Gringley Lodge, the previously mentioned pub/restaurant. On the way home the Inter City 125 developed a fault and was to be 'shedded' at Peterborough where a replacement train would be laid on. This was a brand new diesel unit and I noticed that the bogie rode on rolling lobe air bags. Chatting to the driver revealed that he had an indicator in his cab that showed if a bag burst. If this happened he could continue the journey but had to reduce his speed to 35mph.

The woman sitting opposite was about my age. I admired her beautiful bunch of flowers and we got into conversation. She had been visiting her daughter and grandchildren. Talking about grandchildren (I've got seven) the topic came round to the amount of pocket money they get for doing nothing, when we had had to do jobs for ours. I made the inevitable comment of people of my age about taking wireless accumulator to be charged and getting a ha'penny. She said, "So did I. I still pass the place where the shop used to be, in a hole in a wall. I remember the smell and the funny old chap who ran it. He had a thin pointy nose and always wore a flat cap, even in the summer". I said, "That's a fair description of my Great Uncle Ernie Mitten and his shop in Stroud Green Road!" She told me she had been born and brought up in Blackstock Road and could remember the faded sign over the shop front "Mitten's. Wireless sets bought, sold and repaired". It's a small world as I have mentioned before.

The very last job I did for Jane was to take the Ford Cargo from Gainsborough to Worcester. The job was finished on the East Coast and a new base was being set up in Worcester. The Transport Controller came to Gringley Lodge and it was a hectic night, with him putting a large sum behind the bar. In the morning, I kept well away from the NT men who were driving the other vehicles, I had visions of Mr. Plod saying "Blow into this sir!" so I wended my way cross-country.

Leaving the site at Worcester I had a job to get a taxi so I thumbed a lift. This I got from a car driven by a lorry driver on leave from working for the United Nations in former Yugoslavia. He was earning £700 a week driving those white wagons we saw on TV. I was sorry when that job ended. I travelled everywhere by train and taxi, even to and from my home to the station. I could afford to eat in Motorway Services and Little Chefs. I was so regular on the late afternoon train from Kings Cross I got to know some of the commuters, including the chap who commuted every day from Bradford to the City.

I went to Ellesmere Port, Cardiff, Calne, Thatcham, Ipswich, Norwich, Thetford and, of course, Gainsborough. Always by train in one direction, British Rail let me down just once. The first train from Pitsea was late, so I missed the first train from Paddington, which connected, with the Worcester train at Swindon. When I went to the enquiry window my ticket was endorsed for the non-stop Inter City service to Cardiff, then to travel back to Worcester west of the Severn, but it made me late.

While I was working for the agency I was amazed at the men who, having complained about big mortgages and several kids to feed, turned down a good paying day's work because it was multi-drop or involved South London. Even because it involved getting up to catch the first train. They turned up to do a day round London with little knowledge of London and no A to Z.

At the time I worked for the agency, my son was an owner-driver. To give him a week off I drove his motor on boxes out of Thamesport. One of the jobs I did for him was a load of bikes to a warehouse at Moxley. Following his directions I came off of the M6 at Junction 9, around the edge of Wednesbury to the A41. I recognised that the huge building site on my left was where the Patent Steel Shaft Company factory had been. That firm's origins had been in the days when factories were driven from a single steam engine through a maze of overhead line shafts. It had made a special long grain steel bar with a high torsional resistance. Individual electric motors had killed the line shaft. When I mentioned it at the delivery point, I was told that the site had been donated to the Council for building of a Leisure Centre. When work started it was found to be heavily contaminated, the cost of de-toxifying it was astronomical. Smart move by the donor. The site for the Millennium Dome comes to mind as a similar situation.

Another was a 40' box of imported toys. There was a delay at the dock and when I got to the job there was a crowd of anxious young lads. They tore into the load like loonies and once the load was off they collected their pay, got on their bikes and away. The most casual of casual labour! Shades of the Scottish casual removal porters of the late-40s, early 50s who were only paid for the time at the houses. To and from the yard and between collection and deliveries was a ride (or hurl) to work.

There was even a 40' of pasta made at Lowestoft for export to the Far East. Although the biggest export commodity that I saw during that time and when I had been to Thamesport for Parker Morris was fresh air! Ships departing sitting on top of the water with a full load of empties. I was amazed to see the size of the development at the port when the road in was no better than it had been when I took raw materials for the building of the gas plant and the sealant plant very many years before. A couple of bad bends straightened and a bit of dual carriageway at Chattenden Hill.

During the week I covered a lot of miles and worked a lot of hours. I charged him 60% of what I would have cleared had I done it for the agency. About a month later he said, "I've got the invoices for those jobs you did. With what I paid you I've lost money". No wonder owner-drivers are going to the wall or running bent. My son sold up and went back to being an employee. He is as happy as Larry: no worries and more money.

CHAPTER 17
PILKINGTON'S

The time I spent driving for Haywood's then Pilkington's was pretty enjoyable. South London and the Home Counties I knew well and the other ex-agency driver Ronnie, (before he died) was a mine of information. He could give exact directions to very obscure deliveries, he was known as Mr. A to Z. I was very surprised at the amount of double-glazing firms that existed. A big majority were retail outlets. I suppose that having to work with people all the time calls for a certain attitude. The vast majority were pleasant, helpful people, much the same as I had found many years ago in the retail furniture and TV trade. They were appreciative of good service and grateful if you put yourself out. There were some you could call in on for a cup of tea even if you were not delivering and a few you could 'phone from a previous delivery and tell them to put the kettle on. Had it not been for my health problem I could have finished my time on that job.

There were only a couple of outstanding incidents. One occurred at Tooting. Having made a delivery, I went to drive away but the handbrake would not release. The fitters came and worked on it, I had driven about three-quarters of a mile when the spring brakes came on again. The fitters decided that a rear-end suspended tow was required. The main dealer's wrecker would be sent. A 'phone call to the dealer assured me he had left. After a couple of hours another call confirmed that he was well on his way, they had spoken to him on his mobile phone. Well after dark he arrived. From Basildon he had gone into London on the A13, over London Bridge and down through Brixton and Streatham, no wonder it had taken so long. We hooked it up and I showed him the way back via Croydon, Addington and Bromley to the M25, we were back in the yard in an hour and a half to be greeted by some irate loaders who had been waiting hours to tranship the load. That was all down to a stuck unloader valve which stopped air tanks pressurising.

The other incident occurred at a customer's premises in Sittingbourne. It was a small industrial estate, the yard was very big and the only vehicles were three parked cars right at the far end. The unloading door faced you as you came in, it was necessary to do almost a 'U' turn to the right then come back hard on a left lock, there was still nothing in the yard. I ended up 3' too far to one side of the doorway. I took a shunt forward to move over. I had gone about 6' when there was a terrific crash and the engine stalled. What had I hit? Nothing in front, nothing in the mirrors. As I got up to get out, I could just see the roof of a car through the nearside quarter-light. Looking round the front there was a car diagonally backwards under my nearside front corner. My nearside front wheel was embedded in the nearside front door, the end of the bumper in the nearside door, with the 'B' post and part of the roof, moulded round my nearside front corner.

I asked the woman driver where she had come from and she pointed to the bottom of the yard. Apparently instead of backing out of her parking space and turning to drive out of the estate, she had reversed diagonally up the yard for about 80 yards at some speed until she had hit me. While we were working out how to separate the car from my wagon, she called the police. They came and told her it was none of their business as it was private property and if it had been on a road she would have been done for dangerous driving. With the loan of a crowbar and a hacksaw I got mobile. The car was a write-off; the floor pan and the roof were badly bent and torn where the 'B' post had pulled them in. It was halfway across the passenger seat along with the rear door. To crown it all, she tried to claim that it was my fault because "I hadn't sounded my horn."

There was a glazier's at Folkestone to whom we delivered. The cutter there came from St. Helens and when he was a young man Pilkington's delivered direct to his employer. Crates of window glass down skids from a horse drawn wagon. Another glazier in Eastbourne, Keith Billesness could trace his ancestry to a stranded Dutch pirate. His great grandfather was an itinerant glazier who carried his stock on a 'frail' on his back.

The name 'frail' for a glass-carrying frame was brought to Britain by Flemish glassmakers; it was the old Flemish or High Dutch word for basket. They also brought with them the word 'cullet' for scrap glass; the original Venetian glass makers had given this to them. Probably the word 'pane' for a sheet of glass came from the same source. Rather oddly, in the Brierley Hill area, which once specialised in blowing, cutting and moulding glass, the molten material was always referred to as 'metal'.

The old glass-blowing industry had an unusual system of payment. The firm provided the factory, the material (sand, soda etc.) and the pot arch (furnace). It then bought the saleable pieces from the master blower generally called the Chairman because he sat in a special long-armed chair while he worked. He split the earnings between his teams according to their status. There were similar methods of payment among chain cable makers. Also the hand cut file makers of the Midlands. The latter were also Flemings, the most famous being Peter Stubbs. My uncle, the toolmaker, had a set of Stubbs handcut files of which he was immensely proud, he used them almost with reverence. Stubbs along with Henry Squires locks and Terry springs were some of the first to bring engineering crafts to the Midlands, particularly the Black Country. - More impromptu history.

Going full time with Pilkington's did me a great favour. From the time I collapsed in February until July when my LGV licence was withdrawn, I was able to take advantage of the best sick-pay scheme I had ever had in transport. With termination of full time employment I went to sign on with the Job Centre, for the Job Seeker's Allowance, all £49.15 of it. The interviewer asked me what I could do, I told him "Not much". I had been advised against physical exertion because of blood pressure and heavy lifting or standing too long because of my arthritic back and neck. Both the result of years of driving short wheelbase artic units with stiff springs. She put me down for "Very light labouring" and asked if the Doctor would sign me off as unfit for work.

When I spoke to the Doctor, he said he could not. Because I took tablets, I no longer had blood pressure although exertion would shoot it up. My back and neck were not bad enough to be disabling. The only thing he could put on a certificate was "Old and decrepit" or "Well worn" neither of which were recognised medical conditions. I subsequently went to a chiropractor with my back trouble; he told me that over 50% of his male patients were lorry drivers.

Looking through the job ads certainly brought home, how little age and experience are valued. Once upon a time old drivers ended their time in the office. Their knowledge of geography, loads and customer's foibles was invaluable. Today, the big white box on the desk knows it all, so long as you're young and computer literate you too can be a traffic operator.

The ultimate computer story must be about the 40' load of groupage 'turned out' by HM customs at Dover. When it came to putting it back they had not got the computer generated loading plan. The surplus filled a 17-ton four-wheel van!

CHAPTER 18
DAVIS BROS. and H.T.S.

No story of road haulage can be complete without at least a small mention of Davis Bros. A mention of the name to an old hand will always produce an anecdote. When I came out of Army in 1955 the legend "Yiddle for a Fiddle" was blazoned on every toilet and clearing house waiting room wall!

It was an amalgam of many companies, some with well-established names in haulage. The company itself went back to Ruben Davis with horses and carts. Post nationalisation there were joint enterprises between the brothers and solo efforts by individual family members married in with the whole. John Mollett, in an article in *CVRTC NEWS* in 1984 unravelled some of it. The impact on this group of companies on the haulage scene warrants a book of its own.

One take-over which aroused a lot of comment at the time, was that of Charles Poulter Ltd. Charlie Poulter's was a well-respected old firm best known for its activities around London and St Katherine's Dock and the upriver wharves, local work. Shortly after the take-over there were reports of venerable Poulter wagons in far-flung parts of Britain. Even one report of a Scammell Scarab artic. which usually did bits and pieces around London, being seen in Ramsgate. The take-over also led to the famous (or infamous?) depot in The Highway, London E.1. In reply to a question "Whereabouts in The Highway is Davis' depot?" came the reply "Anywhere along the kerb there is a space!" Changing engines, gearboxes and diffs. in the street was a common sight.

I was given a lift by a Davis black oil tanker (a Leyland Octopus) and as I got in the driver said, "Don't step on the night man", and there he was, fast asleep on the floor on the passenger side, on top of all the fittings!

When I worked for BRS we used to load palletised cartons out of Thames Board Mills. Each afternoon a Davis' Ford Trader artic used to collect six ton of cartons for Liverpool. These were loaded on top of 16 tons of boilerplate already on the floor. Subsequently on nights for Morton's I often passed this vehicle going up the hill on the Coventry by-pass past the Jaguar dealers. It needed a close study of the wheel nuts to see that it was moving! How it got out of Hockliffe or up Weedon I don't know, I am sure with that weight it would have kept away from the M1 motorway.

Maintenance never seemed to be a strong point. When an MoT examiner visited their Moxley depot he remarked in his report "I didn't know if I was entering a haulage depot or a breaker's yard." Ubby is reported to have said to another MoT man who was talking about preventative maintenance "We don't mend 'em 'til they're broke and then we don't mend 'em too much". Then there were the Turkish fitters who were 'imported' somewhere about 1965 or 1966. They could speak little or no English and lived in redundant ISO containers at the top of the yard in Mint Street. They had a weekly delivery of halal foodstuffs specially brought over from Turkey.

The notorious dog ringing case got the firm a mention in the national press. A white greyhound was dyed brown and substituted; the colour coming off gave the game away. Dog-racing aficionados tell me that the brown dog that was replaced was good enough to have won anyway. One of the drivers from BRS Grays had been in some way involved, when he worked for Davis. He was arrested by the Flying Squad in the middle of the yard when he came in off a trip! Just to digress a moment; that driver had been divorced and his ex-wife had an injunction which prevented him from going within 500 yards of the marital home. Unfortunately this was just behind the A13 when it was the main road out of Tilbury Dock. One day his 'ex' saw him driving along the A13 and reported him to the Court for breaking the injunction. After that he had to leave the Dock either through Chadwell St Mary or Little Thurrock and Grays.

When the Commercial Motor Show was at Earls Court, a security company fitted an assortment of its devices to a new Ford Transit van. It then threw out a challenge; anyone who could drive it away could have it. The Davis Brothers' team duly arrived complete with metal cutters and oxy-acetylene gear. They eventually got in and drove it away, but it was only fit for scrap.

An event at South Mimms, which I witnessed, involved a Davis night trunk motor that had a trailer tyre on fire. The driver dropped off the unit and other drivers helped save part of the load. One of the brothers arrived, pulled out a large 'wedge' and gave all concerned a drink. The following week the driver said that it had been stopped out of his wages, Sammy reckoned the fire was his fault for running on a flat.

There was another incident at South Mimms involving a Davis motor, in the days when Mutton Lane crossed the Barnet by-pass at a halt sign and joined the A5 at a T-junction. A wagon came out of the junction without stopping, forcing a Davis' wagon and drag off the road into a field. The drag went right over the wagon landing in front of it. The trailer boy was killed. At the subsequent court case when his widow was claiming damages, she was told her damages would be reduced because "-- you are young enough and good looking enough to be able to easily remarry". Such a consideration was perfectly legal at that time.

Sometime early in 1970 I was at a meeting with a group of hauliers. The conversation came round to the demise of the Davis Empire. Many were of the opinion that had it been run straight the organisation could have been one of the most powerful in the industry. Someone commented that we would never see the like of Davis Brothers again, to which one very old East End haulier replied, "Thank God, no industry could stand more than one Davis family in its history".

Davis' had a country depot at Warley Street in Essex, commonly known as The Ranch. That was taken over by George Davis and Sons Ltd., which later became Dual Carriage, which were mostly owner-drivers. It is now a GKN-Chep pallet depot.

Strangely enough the first picture that comes into my mind on the mention of Davis Bros. is the waiting room of Tower Hill Transport's clearing house at Nottingham. There was an old sofa there, which contained enough oil and grease to lubricate an eight-wheeler.

HTS was a company that some people referred to as the modern 'Yiddle.' The boss, Ralph Hilton made the ultimate move to evade justice; he died in the middle of the case. WBS, which was its successor succeeded in going spectacularly skint just after receiving a huge sum to move from Rotherhithe to West Thurrock. I was told that the irate drivers played dodgems with the fleet the night they got their notice. There was a report of a unit being driven through a warehouse wall.

One HTS story. When I worked for Morton's we collected groupage for Ford from a firm at Charlton. They were having a party for the accountant who was leaving to become Chief Accountant at HTS. By the following Tuesday he was back at his desk. When he had taken his new post he asked for the company accounts. He was given a pile of exercise books, old circulars and envelopes spread out flat. He had visions of Pentonville or the 'Scrubs and resigned on the spot. As events evolved, that turned out to be a very wise move.

CHAPTER 19
GOING WEST

Road haulage recollections certainly must include a mention of cafés, once mainstays of the industry. While a significant facet of transport café life was the 'regular', which died out towards the end of the '70's. Drivers and staff would all be on first name terms; wives and children would be known from summer rides. Some of the old time landladies would make arrangements for wives and children to stay overnight. When I started driving, I was known as "Bert's Boy" in many London and West of England cafés for a long time.

Having a quick reckon up, when I started, between the A406 and The Glue Pot (where the Milton Keynes Bowl now stands) there were five tea stalls, sixteen cafes and six B & B houses. Today, the equivalent stretch of the Ml motorway has three (Scratchwood, Toddington and Newport Pagnell).

When I set off on my first solo trip, Dad said to me "You should be well towards 'Brum by dinnertime, go into the Meriden Cafe, they do a good dinner". So they did: roast pork, crackling, stuffing, baked and boiled spuds, carrots; fruit pudding and custard, two teas and two buttered slices (real bread) all for 2/3d (11½p). At that time: egg, bacon, sausage, mushrooms and a fried slice, two teas and a buttered slice cost 1/11d (10p) at Fred Saltmarsh's Cafe in the middle of London Colney.

That is jumping ahead. My first contact with transport cafés was as a child, when most of the runs I first remember were to the West Country. Many of the cafés, I went on to use as an adult. Dad used to start his day with a tea and two slices of bread and jam, get out of London and then stop for breakfast. Thus the first stop was often the Silver Grill opposite Ashford (Middlesex) Cemetery, it often meant waiting for the frying pan to heat up. Then came Bert's at the start of the Bagshot by-pass. This became well known as 'Bert's Gone Mad' a slogan he had painted on the gable wall under which he advertised today's cut-price offer. Just along the road was the middle class bungalow tearoom where Dougie Bader met his wife.

The next place of note was The Blue Hut at the western end of what was then the Basingstoke by-pass. When I first knew it, it was indeed a blue painted wooden hut. Cyril, an elderly chap with a humped back, ran it. My Dad told me that Cyril was a veteran of WWI. When he (Dad) had first used the place it was a tarpaulin over a rope stretched between two trees, the furniture was ex-WD folding tables and forms and the cooking was on paraffin stoves. It still was in the late 1940's. It sticks in my mind as the first place I had a Lyons Individual Fruit Pie. They were not in a box at that time but a cellophane bag. Filled with real fruit; apple, strawberry, raspberry and blackberry. When you took the top off there it was clearly recognisable. Not the anonymous sticky sludge to which their filling degenerated. Their outstanding feature was that they were square shaped.

Going down that road between Bert's and The Blue Hut was Blackbushe Aerodrome, a WWII bomber base. During the war the A30 was closed if they were flying. Doing that run at night involved a long diversion round narrow winding lanes.

Just before where the A33 forked off to the left for Southampton were two pubs. The Wheatsheaf and The Rising Sun, the latter had a tea stall, OK for a quick cuppa. By the Wheatsheaf was a brook, which was handy for filling radiators, that old pool petrol, made engines run hot!

A bit further on the A303 (which everyone used) turned right off the A30. Right in the corner was a bungalow. All through the war, every night the people who lived there put a nightlight on the sideboard at the back of the room and left the curtains open about an inch. That tiny light saved many westbound drivers from overshooting the corner. Those Hartley Masks did not let out a lot of light!

The next was the Blinking Owl at Andover. This is still visible from the new A303. We sat outside there and watched the gliders going over to Arnhem from Thruxton aerodrome (now a motor racing circuit). Just after the Blinking Owl was Stan's of Weyhill, in the corner of the Ludgershall road. It had a most impressive facade that hid a large Nissen hut, but did good grub despite the sham.

There was a cafe in Amesbury, which I think was called The Countess. It had a huge wooden building at the back, which was used as digs. That was one I used as a last resort, when time had well run out.

Coming down the hill after Amesbury I had my first view of Stonehenge. All through the war this was a private tea stop. On the left was a worked out quarry, we used to stop there and brew tea on a Primus. If the weather was nice we used to walk over to The Stones (English Heritage had not yet turned it into a "nice little earner") and brew our tea in the lee of one of the trilithons.

Between Chicklade and Mere was a well-used cafe on the corner of the B-road from Wilton. That road caused a big headache for one of my mates Johnny the Shop Steward. If he were delivering in the Salisbury area, he would use it to reach that cafe and get back on the A303. One winter he was going to Bodmin. Instead of leaving on Sunday morning, he had a day at home and went in the early hours of Monday. He stopped for tea at the Rising Sun, to be told that the A303 was closed at Wylye due to a blizzard. He went down the A30 to Salisbury only to be told by the police that the same blizzard had closed Shaftesbury. As he had a double-drive Leyland Octopus he decided to give the B3089 a go. With almost virgin snow and no abandoned vehicles he got through to the cafe to find a huge eastbound queue and an empty, lightly powdered road to the west. He was thus able to go on and do his delivery and reload. On the way home he met the others who had left on time on the Sunday morning still heading west having been held up for nearly two days. Fortunately, back at the depot, the management chose not to press him too hard as to how he had not been snowed in with the others!

He had another adventure in the snow the following year. On the same run, going round the north side of Dartmoor, he, along with many others became snowed in at Whiddon Down. Really snowed in, only cab roofs and high loads sticking up out of an unbroken snowfield. The drivers were given shelter in pubs, church and school halls in the village. Those drivers carrying foodstuffs gave up part of their loads to supplement the village's stocks. By the time the road was re-opened, two full pallets of marg. and cooking fat off of the back of the load had been eaten. The argument about who should pay for them rumbled on for ages. Should it be Devon Police, BRS, V.d.J. or the Goods-in-transit insurance? Johnny survived the Palestine trouble pre-war, the Dunkirk evacuation, the Normandy landings and being blown up by a Teller mine. Although he still had bits of shrapnel coming out of his body in the early nineties. He died in 2005 at the age of 81; he lied about his age to get into the army and was in fact only 16 when he queued in the water to get off of the beach at Dunkirk.

Enough about Johnny's troubles! The next cafe of note from my childhood was Mrs Howard's. This was a couple of old World War I Army huts just on the western edge of the R.N.A.S./F.A.A. aerodrome at Yeovilton. The toilet was a shed up the garden, but it boasted a "Willow Pattern" pan. She had a heart of gold and a huge brood of children. There never seemed to be a Mr Howard and their assorted features caused much conjecture among the regulars. Nevertheless even in the worst of rationing you always got a good feed. As far as I can work out it was superseded by the Frying Pan, which warrants an aside.

Sam 'Bowler' Tyson was doing the Bodmin marg. run. He had had a Sunday indoors and an early start on Monday and dropped in at the Frying Pan for breakfast. Unknown to him the nearside drive axle inner tyre had punctured and run very hot. While he was eating, it caught fire and set fire to the wagon. The load melted and ran down the sloping car park forming a lake of molten margarine on the A303. The road was closed for ages, while it was allowed to reset and could be shovelled up. Naturally, he swore that he had had a night out at Wincanton, BRS engineers were positive that running that short distance would not have heated the tyre that much. Eventually he appeared before Bernard Ridley, the District Manager, and was given seven days suspension.

Past Ilchester on the left was a red brick house The Fosseway Cafe, run by a funny old lady Mrs Evans. This was a good digs, lit by oil lamps, but always with steak for your evening meal. The car park, which was part of the verge, was a bit of rough hardstanding on the opposite side of the road.

After climbing Yarcombe Hill, which in the early days was quite formidable, you dropped down to a river bridge, which was the Somerset-Devon border. As a small boy I remember lowering a water can on a very long rope to get water for the rad. Not far past that was Kay's Cottage, the first house and cafe in Devon.

Next was the Cosy Cafe in the High Street Honiton; imagine parking along the High Street to use a cafe. This had a regular clientele; Alan Spillett has an evocative painting of Arnold's wagons parked there. My Dad and I used Tiny's, on the left at the western edge of the town. The lady behind the counter knew all the regulars by their surname. The cafe did beds, but with all the family my Dad could not afford it, so we slept in the van in the lorry-park, which was down a lane opposite. We were there the night of the Honiton Air Raid. A Jerry returning from Exeter jettisoned a bomb, which exploded in a field killing a bull. It was still being talked about in the late '60's. Percy Mitchell the Grays Superintendent had Tiny's pony trap transported to Stanford le Hope to be repaired by a local cartwright and wagon builder.

Early in the war we used Paris's in Exeter. When I went looking for it during a cycling holiday in 1949 I found it had been annihilated during the Exeter blitz.

Going west on the A30, there was the White House Cafe at Tongue End near Sticklepath. I cannot remember the woman's name but that was a large home from home used regularly by Tate & Lyle's men. One of them was taken ill on the road, and managed to get to the White House where she made all the arrangements to get his wagon collected and then nursed him for a fortnight. She even arranged for his wife to come and visit him.

The only other café I remember going that way, was the BRS digs in St. Austell, very exotic, palm trees outside and peaches growing in a conservatory at the end.

Going out of Exeter the other way on the A38 during the early years you had a choice between going over Telegraph Hill or forking left on the easier road into Newton Abbot and rejoining the A38 towards Ashburton. There was a rough car park at the top of Telegraph Hill, which had a 45-gallon drum of water courtesy of the A.A. The right place to let the engine cool and top up the radiator. There was a similar site on Carter Bar. Telegraph Hill was supposed to be the site of the first beacon in the chain, which signalled the arrival of the Spanish Armada, also a military mechanical semaphore station.

The major cafe on this road was at Plympton. I can't remember the name; it was just on the right at the top of a hill with a big car park. This was another place where we sat and watched a town being bombed, just after we had delivered a load of textiles evacuated from London "for safety?" in this case Plymouth. I used that place in the early '70's while delivering tractors to Plymstock.

There was an incident involving that run to The West that happened in my BRS days. There was a company rule: "A driver is entitled to use the nearest 'suitable accommodation' to the point where his time runs out. If the charge is more than the subsistence allowance, the company will pay the difference, on the production of receipts".

The driver involved was sent with an imported removal in a large packing case. He was to be met at the house by Pickfords' porters who would do the actual delivery. Having crawled through the lanes of "millionaire land" behind Sunningdale, he had to reverse into the job, (the gate was too narrow to drive in) and about a quarter of a mile up a gravel drive, which his double-drive Octopus did the world of no good. The house was in darkness and there was a note on the door saying that the porters would be there at 9 o'clock the next day. When he got back to his wagon it had sunk up to the axles. He got his case and walked into Ascot. The only available accommodation was The Berystede; a five-star place patronised by celebrities using the nearby golf courses. The bill came to just over £15 (night out money was 17/6d).

It took the weight of the London District Staff Officer to get him the money back. The bill for repairing the drive would have bought a new eight-wheeler.

Everyone in the depot found this hilarious, the more so because the driver was noted for being tight. He came from the island of Foula (the most northerly of the Shetlands), when he went on holiday we never knew when he was coming back; it depended on when the next boat could dock. He was known as 'Saxpence', because of his pronunciation. Five of us were waiting to load at Empire Paper Mills in Gravesend, taking turns to buy the teas from the stall. When it came to 'Saxpence's' turn, he came back with five hot Oxos. The uproar subsided and he explained "Weel ye ken, they teas were thruppence, Oxo was ony tuppence ha'penny".

The early days of heavy haulage, ex-Midland Road Services, nationalised into Pickfords. One of two solid tyred 100-ton Scammells. (Drawing by Chris Salaman)

CHAPTER 20
THE MIDLANDS

The Midlands and the North were my personal early runs. As a well-established route since the beginnings of road haulage it was dotted with many cafes enough to fill a separate book. I have picked out some of the better known, some of which I had been going into since I was a child.

The first big one coming out of London was the Beacon at Bignall's Corner. It belonged to Bobby Deard; the haulage contractor. There were beds, a clearing house and a filling station. It was used as a layover point for Abnormal Indivisible loads, as is its successor (still in the same building) the BP Truckstop. It was always a dismal place. The Good Companions just up the road at South Mimms was a much nicer place, but not 24-hour and with little parking.

The next (pre- bypass) was the Farm just over the bridge in London Colney. It was next door to the Water Splash pub and roadhouse, now the site of an industrial estate. There was a small one on the left, the Cottage, I think, but the most popular was 'Fred's 18 mile,' run by Fred Saltmarsh. The car park was not very big and anyone not parking tight and tidy would get a rucking from Fred. I was in there the morning of the first big pile up on the Ml motorway. A policeman came and called out "Anyone going north, use the A5, the Ml is shut, and it looks like Cohen's yard". George Cohen was a famous scrap metal man at the time and was known as The 600 Group.

Still travelling north, there was the Redbourn Cafe just by the railway bridge, used by Tate & Lyle to change over. That is now inside the St. Albans 7.5 tonne exclusion zone. Then comes a very famous cafe, the Watling Street. I first went in there as a very small boy. It has recently all been done up, with a nice Tarmac lorry-park. I best remember it with a lorry-park like a ploughed field. The fuel pumps right on the edge of the road, with two large overhead diesel tanks. It was a job to tell at this point where the park finished and the road began as the edge of the road was badly pot-holed probably by spilt diesel. It had one of the first public TV sets. A big heavyweight-boxing match resulted in not being able to get on the park or into the cafe. Just past that was a small green wooden hut cafe with a steeply sloping lorry-park, a popular place with tanker men. This is now a Little Chef. After that came the Three Sisters, a large house lying back from the road. This did beds and has already been mentioned, its site now holds a huge hotel.

Just coming into Markyate, on the right was a small café, which survived for many years after the by-pass. The village was subject to a 15 mph speed limit, it was extremely narrow, and most of the houses bore the scars of being scraped by passing lorries. It was on the newly opened bypass that George Wright of BRS Parcels had the spectacular engine run-away (the governor broke!) mentioned earlier.

Beyond Markyate was another well-known cafe, the Pack Horse, next door to the 15th century Pack Horse pub. This later became a depot of J & H Transport of Peckham. It is now a warehouse complex. S.W. Steven-Stratten's book "British Lorries 1945-75" has a photo of J & H's Diamond T breakdown parked outside. This was the location of Jim Spring's fatal accident involving 14 tons of carrots.

Through Dunstable and down the cutting was the Sentinel, an old railway carriage. This was picked up and moved bodily to a site nearer Hockliffe sometime in the late 1940's. The hedge, which backed the original site, can just be seen by the new roundabout for the Stanbridge Road. Like so many A5 cafes, the Ml closed it and the site became a tyre depot. It is now a motel, which, according to local man Joe Greenwood, older residents still refer to as The Sentinel. Just after the war my Dad was off to Brum, it was a very foggy day, typical of November at that time. He decided to pull in at the Sentinel and give his eyes a rest. He went to the back of the park right by the cafe. As he got out a man ran up to him and said, "You can't leave that there in this weather". Dad was just going to ask why not, when he looked back across the park and saw a line of sidelights vanishing into the fog. He had picked up a convoy of cars going through Dunstable; they had followed him off the road and into the cafe.

In Hockliffe was the Manor House, mentioned earlier in my brush with the local greengrocer. The site is now a cul-de-sac of smart houses. Even the old pub up the hill, The Grapes, is now just a house.

Just before the Manor House the A5 forked off to the right. In the pre-Motorway era the route for Northampton via Newport Pagnell. If I had to stay in Northampton I used Johnny's in The Causeway, which was just an ordinary town centre working men's plus transport café, which had a few beds. My main excuse for diverting off to Northampton was to mention another feature. At the bus terminal in the town centre was a gas lamp with a little machine on the side. If you put a penny (1d) in the slot, a pint of boiling water came out of a spout. Ideal for the times when many workmen and bus drivers carried a tea-can complete with some dry tea and a couple of spoonfuls of sweetened condensed milk.

Back on the A5 it was over The Sandhills and along Mickey's Mile into Little Brickhill and the Brickhill Cafe, which figured large in my days at BRS Kentish Town. My friend Joe Greenwood, who lives in the village did a lot of research into the Mickey of Mickey's Mile fame and came up with two theories, a highwayman or a toll keeper/lengthman. Another friend had researched the highwayman theory and had drawn a blank so it seems that Mickey was an early roadworker. When I started driving, the end of Mickey's Mile did a peculiar right and left kink through an orchard. In those days there was a derelict cottage in the orchard, which I was told was a Telford tollhouse. This was lost when the kink was straightened.

Joe found that Telford's Holyhead Road followed the line of the Roman Road (which ran to the west of the village) The kink being the result of Telford diverting east off of the line of the Roman Road to go through the village, which became a major coaching station. So the story of the cottage is probably true and may even have been Mickey's home. According to Joe, in the 18th Century it contained fourteen pubs and traveller's lodgings, and saw between 40 and 60 coaches a day passing through. Talking of coaching – Stony Stratford was home to two coaching inns, The Cock and The Bull, where travellers gathered to tell tall tales of their experiences, hence "A Cock and Bull Story". While in Dunstable was The Sugarloaf, well known for its enormous meals.

At the bottom of Brickhill was another railway coach cafe, The Pullman. Again, thanks to Joe's information, I know that this was brought from Wolverton carriage works by traction engine. It was rebuilt as a brick building around 1950 and is currently a farm shop. It marks the start of the very recent Brickhill by-pass, which now runs east of the village.

Still going north, after the Denby Hall bridge was the 46 Mile Café. Run by a formidable blonde lady, known as The Duchess, in fact the cafe was often known as The Duchess'. This is now part of the "Sizzling Sausage" chain.

After that came the famous (or infamous) 48 Mile Café, universally known as The Glue Pot. When I went with Dad a real character called Bill Spittles ran it! Even in the worst depths of rationing he always had meat, even steak. I used it for many years, until the advent of Milton Keynes when it finally disappeared under The Bowl. The Glue Pot was a legend. It was an operating centre for the not very ladylike "ladies of the road", particularly Sadie. Behind the cafe was the washroom, which also served the digs. In the early days one wall would often have several wheels with registration numbers chalked on them. If you were lightly loaded and came across someone with a double 'blow out' it was common practice to lend him your spare. This would then be left at The Glue Pot to be collected. The 'fourpenny tool kit' ended that practice.

At night in those early days it was the gathering point for BRS Meat Pool drivers, who had a large card school, the kitties were astronomical, piles of notes under an ashtray. It was common for one of them to call out "I've got a change-over and I'm on a winning streak, who wants to earn a fiver running up to the Pot Thrower?" As that was a third of a week's wages I have done it more than once. It was 120 miles of hard work. The double bend over the canal at Long Buckby, the right angle bend at the bottom of Kilsby and the narrow railway bridges, and still 95 miles home afterwards, times were hard.

One of the funniest things I ever saw was at the Glue Pot. The card school was in full swing when a driver stuck his head round the door. "Would BRS Meat number so and so please let me out?" A voice replied, "Wait 'til we finish the hand". About half-an-hour later same driver, same response. At that moment I went out. This driver had a low loader carrying a mobile crane. As I came out of the door he was getting up into the crane which he started. His mate put a set of chains on the offending motor and he picked it up. Further up the park was an empty Pickfords' low loader. The mate drove the low loader carrying the crane alongside it, with the Meat Pool motor dangling over the back. The driver and his mate then dropped it on to the empty Pickfords. I sat in my cab to watch what happened.

Eventually the card school rolled out, Pickfords' driver included. They were hysterical. When the laughter subsided, the driver whose motor it was, said to the Pickfords' man, "I'll help you chain it down, you can drop it off at Cotton Street on your way to Bow."

Mentioning Long Buckby reminded me of an equally funny incident, which could have been a tragedy. Coming south, the A5 ran alongside the Grand Union Canal in a long, straight. It then did a sharp right over the canal and a sharp left at a pub to run on the other side of the canal. I was following an eight-wheeler and we were both slowing for the turn. A USAF artic passed us both. I saw him go over the bridge in the wheeler's lights, and then there was a cloud of dust and a crash. We stopped on the bridge; the artic was in the pub car park. There was a lot of screaming and we found an old lady running round with a doorknob in her hand. She had been coming out of the outside toilets, as she shut the door the artic demolished the lot and left her holding the doorknob. Fortunately, neither she nor the driver was hurt. The old bridge went with the road improvements that left the road straight. But the last time I was past, the sign for "Pedigree Fresian Herd" which we used as a braking point was still visible in the nearside hedge.

I was supposed to be talking about cafés, but these little asides are just as interesting.

In Towcester was Albert's Café, which was investigated by BRS because it gave out car park tickets when it did not have a car park! Just north of Towcester was the Tower Café (one of a chain) now called Jack's Hill; the southbound queue for the Towcester lights used to start there at busy times. Forking left for Brum on the A45, the first cafe at the top of the hill was The Ace, Weedon. This is now a brick building; it used to be a wooden place. There is a story that a burned out McNamara's Scammell was buried at the back (north side) of the park in an earlier expansion. My Dad stopped there with a steamer, when Weedon Barracks was a remount centre for the cavalry. A long series of low jumps for schooling young horses is still called "A Weedon Lane" by riding instructors.

On the new Daventry by-pass will be found the Royal Oak Roundabout. At one time this was the site of the Royal Oak pub, which did beds for drivers, the guvnor, Tom was a nice old boy.

Further along were the Green Hut and Sid's Wood Farm Café. In the days of solid tyres a full day's work from London. Dad used it regularly while on the Aston Vinegar job. It was one of the old glorified sheds.

After the drop down Braunstone Hill, came Tubby's at Willoughby and across the road the Four Crosses pub and digs. Tubby's was well named; his huge belly was always visible under the grubby vest, well soaked in fat flying out of the egg pan. It was a regular comment, always accepted without rancour, "Better ring your vest out Tubby the egg pan's getting low". He married a woman off the canal boats, always known as Cock-eyed Sarah for obvious reasons. When things 'fell off the back of lorries' they often landed in Tubby's. One night some zealous young PC decided to have a nose round. A driver pulling in spotted him and told Tubby who marched out, grabbed the copper by the seat of his trousers and his collar. He carried him out and dropped him on the road saying, "This is public property. Where you were is private property, my private property and you were definitely not invited". At the same time any PC who openly drove or rode in and parked round the back got a tea and a sandwich. Sadly, another legend that has fallen to the demolition man.

Past the Laughing Dog Brand pet food factory, near where the M45 roundabout was finally built, came the A45 Blue Boar, (its name commemorates an old coaching inn) turn left for Leamington via Princethorpe. It's the ancestor of the one over on the A5 and the name lives on with the Watford Gap Services. That was a well-used cafe day and night. Today it is another Little Chef. In the '60s it had a resident tyre fitter, Eric, an ex-German PoW who stayed. One of the few men I have met, who I could not get on with under any circumstances.

On the right was The Autos. The most spotlessly clean transport café I have ever been in. This was run and staffed entirely by women. I was told that they were ex-WAAF cookhouse staff from the nearby aerodrome, subsequently used by Export Packers & Shippers. By the time I had heard the story and got up that way to ask, it had shut.

Bob's of Stretton was another well-known, well-used café. On the night of 14th November 1940 we were asleep in the van on its lorry-park. We were woken by the noise of the bombing and watched Coventry burn. We had just delivered a load of textiles to the Co-op warehouse in Spon Street. We were held up because the A45 and A5 were closed to allow the free movement of emergency vehicles. When I used the cafe regularly in the '60s and '70s, the night staff was a Swiss couple Trudy and Bernie. When I went past in October 1997 it was still open, advertising itself as a Family Restaurant. Looking from the road the lorry-park did not seem to have improved much in the last 57 years. Sadly it is closed and up for sale.

If I had to go into Coventry and could not get back to Bob's, I stayed at Lee's Transport House at 46 Holyhead Road. This was right on a corner at some lights, with a fair bit of heavy traffic all night. I had noticed, and heard other drivers remark that so long as the traffic flowed normally you never noticed it and slept well. But a skid or someone making a mess of a gearbox would upset the routine waking you to wonder why. The Meriden Café, I mentioned at the beginning. I used it quite a few times over the years, even after the by-pass opened. But I lost track of its fate when I went on to regular nights. The last café going into Brum was Anne's Pantry which was a teashop in a parade, but popular with drivers.

When I stayed in Brum I used the Dolphin Café in Meriden Street, a turning off the Digbeth, up to the mid '60s, when it closed with the start of the Bull Ring redevelopment. It was a very old run down building, but the food was good and the beds clean. The place was so dilapidated, that if you dropped your shaving brush in the long washroom it would roll down the sloping floor to the end!

The last time I stayed there I was delivering 50-ft. 12" x 12"s to the site of the Birmingham Post Office Tower. It was very foggy. I was to be unloaded by a 100-ft. crawler crane, which stood at the bottom of an 80-ft. hole, but the driver could not see the banksman standing beside the trailer, so I was told to go away and come back when the fog went. I wended my way round into Sherlock Street, which before the building of the new wholesale market went to the lights on the Digbeth, with Meriden Street straight ahead. I was about 8 or 9 to go at the lights and it took me exactly one hour to get across those lights.

When I came to park up I had to leave the wagon as best I could get it into the kerb (on-street parking), I could only see about half way down the trailer.

BRS Bromford Lane had two regular digs. One was above a fish and chip shop just across the road. It wasn't bad, but it took as far as North London for the smell of chip fat to leave your clothes. The other one was a big private house in the Tyburn Road. The beds and the food were good but it was a good walk from the depot. The owner was a builder and I must have heard the story of how he installed his central heating system (all screwed iron) only having to take up two floorboards on each floor, at least thirty times.

My depot started to do many loads of tyres out of Bushbury through BRS Wolverhampton. My request to have a bed booked introduced me to what I reckoned to be the best digs in England, Molly Potts, 102 Wellington Road, Bilston. We used to park-up in Jenner Street depot under the watchful eye of Old Jack and Noggy, then catch the trolleybus to the digs. It was a real home from home, a big pot of tea always on the go. Drivers, who had kids of their own, were left in charge of hers so that she and her husband could have an evening off.

There was a driver for Rakusen's of Leeds (the matzo makers) who had stayed there so regularly over the years that kids called him Uncle George. Molly actually closed once, then reopened in a house directly opposite. If Molly was full, (you had to book early) there was another good digs at West Bromwich. Where this once stood is now an empty site just across from the Junction 1 Truckstop. It took a couple of visits to the latter to recognise the connection with former times. Then only from the little open all hours corner shop opposite, which is still standing.

On the other side of the Midlands i.e. Leicester and Nottingham there were two good digs and a café I used regularly. The café lay between Leicester and Mountsorrel and was used when loading 'Alice's loads'. It was run by a little old lady, about as fat as a broomstick, known to all and sundry as Ma. She did all the cooking on a coal range and used those old cast-iron saucepans with the tubular handles. The big ones when full must have weighed as much as her. When she lifted them the veins stood out in her neck. It was a place I won't forget. The path to the front door was below the road and protected by a guardrail. On a very foggy morning a London Carrier's driver mistook the car park for the road and ran into the end of the barrier with fatal results.

In Leicester it was The Gate in Humberstone Gate near the clock. The woman there had her old uncle living with her. He had worked in the pits as a checker. He had us in fits with his tales. His favourite was about his job. When the pits were private, he went round three pits on a bike and did all his books in a shed by the offices. When they were nationalised, the NCB built him an office and gave him a van. By the time he retired he had three typists to do the figures and a chauffeur driven car to take him round the pits. When I went on to BRS we were always booked in at The Engine which was a pub. Not as good as The Gate, although BRS approved.

In Nottingham it was Alice's, 124 London Road. This was an enormous old Victorian house. It was almost as good as Molly's. In those days it was common for landladies to chuck you out for the evening. Not Alice Herbert, she had a comfortable big sitting room, she would sit and join in the conversation and knew as much about transport as we did. At bed time there was always a huge cold supper. Fresh bread, cold meat, cheese and pickles. She had a live-in helper, Sarah, who was a dead ringer for Dame Edna Evarage's bridesmaid Madge. When trade started to drop, Alice moved a few doors up the road so that her house directly faced the exit from the Cattle Market where we parked. The last time I was in Nottingham, all those well-built Victorian houses had gone, and had been replaced by a line of modern rabbit hutches.

On the other side of the Midlands was Evesham. This was a place you went to for a reason, it was not on a direct route to or from anywhere. I had done TV deliveries there but started going regularly when Van den Burgh & Jurgens of Purfleet launched its own label squash called 'Tree Tops'. Beaches of Evesham made this under contract. As BRS Grays had the bulk storage contract we did many loads each week. I saw a most spectacular sight on that work. A British Sugar man was delivering a load of hot sugar syrup when his hose burst. A fan shaped spout of liquid went about eight feet in the air and set as it started to fall. In about a minute it was like an ice fountain. It had to be broken up with sledgehammers.

Our regular digs was Mrs Icke's in Merstow Place. One afternoon one of the other regulars said to me, "You go home Stratford – Banbury (some went Broadway – Oxford) come with me to Bridies". When we went in Bridie said "Hello Ronnie! The usual?" adding, "It's gone up to 32/6d (£1.62½p). Ronnie paid up and then she said to me "Your unlucky my dear, they've all gone, that'll be 17/6 (87½p)". When we were washing I asked Ronnie about the 15/0-(75p) difference, and what had all gone? He replied "Didn't you know? A waitress or a room maid. Bridie fetches them over from Ireland and sends them back when they get pregnant. I don't think there are any staff bedrooms". Towards the end of that job we all had to stay at Bridie's after Mrs Icke caught two male drivers in bed together and we were banished. Bridie's was a nice purpose built place with a very big car park. The last time I was past it was a derelict shell.

While on that side of the Midlands on the odd occasions I visited the Droitwich – Worcester area on the A38 near Wychbold I used was a very good old-style café. It had a big car park, which always seemed to be overflowing. The last time I was in there it was overshadowed by the then newly built M5. It advertised in *Headlight* for many years after the Motorway opened as it was near Junction 5.

Mentioning the A38 made me think of another well-known café in the west on the A38, Wood's at North Petherton. I only went there once. It was Christmas Eve, a normal working day at that time. They were giving a free Christmas dinner with a bottle of beer to everyone. That was a fairly common practice at one time, but usually confined to known regulars.

Talking of working on Christmas Eve reminded me of two things not connected with cafés.

In my van days we would be put on hire to the Royal Mail for the Christmas rush. This involved working until 1 o'clock Christmas Day delivering parcels.

While when I was on night trunk for BRS and Morton's, the last working day before the holiday was Christmas Eve, thus the shift finished at 6.30am on Christmas morning. Christmas Eve '70 particularly stood out. I was coming home from Brum and there wasn't a soul about. As I came on to the London Colney by-pass, there was a BRS Parcels wagon in the lay-by, the driver who I knew as Little George was leaping up and down in the middle of the road. He had stopped for a kip, got down to have a pee and forgotten to release the slam lock. He was locked out, with keys and tools in the cab. It took a lot of wangling with my screwdriver and a piece of box banding off my load to get him back in. He was having visions of trying to get the breakdown crew out from Walnut Tree Walk workshops on Christmas Day.

There was another Bridies on that run. A small place at Aynho on the A41. It was a favourite haunt of BRS men doing the pig iron run from Fords at Dagenham to the Leamington Foundry, it went back as far as General Roadways days when its drivers went straight through to Liverpool making use of the Birmingham New Road. It closed and reopened a few times, the last time I was up that road it was a haulage contractor's office. Anyone digging down in the car park would find large quantities of pig iron used to fill big potholes.

The two horse power of Grandad's day, waiting to take part in a recent annual cart marking ceremony.

BRS men all. John, Chris Salaman, the author, and Stan Bird who was nationalised with General Roadways.

Membership card from September 1955. An attempt by Harry Kelson, Editor of 'Headlight' magazine, which provided advice and assistance for lorry drivers to foster some of the old Bedford Drivers' Club spirit.

Headlight Drivers Club

MEMBERSHIP CARD

No. 2542

This is to Certify

that Mr R. F. Raol

of

has this day been elected to membership of

THE HEADLIGHT DRIVERS CLUB

Dated 1 XI 1955

J. Burgess

Secretary

NOTE: YOUR ANNUAL SUBSCRIPTION IS PAYABLE ON

THE 1st DAY OF September IN EACH YEAR.

The objects of the club are :—

(a) To promote and maintain a spirit of comradeship and good fellowship among all persons employed as drivers or drivers' mates in the road haulage industry.

(b) To ensure that proper regard is had to the needs and comfort of drivers and their mates by manufacturers of commercial vehicles.

(c) To lay down standards of cleanliness and comfort for cafes and hotels catering for drivers and their mates.

(d) To provide as far as practicable free legal and technical advice for drivers and their mates on questions of wages, hours and loads.

(e) To effect insurance of the members.

(f) To promote and conduct examinations for testing the efficiency of commercial drivers and to award certificates to be known as " Headlight Proficiency Certificates " to successful candidates.

(Top) A modern van belonging to The Pantechnicon. When the picture was taken (early '90s) the firm was being run by a descendant of Seth Smith.

(Bottom) A genuine 2,000 cubic foot Leyland Luton van with crew cab and sleeping quarters in the Luton.

A Scania removal van from a firm which dates back to horses. The Luton "bedroom" even has a window!

A beutifully restored BRS Bristol belonging to Robin Masters, also waiting for a recent cart marking ceremony.

An Alan Spillett painting of the author with his Bristol at work on the A30.

Also by Alan, a painting of the Tuffley Steeple waiting at the Windrush Cafe for the police escort to arrive.

Another AS painting of a Welsh Leyland back loading at the Old Covent Garden Market.

A fine AS painting of an AEC Mandator climbing The Devil's Punchbowl on the A3.

(Top) A Liverpool Foden FG being prepared for trunk. This model always brings back memories for me of being stuck in low reverse. Sheeting and roping, ropes in a tangle, drivers wearing old suit or sports jackets, a younger "teddy-boy" looking on. marvellous memories. (Photo: Peter J. Davies)
(Bottom) A convoy of AECs on a fine autumn evening, obviously just come down from Shotton via the M1 and heading west on the A505 with steel to Vauxhall's. Almost ready to park up in Dunstable BRS Depot for a night out. (Photo: Peter J. Davies)

(Left) Traditional glass carrying style of body on a Volvo FL6. It has a side frail for securing very large panes of glass.

(Below) The author in relaxed mode whilst shunting at the Basildon tractor plant.

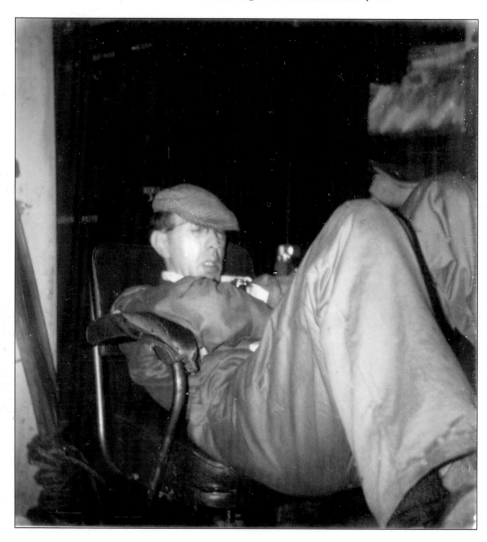

CHAPTER 21
THE NORTH WEST

The first part of this trip was exactly the same as going to the Midlands. Going to the North West meant staying on the A5 at Weedon. Although it was the A45, which crossed, this actually involved a right turn. Going south it was the main A5 that had a Halt sign.

The first café was the Blue Boar, owned by the same company that owned the original Blue Boar on the A45. This firm later went on to run the Watford Gap Service Area on the M1 under that famous name. This could actually be reached from the lane opposite the A5 place. There was a timber yard in that lane and if you were prepared to overlook the "No Entry except for service vehicles" signs it was possible to deliver there via the M1 services.

Before the Ml was built, the first landmark was a sharp left, followed by a sharp right and almost immediately by a sign saying 'Steep hill, engage low gear now'. At the bottom of the hill was another sharp right with the George Garage facing and the George pub next door and straight away a narrow railway bridge. A bit farther on the A5 took a sharp left turn where it met the A428 from Northampton. Up on the right was The Rendezvous, which is the site of the Crick BP Truckstop.

The next landmark was another funny road junction. The A46 from Leicester came out to a T-junction on your right. Up the hill past that, the A46 swung away to the left. Staying on the A5 meant doing a right and left at an island.

The first café I used was the Birdcage, which was a bungalow up a garden path. The old lady made delicious fruit bread in round cake tins. All the slices were different shapes and thicknesses but all were the same weight as she proved more than once to sceptical drivers.

After that was one I think called the Coppice, I know I was its first customer. I was going along thinking of tea, when I saw a neon sign come on, so I pulled in. I had my breakfast, as I got to my second tea I asked "How much?" and the woman replied "That one is on us, we've just opened. You are our first customer. Keep on coming in and tell all your mates."

Then came the long established Pot Thrower, just past the Reliant works. Next door was a place that made insulators for grid pylons. I collected these and had a demonstration of a machine that made artificial lightning.

We used to turn right on to the B5404 to cut through to the A51. This crossed the A458. There was a two-wagon crash at this crossroads; one wagon went into a garden. The retired miner who lived in the bungalow said to the driver "Bloody hell, forty-two years down the pit with only a cut or two and you bloody near killed me sitting in a deckchair in my own back garden."

The St Michael's in Lichfield I've mentioned. The next was the Farm in Rugeley.

You came to the Farm Café over a railway bridge, looking down into the lorry-park. It was used by lime wagons from Buxton, DG and FG Fodens. Sometimes a brake drum could be seen glowing; even if they did not glow you could light a fag on a front steer drum through the vent hole in the wheel. No wonder Ferodo built its factory at Chapel en le Frith! Just up the road was Hixon where the Wynn's Pacific low loader and transformer were written off after being hit by an express train on an automatic level crossing. This resulted in all those signs about informing the signalman before and after crossing the line that appeared at level crossings.

Mentioning Rugeley brought to mind Ted Murphy. This is one of his stories and every time I went through Rugeley I would picture the scene and laugh. Ted was going south with a load of soap flakes out of Port Sunlight. That old A51 through Weston, Great Heywood and Colwich was very winding. It had two places with huge signs, ***"Beware Skew Bridge. Dead Slow"***, where the road changed to the other side of the railway. Somewhere along there Ted's load shot, when he got into Rugeley where there was a bit of light, he stopped and unsheeted part of it to re-stack it. No sooner was the sheet off, than there was a cloudburst. In no time the street was full from end to end with soapsuds up to the eaves. Drivers coming into the town were confronted with a wall of foam. The fire brigade had to wash it away.

My Dad did much the same with our kitchen when trying out a new washing machine, although he did not need the fire brigade.

We joined the A34 at Stone. Past Bassett's yard, and Trentham Gardens to skirt the Five Towns. Along by Trentham there were massive roadworks (pre-cone) I think they were dualling the A34. For miles I was stuck behind a four-wheeler carrying a single 8ft diameter spun concrete pipe. We came to a 'Ramp' sign and I saw him drop, then a cloud of dust. When this cleared, there was the four-wheeler, but no pipe! The driver got out and stood staring at the bed of his wagon. When I got out I could see it was covered in hard-core and loose ropes, the pipe had collapsed. He said to me "I might as well go home, I've got bugger all to deliver!" We all helped him clean off his wagon (the biggest bit was only a foot square) and skein up his ropes. He went on a bit 'til we came to the park gate, where I held back and made a space, he turned round, joined the southbound stream and was gone.

Woodley's came next. A real old-fashioned transport café, pints of tea and huge meals. It dated back to my Dad's days. Just before Woodley's was where the A52 forked left for the "Salt Mines", Crewe. When I was sent there on BRS we were always booked into the Iron Grey Inn which was a typical pub digs.

On the A34 was a little roundabout, a lot of the drivers called the Silverdale roundabout because of the branch of the Co-op of that name which stood on one corner. Then there was Smith's Café another old time place. It was good but I preferred Woodley's. A bit further on was Richardson's Metallic Tile Works, right up to the '70's it was still using traditional coal fired brick kilns.

Beyond there some drivers kept to the A34 going via Congleton and Wilmslow to Manchester. Many stuck by the belief that the best way in to Manchester was via Altrincham so went A50 through Holmes Chapel and Knutsford. Altrincham was on the A56; it was possible to fork at Tatton Park through a narrow road or go up to Mere Corner and turn right. If you stayed on the A50 for Warrington there was the Poplars Café, with Poplar Motor Transport behind it. It was possible to get a meal and a back-load without moving.

In Warrington I stayed in Hitchison's on Wilderspool Causeway. This was a café and digs and used by Davis Bros. drivers. There was an Indian mynah bird in the dining room which had the largest vocabulary of swear words you can imagine, all taught to it by Davis' day sleepers.

There was a strange arrangement. As the day sleepers got up to do their night runs they got an egg, bacon and sausage breakfast. While the day men just booking in had a traditional roast dinner. In the morning the meals were reversed.

BRS booked its drivers into Mrs Jeffries in Scott Street near the depot. She had a beautiful daughter aged about nineteen, (in the late '60s) who set all the young drivers hearts a flutter. After much cross-examination Mrs Jeffries selected one to take her daughter out for the evening. She guarded her daughter's innocence like a Mother Superior. Little did she know that the reward for a night away from

Mum, at a dance or the pictures, was a 'knee trembler' in the entry at the side of the house!

Liverpool was no problem on BRS; we parked in the depot and stayed in the Sally Ann or Arden House. On Noble's we got out of the town if possible. If not it was a case of finding a bombsite lorry park, which had a big team of juvenile 'Motor Minders'. We were actually given four half-crowns in an envelope, which were only to be used to pay these junior protection racketeers. Most were good, once you had paid they would shed blood to stop your wagon being damaged or broken into.

On Osborne's my porter had a cousin several times removed who ran digs on the Dingle. A street just like the one in *'Bread'* with the Mersey at the bottom. She took a lot of Irish building workers. She only served stew, which was prepared in a way that would horrify modern PHO's. She had two huge cast-iron fish kettles one held about 3 gallons, the other held 2 gallons. When you got in at night, the big one was full to the top with stew, which was covered with dumplings, this sat at the back of the coal-fired range. The other was full of potatoes boiling on the hot-spot. In the morning she prepared a heap of carrots, onions, turnips and stewing beef which was added to the remains of the previous night's brew together with a dozen Oxos. The pot was filled with water, put on the hot-spot and brought to the boil, then put to the back of the range. She then peeled enough potatoes to fill the other pot, covered them with water and stood the pot in the hearth. She then stripped all the drivers' beds and washed the sheets by hand. About 4.00pm she made a load of dumplings which went in on top of the stew and put the potatoes on to boil. Maginty (the porter) told me that this was her routine seven days a week. In all the years he had been going there (he also stayed socially) he had never seen the stew pot emptied and washed-up.

When I went to Manchester I stayed at Mrs Brady's on the corner of Ardwick Green. It was opposite the Ardwick Empire and when I first went in the late '50's she was still taking in a few 'theatricals'. Sometimes I stayed with an old Army mate Roy Burroughs who lived at Newton Heath. The houses were arranged in a way I have only seen in the north. There were four terraces making a big hollow square behind the houses, which fronted the pavement. The square was roughly grassed and used as a playground and drying area. Ray's Mum taught in a special school for Down's Syndrome children, some of whom she had home to tea. When I walked in I was always greeted with "Look, it's Uncle Bob, please say something in Cockney Uncle Bob".

When I was over the West Side I used the Rose Lea in City Road, Old Trafford. This was a really old fashioned place. Parking was on a bombsite round the back.

Margam earned a comment for being the second digs I would not stay in again. The first was in Cheetham Hill Road, Manchester. I was stuck in that area with a delivery, which I had just missed and that had to be done at 08.00 sharp. It was a cold, wet, foggy November night (who said normal for Manchester) so I did not fancy cabbing it. I asked a passing policeman (yes they did use to exist) who directed me to a house, with the comment "I would not recommend it, but it is better than sleeping in the cab. Just!"

The beds were about a foot apart and there was only cold water in a bowl to wash. She did not do evening meals, but pointed me to a snack bar at the crossroads. That turned out to be the operating centre for the local 'ladies of the night', who were all inside sheltering from the cold. The locals must have been desperate; they would have had to pay me to get into bed with them. Back at the digs, I was going to get undressed when the bloke in the next bed said "Don't bother mate and put the bed legs in yer boots". There were only blankets with brown paper under the bottom one and between the top two. Good job I had a big overcoat, the room was like a 'fridge box and the bed was damp. Breakfast (in bed) was a fish-paste sandwich and a cup of 'three leaves' tea. At 4/6d (22½p) it was about 4/- (20p) too dear.

On BRS I never stayed in Manchester, I always got sent to Bolton, Bury, Blackburn or Preston. The only digs I can remember are Mrs. Smith's in Pilkington Street, Blackburn a private house where a widow took in drivers. The other was the Café Roma in Bond Street, Bury. This was a digs over a street café. I also used this on Osborne's. There were others, mostly a couple of beds in a private house.

When it was unavoidable, it was necessary to go north from the Manchester area on the A6 via Lancaster for The Lake District or Scotland via Shap. There was a parking place in Kendal right beside the river and the corner was a three-storey house where an old lady ran a digs. She was another of the old fashioned landladies who never turned any one away. When things have been bad on Shap I have slept on the turn landing of the stairs, while others have slept on mattresses actually laid up the stairs. I have even been sent to a friend of her's to have a wash and get breakfast.

A couple of aerial views of Shap in winter when it was the main West Coast trunk road (A6) between England and Scotland. These scenes on Shap itself and Shap village were guaranteed at least once a year, and in most winters on several occasions. Local residents in the village and neighbouring farms rallied round to provide stranded drivers with food and shelter. Remember, no sleeper cabs with night heaters in those days.

(Photos: Courtesy of Gordon Baron sourced from Cumbrian Newspapers but originally supplied by an unrecorded News Agency)

CHAPTER 22
TO THE FAR NORTH

It's back to London now to start a trip to the northeast and Scotland via one of England's oldest major routes, the Great North Road. As such, at one time it was well supplied with cafes and digs, more even than Telford's Holyhead Road or as the Romans called it, Watling Street. From Northeast London there were two choices, Whetstone, Potters Bar, Hatfield straight onto the Al. Or, Great Cambridge Road (the A10) to Royston then old A14 to Alconbury.

Coming on to the Al at Whetstone at the lights by the pub of that name. You passed the actual whetstone that gave the place its name. It was used to sharpen the swords and pikes used in the Battle of Barnet in 1471. There was a tea stall outside a pub on the right. It was common practice for some years for retired drivers to go to this stall by bus to have a yarn with southbound drivers and get a ride back into London.

The first real café was Mrs Seeley's. On the left opposite Lyonsdown Road was a big hoarding. In the middle were a door and a window, once through the door you were into a large Army hut. This dated back to steam days, the hoarding being built in front of it. It was well used by local drivers and was still open recently (1998).

Further north was the Odeon, Barnet, with a service road outside. In the morning, in the '60's this would be full of Bowater's wagons. Their time ran out there and relief drivers were sent out in cars to change over. Up Barnet Hill, my Dad was fined 5/- (25p) for "Emitting Sparks" with an over-type Foden. Once into the village and through the High Street was the start of the A6, which, forked left and with it traffic for Brum and the Northwest. Keeping on the Al took you over Hadley Common, once a major operating centre for highwaymen. In Potters Bar were the lights at the Greyhound Garage where the other route to the Midlands crossed. Through Potters Bar was the Cock of the North pub, next door to which was the depot of Rand & Brunt, haulage contractors and coach operators. In a side road was the depot of Freddy Forest who was the start of Merchandise Transport, the A-licensed arm of Lebus. Then came the Rookery Café. It has been there as long as I can remember; in its time it has been a cyclist's and motorcyclist's meeting place as well as a transport café. So far as I know it is still going.

Today you bear off left over a bridge to the new industry of Welham Green. This used to be a lane over a level crossing the scene of a spectacular railway accident. In the old days it was straight on into Hatfield, which had a digs. Over The Wrestlers' Bridge, (which fell down) to what I first knew as the Al and is now the A1000 and a dead end. In Hatfield used to be a well-known grain and flour haulier Sheriff's.

The next major one was Jack's Hill at Gravely just past Stevenage. This was a heavily used old style place related in later days to the one at Towcester. Going into Baldock was the double-bend round the Kayser-Bondor stocking factory. This has an art-noveau façade, which is listed and has survived the conversion into a Tesco's store. In the High Street was a teashop in a parade, well used by drivers when it was possible to park along the street. Micky (the driver involved with Davis' dog) had a very colourful accident on the bend just past the tearooms. He turned over a trailer load of paint.

At Sandy was an unusual modern cafe. This was a Portakabin on a 40' trailer. It was sited on a bit of the old road, which had been left as a lay-by by road straightening. I remember the owner having a lot of trouble with the local planners. I never knew the outcome.

Mac's at Alconbury was another old and well-known cafe. Good meals and 24-hour. Many of the furniture men coming out of London on the original A14 made for Mac's in preference to the Afton. This is another Little Chef.

Today (2000) the A1 follows a brand new course from Brampton Hut to the north of Peterborough, bypassing landmarks like Mac's, Stangate Hill and Norman Cross.

Norman Cross used to be the place to turn right for Peterborough, through Yaxley, HQ of Peterborough Heavy Haulage. With the bypass, drivers go a bit further north and use the posh dual carriageway into the town, this is the place that the Mermaids and Nuts and Bolts lurk. At Norman Cross there used to be a memorial on the left (going north) surmounted by a bronze eagle, it must have puzzled many drivers. Even my old Dad didn't know that one. It is a memorial to the many French POWs from the Napoleonic Wars who died in the camps round about Peterborough. They were the ones who made those marvellous toys and ships out of mutton bones. The memorial got damaged in an accident and two 'Herberts' came along with a lorry and nicked the eagle. Some local associations are trying to restore the whole thing.

One cafe synonymous with the Al was Kate's Cabin, now called K.C.'s Diner. So many drivers believe that the cafe was originally a cabin run by a woman called Kate. In fact, the area is called Kate's Cabin and the cafe was named after it. It is believed that the cabin referred to was a hunting lodge owned by one Sydney Kate. There is a similar situation further south with the Brampton Hut, where the new A14 interchange was built. While the A5 has Foster's Booth, although that was probably a tollhouse.

Going into Stamford (pre-by-pass) many drivers sitting in the queue created by the lights and the bad bends at the church must have had a very wry smile at the sign "Welcome to Stamford. Stay a while amid its ancient charm." For a few days there was a small sign added by some disgruntled driver which said "What alternative is on offer?" Stamford was a major coaching centre. In my early years there used to be a tiny café in the square beyond the church.

The Compass Cafe at Colsterworth was a major transport stop for many years. It boasted a big car park and had a shed/office for a BRS Foreman. This is now under a motel.

Margaret Roberts, the grocer's daughter, may think she put Grantham on the map in her married name of Thatcher. But Tony Wakefield and his Mum preceded her by many years. 'Tony's of Grantham' was a by-word for well-cooked big meals. The old place at the top of Spittlegate Hill, not the gin palace on the by-pass. In the winter, going north you would find motors parked up on the side of the road before you got to Tony's. This spelt trouble. You joined the back of the line and walked up to the cafe. The lorry-park would be "two high and a binder", the cafe the same. The air had been breathed so many times much of the oxygen had gone. Even non-smokers had 'smoked' ten Woodbines before getting to the counter! The usual story was that Gonerby was shut. It was usually a wagon and drag from Bout's or Holdsworth's causing the problem. Then the faces of the regulars going south would appear an indication that the road was open. Usually sorted by a double-drive Leyland from Sheffield or Rotherham loaded with sixteen tons of steel and equipped with a tow chain.

Then it was back to work out in the cold. All the Gardners that had been idling for two hours or more were revved up; the result was more smoke than there had been in the cafe. By the time you got back to your wagon the tears were running down your cheeks. A cold Gardner could sell a lot of Kleenex!

Ford's of Long Bennington was a digs more commonly known as 'The Piggery'. Part of the accommodation was an old chapel, a high barn of a place heated only by Valor paraffin stoves. Nonetheless it was very popular with Scots drivers.

Coming into Newark, on the left was a food café, which I knew from childhood as the New Ark. The main place was the Wharf, right in the town centre by the bridge over the Trent. The river was one boundary of the car park. When staying overnight, you ate in the cafe. The accommodation, washroom, TV room etc. were in a couple of houses next door but one. Reminiscent of the Capesthorne Hotel in

142

Stoke, which I mentioned in my account of my BRS days.

Just north of Newark is North Muskham with the Newcastle Arms a historic riverside pub, which did beds for drivers. It was well off the Al but very popular. The couple who ran it in the late '60's were two of the most obliging people I have ever met.

Next came Markham Moor, currently the site of a truckstop. In the days when I remember it well it was a major crossroads, Lincoln to the right, turn left for Sheffield via Worksop. There were two good cafés. One looked like a middle class tearoom but was happy to feed drivers. I spent a lot of time there one winter when my van was blown into a snowdrift. There was a waiting list for the wrecker from the village garage. Nowadays, the Al is signed up what used to be the A57 to meet the Doncaster by-pass at Blyth.

Staying on what was the Al and is now the A638, you came to Retford. Officially East Retford, no one knows where or if there was a West Retford. On the left was a big white house; known as the Guest House, its phone number was Retford 91. The woman who ran it must have been an ex-ATS Sergeant Major, but the beds were clean and the food excellent. This is now a saddlery. I became very familiar with Retford while on the Northern Telecom job. I found the all-night café near the station, which we used. This is now a taxi office. Also the street where we parked to cab it when the digs were full. The town no longer smells of the maltings, Gilstrup, Earp as I remember.

In Bawtry was a BRS depot; right next door was a café and digs. It was a pair of semis, only joined by a door on the first floor landing. It was most confusing; to go from the dining room to the washroom and TV room (all on the ground floor) you had to go upstairs along the landing and down the other stairs. The BRS depot was a redistribution point for TVs and new furniture. I was introduced to the café by Jack Bawling who drove the only Jensen Luton on Cambridge BRS, we were doing TVs for Pyc. One night about 9 o'clock the depot had a colossal fire. Strangely enough the auditors were en-route to do an unannounced stock check the following day. I actually met George the auditor at an NFC shareholder's meeting. The alleged discrepancy was large but nothing was ever proved.

The old A1 went straight through Doncaster where there were several pull up outside cafés, some of them 24-hour. The digs I used (along with many furniture men) was Mrs Oakes in Waterdale. She had the biggest, meanest parrot I have ever seen. That was a happy house, most of the old furniture men were good company. Waterdale was very wide and we parked in a line down the middle like traffic islands. Going north out of Doncaster the tramlines finished at Bentley. There was The Aero (it had a propeller across the front over the door). I started going there with my Dad. It was famous for its Yorkshire teacakes. They were about eight inches across and an inch thick, nearly a meal on their own, toasted with lots of butter. After a long break, I went in and ordered a mug of tea and a tea cake, only to be told "We don't do 'em anymore love, we've done away with the coal range and they won't fit in the toaster". Another bit of history gone in the name of progress.

Just north of Doncaster were a couple of options for forking left for Leeds. The A639 via Pontefract and Castleford was the favourite way with furniture men: while the latter was a loading place for bottles on BRS. The digs were in Leeds itself Mrs Wilson's in Spencer Place off the Roundhay Road. This digs provided a transport service. After parking in the lorry-park, you 'phoned the digs and were collected in a large American car. To be taken back in the morning. Spencer Place was in the news as the operating centre of Julie Dart; the prostitute murdered by Michael Sams the kidnapper.

The next one north on the A1 was the café next door to The Fox at Brotherton (fork right for Tadcaster and Smith's Brewery) this was another long-standing place. At one time its neon sign could be seen from the new road when Brotherton was by-passed. Just before Brotherton we used to cross the Aire and

Calder Navigation on an old stone bridge at Ferrybridge. I was surprised to learn from a TV programme on canals that this is now scheduled as an ancient monument. I delivered many loads of 50ft rebar for the cooling towers of Ferrybridge power station and the nearby one at Eggborough. Both of these had their coal delivered by water back then.

Micklefield was the site of a very big café and digs known as The First 'Un. Holdsworth & Hanson at one time owned this. There was a plan to have similar places at strategic locations all over the country to fit in with H & H's operations. Good food, good beds and secure parking all on a company site. This was strongly resisted by the Union and never went ahead. I have been told this is now a truckstop.

One thing, which sticks in my mind from this area, was Bramham Crossroads (A64) which had lights. If inexperienced drivers asked "How do I get to York?" we would tell them to "Go up the Al, when you come to a set of lights in the middle of nowhere turn right any you'll come to it".

Lawsons of Londonderry was another famous Great North Road cafe and digs. The car park was vast. It had the disadvantage of being beside the airfield known as RAF Leeming Bar. If they were night flying it could make sleeping a bit difficult. Also in Londonderry was a garage proprietor who had one of the first heavy wreckers in that part of the country

Up the Catterick Straight past the airfield, at that time home of the RAF Regiment. That was a certain blow-over spot for furniture vans. There was a marvellous aerial shot in the dailies one winter a whole line of furniture vans all on their side, an advert for the north London furniture trade. Into Catterick and the Tudor Café, another Scots driver's haven. It was not until I saw it on TV recently that I realised how sharp a bend the old Catterick Bridge was; the same programme mentioned the Londonderry wrecker.

There was and is a café at Scotch Corner, for some reason I never used it. This is now a money-spinner taking money off of motorists and coach passengers. There it is left on to the A66. The first time I went up that road, there was a filling station at Greta Bridge which had a petrol pump with two 1gallon, glass jars. You filled one with a semi-rotary hand pump, while that drained into the tank you filled the other. Good job tanks didn't hold a hundred and twenty gallons. That little 'bosky glen' has been by-passed along with the infamous 'Steep hill many corners'.

Eventually you came to Sayer's of Brough a famous café and filling station, which was very welcome in the winter. Just before the Countess Pillar and the open air swimming pool on the River Eamont was one of my favourite cafés, The Beacon. It was one of the first Bedford Driver's Club approved sites and still had the original enamel BDC steering wheel sign. Bette Sanderson would never turn anyone away. I've slept on the lounge floor more than once. One winter in the early '50's she had 60+ drivers marooned there. Each autumn she stocked up for a siege with cases of tins, sacks of flour and sugar, sides of bacon etc. She had drivers cooking and making bread. She used 3 cwt of flour before the snowploughs got through. She was the daughter of the original owner. Her sister Molly was married to a Scots Lebus driver and lived in Glasgow. Her sister Joan was married to another Lebus driver and lived in Brough and worked for Sayer's until he died, when she moved back to the Beacon. Bette was an authority on van haulage. She and her sister were still running the café in '94 when my son called in.

From the Beacon it was into Penrith to a Halt sign to turn right on the A6. There was a house at Plumpton right by the road. If the sign outside offered 'Fresh Eggs for Sale', it meant that the ladies of easy virtue who lived there were available for business.

Carlisle had a very big café and digs; my mind is completely blank as to the name. I understand this was taken over by Jimmy Bell an owner driver turned haulier who wanted to make it into the sort of place we all knew and loved. My son thought it was a plastic truckstop the last time he was up that way.

Lockerbie must be a name known around the world. I remember it was a pleasant little place that you passed through. The target was the Beattock Summit café, which I can remember being rebuilt to make it impervious to the weather; the windows were small and right up by the eaves. It was the site of many spectacular maroonings with the road snowed in for days. There was one well-reported event, early '60s I think. A large number of drivers were marooned in the café. Davis Bros. organised a helicopter to lift out its men and offered to do the same for anyone who chipped in. The Davis men found out that they were 'chipping in' when they got their wages!

Somewhere along the A74, I think on Douglas Moor, was a sharp right hand downhill bend. As you approached the bend, facing you on the hillside was a hoarding with a religious message. It always seemed to be in the vein of "The end is nigh" or "Prepare to meet thy maker". Not very inspiring on a dismal stretch of road. From there it was through Hamilton and into Glasgow at the Gallowgate Clock.

In the furniture days there were always 'runners' sitting on the wall waiting to help furniture drivers. Just round the corner in the Gallowgate was the National Café. All the best 'runners' used this as an HQ. It was possible to send a telegram giving your ETA and book your favourite man. A good runner could save a full day delivering round the town. The first words were always "Gi us your lines Jimmy, let's see where we're for".

I mentioned earlier that I did an exhibition van job round Glasgow. As the van had to be securely parked, I spent the week in the Bellgrove 'Hotel!', which had a locked yard. It was right opposite the infamous Barrowlands. It was a weird place reminiscent of those places you see in American films about New York. The lower floors were single rooms exclusively for down and outs. The lowest was a dormitory for one nighters. Then there were rooms rented by the week. The top floor was single rooms exclusively for drivers.

You got tickets to get your meals, which were taken, in a big dining hall in the basement. Shades of St. Martin's in the Fields crypt. That week was in the days of the one-hour pub opening, I went over the road for a pint and was amazed to see the whole bar covered in full pint glasses, which were being downed and refilled as fast as the barmen could go.

The only other place further north that I stayed was the guardroom of the FAA base at Lossiemouth. When we were delivering the Navy furniture, picked up from the Royal Victoria Victualling Yard at Deptford (next door to Convoy's). The sailors used to put us up for the night.

We will now nip across the A8 to Edinburgh. The only digs I stopped in Edinburgh was in a Victorian square just off Leith Walk. I have not the name or address. I was led there the first time I went, so I knew where I was going. When I went for whisky on BRS, the depot did the business on being told "The one off Leith Walk". I went there with the old Albion when I was on Osborne's (Bell's). It was so long since I had been that I forgot about the steep camber and the fact that the van leaned over. As I pulled up there was a crash and the top of the lamppost fell to the ground. The woman came out and said "Don't worry driver, that's the second time this week and nearly 50 this year. I keep telling them the post needs moving. They just come and put the top back".

We are going south now, round the back of Arthur's Seat on to the A68 over Carter Bar with its fantastic views from the car park at the top, to the A696 to top end of Newcastle.

There was a good private house digs in Race Street and many cafés throughout the town. Particularly down on the Quays. It was even possible to use the staff canteen in the Central Station, which was open 24 hours a day 365 days a year. Geordie dockers were very good. If there were two or three wagons waiting they would send you off to the café. When you got back, the wagon would be empty all the sheets properly folded and the ropes skeined. We went to Newcastle in '93 for the start of the Tall Ships race. Everything along the Quays was gone; it was like a bombsite. We went round on the south side of the Tyne; Harland & Wolf's and the other shipyards were housing estates.

My mate Stan (on Noble's) had a bad experience in Newcastle. He was arrested at home in London by the Newcastle police, accused of stealing a load of furniture. When he was taken back he found a lot of other furniture men in adjoining cells. They had all been taken in by the oldest trick in the book. Delivering to the back of a big shop in Northumberland Street they had been met by a man who re-directed them to the 'overflow' warehouse.

When they took the police to the warehouse it was empty. A neighbour said she had seen all the vans delivering and then on Saturday afternoon a fleet of vans came and cleared out the place.

South over the Tyne Bridge into Gateshead would mean one of two things. Straight home via Chester le Street, going over the level crossing where a woman was whipped off of her bike and killed by the loose ends of a load of random timber. Then up the long drag to the quaintly named Pity Me. Round the Durham by-pass, looking out for the trainee policemen who stopped you and then measured everything, even the height of the sidelights. Past the old Army camp at Spennymoor which became a vast industrial estate. Through Newton Aycliffe which became a new town, on through Darlington to Scotch Corner.

Alternatively you could turn left for Sunderland to pick up the A19 for Stockton on Tees and Middlesborough. In my BRS days I paid many visits to this area. With the I.C.I. at Billingham, Yarm and Redcar there were always back-loads when all kinds of materials were going into the building of the huge chemical complex at Port Clarence.

When in that area I stayed with Mrs Bray in Ayersome Grange Road (it must have been knocked down, its not on modern maps!). That was a happy family house, where drivers baby-sat. Her youngest is the same age as my youngest. His nappy rash was cured when I told her about the cream we had for our daughter. She moved from 11 to 19 (an identical house) "For a change". Number 11 had a re-direction notice on the door for years.

From Teesside it was down to Thirsk and the Central Café, which was a good old-fashioned place. It was one of the first to advertise in the *Headlight* when Harry Kelson published that. Just outside Thirsk was the notorious Sutton Bank on the way to Pickering and Scarborough. I did my driver training along that road in 1952 when I was stationed at Catterick.

As we have already explored the A1, I am going via York (I only went to deliver there twice in 42 years!), Barnby Moor and Market Weighton to Kingston upon Hull. Specifically to 150 Anlaby Road. The digs of Mrs Waytzman, a wartime Polish refugee who spoke fractured English with a Yorkshire accent. It had a bombsite lorry-park next door, and was noted for its cleanliness and good food. Breakfast was an experience, a huge dinner plate with egg, bacon, sausage and a fried slice (about an inch thick) with a choice of beans, tomatoes or mushrooms. Loaves to cut your own bread and two pound jars of marmalade. Halfway through Mrs Waytzman would bring in two oval meat dishes, one piled with eggs, the other bacon so you could top up your plate. When everyone was finished, she made up sandwiches with the leftover eggs and bacon. You all got one to take away. Another long serving driver (I won't say old, he'd hit me with his Zimmer frame) reminded me that she was known as Doris Day, presumably because she was always singing.

Leaving Hull it was A63 and A614 across Thorne Waste to rejoin the A1 at Bawtry. There used to be a joke in the furniture trade "Sorry to hear about the fire, Solly", "Shut up you fool, that's next week".

Slow moving stock and their finances often resulted in the insurance fire. This also applied to the transport side. A rough old van would be loaded with old stock or stuff from junk shops. It would then be sent to Hull. Halfway across Thorne Waste it would catch fire. It was miles to a phone and even further to a fire station; hence the van was totally destroyed. The insurance man would count the castors and divide by twelve or count the knobs and hinges. After being assured by the driver that the wagon was the pride of the fleet and going like a bird and it must have been a flat tyre, they paid out!

As we went up the Al we'll come home via the original A14 and A10. After leaving Alconbury the first café was in Godmanchester (pronounced locally as Gumster). More of a tearoom. There is a crossroads called Kilsby's Hut obviously another lengthman's cottage. At the Caxton Gibbet where the A45 crosses, there was a café behind the pub. At the Cambridge end of the A45 was the Enterprise Café, well known and still well used. Not far from Rayner's depot, an old firm now defunct, which, towards the end ran an entire fleet of Barreiros Dodges. The A603 Cambridge - Sandy road used to cross the A14 at Wimpole. Today the Wimpole - Sandy stretch is the B1042.

There were two cafés actually in Royston, but the best known was the Silver Ball just to the south on the A10. This featured in the Bob Hoskins film *'Mona Lisa'*. There was no Buntingford by-pass and Sainsbury's RDC was only being built in the late '60s. Just before Puckeridge was Eddy's Café with its rough, sloping car park and the filling station next door. The girl on the till in the filling station had her own form of bonus for big fill-ups! What she gave and how she gave it would get this book an X rating. While I was at Coppetts Road, Eddy's car park gave us a major headache. The van trailer for the Edinburgh trunk was not available so about 14 tons of parcels were loaded on a tandem axle flat. The driver took it to the top of the car park and did a jack-knife turn across the slope. The load did not just shoot; it fell right off! A quarter of the bank staff was loaded into a hastily hired minibus and shipped off to reload it. In the best trunking tradition the service got through albeit a bit late.

Puckeridge village was narrow and winding. A driver from Mason's of Rotherham had a spectacular and unexplained accident there. He went through the parapet of the river bridge that was between two houses. The entire wagon, an artic with an extra long trailer, finished up lying in the riverbed behind the houses totally off the road. Unfortunately the driver was killed under the load of rebar.

The next café was the New Tram between Hoddesdon and Wormley. The original Tram was just that, an old London tram dropped at the edge of the road. When there was racing at Newmarket, that famous old racing tipster Prince Raz Monolulu ("I've got a horse") used to hang about there looking for a lift.

CHAPTER 23
TO THE WEST AND WALES

From my part of London setting out for either Bristol or Wales meant the North Circular Road. Even from Grays we used that route unless we left very early when we used the A13 and the Embankment. Until the ban it was even possible to go round Parliament Square.

The first tea stop was a small café at Staples Corner; this was open 24 hours a day, 364 days a year. It was swept away with the building of the flyover. At one time Hallet, Silberman had a sub-depot under the railway arches opposite, it employed a full-blooded American Indian as an eight-wheeler driver.

The next one was the Highland Glen, just past the lights at Brentfield Road. This was run by the wife of the foreman of Albion Motors, just around the corner. They had moved to England when Albion set up. The café is still there, but the works is now the site of a quite famous Hindu temple, apparently the architecture makes it well worth a visit.

Under the seven bridges was The Ace, Stonebridge Park. A good transport café and a motorcycling legend. It appeared in several '60s films. It closed and became a tyre depot, but now that it is sidelined by road improvements it has re-opened as a cafe using much of the original decor found stored upstairs.

I always turned right at what is now the Hanger Lane Gyratory to pick up the A40 even when aiming for the A4, which was reached by crossing Iver Heath into Slough. But as we are looking at cafés we will go over Hanger Hill past the air-raid shelter that received a direct hit by a bomb during the war. There was a small café at Chiswick roundabout this went when the flyover was built. Off the roundabout in Chiswick High Road were two cafés, which served the Brentford Market, now a Leisure Centre. I took my nine-year-old daughter with me to Heathrow at night in the '70s; over thirty years later her most vivid memory of that trip is the smell of citrus fruit wafting over the M4 elevated from the market. If she comes in and smells grapefruit she will always reminisce about, "The night we went to the airport". It impressed her more than all the Jumbo jets at the Cargo Terminal. No! She did not become a lorry driver, she married one.

Along the Great West Road, outside the Firestone factory was a very popular tea stall. Imagine parking in the road at that spot today. On the opposite corner to Gillette's was the Better 'Ole, named from Bruce Barnfather's 'Old Bill' cartoons from WWI.

Just across the road in Syon Lane is the Station Café. All my life it has been a tipper man's and dustman's café. The wagons outside today are Fodens and Hinos instead of the 5-yard Bedford OSTs but the café is unchanged.

Over Hounslow Heath, past Heathrow you come to Jock's probably as well known for the old wagons dumped at the back as for being a good café. My brother used it regularly until very recently; he first went as a toddler. At one time it was a digs. Past Jock's the MoT was experimenting with a weighbridge, which would automatically weigh vehicles as they passed. That was over thirty-five years ago and they still have not cracked it.

Right in the centre of Slough was a digs called Baltic House in Wellington Street. This used to be the last turning on the right off the Uxbridge Road before the lights in the High Street. Today, Wellington Street is the town-centre by-pass and Baltic House is under the eastbound carriageway. When I stayed there we used to collect dyes, saccharin and other coal tar by-products from Slough Gas Works. This is now I.C.I.'s dyestuff division.

An arm of the Grand Union Canal, which took coal to the gasworks, served Slough at one time. Leaving Slough you passed one of the first purpose built industrial estate in Britain. The many sets of traffic lights were linked so that it you maintained the advised speed you got greens all the way through.

Heading for Maidenhead, before the railway bridge at Taplow, National Carriers had one of the first, if not the first, HGV driving school. It used Morris Commercial artics., which had a sliding driver's door, which were on runners, which went behind the cab.

When I started we went over the stone bridge across the Thames and right through the middle of Maidenhead. There was a posh riverside hotel by the bridge called Skindles. The building still stands but has been boarded up for some years. My old mate Rodney wrote off a nearly new Rover outside there, severely injuring all the passengers. They had been to a do in the hotel; the driver was so drunk his injuries could not be treated until his blood alcohol level had reduced. The Maidenhead by-pass was the first section of the M4 to be opened.

Beyond Maidenhead Thicket was the Seven Stars pub close by which was the Square Deal café, which was very popular. I never used it, I preferred the next one, which I don't think had a name. It was a wooden building in a garden, run by Chris. His mother-in-law was constantly harassing him, but he did good grub in spite of her. Past that lay Waterer's Floral Mile, the seed company's trial ground.

At Twyford was the 'Wee Waif' run by a Scots couple and very popular with their countrymen. It was well used by furniture drivers collecting soft suites from the nearby Lebus upholstery factory. Approaching Reading was Suttons Seeds trial ground, which is now an industrial estate served by a spur off of the M4.

Going into Reading there were lights at Cemetery Junction. There used to be a choice between going left past the Royal Berkshire Hospital or forking right for the town centre. Then round by the prison and the railway station to the BRS depot in Cardiff Road, which had a superb canteen and was a compulsory stop when taking cigarettes to Bristol. We also went that way to load biscuits from Huntley & Palmers. A group of us went to load there. After tea break the driver of the Albion four-wheeler could not find his wagon and it was presumed stolen. The rest of us loaded and took him home. The next day Reading 'phoned to say the Albion had been found, by a boat running into it. The handbrake had failed and it had run off the lorry-park into the Kennet.

After Reading came Theale, with two teashops. But the transport cafés were further west. First we had the very famous Mac's at Beenham. I was never sure whether the huge teapot over the door or the even bigger potholes in the car park was what made it famous. It had sleeping quarters consisting of old railway coaches. These were heated by a slow combustion stove; regulars used to climb on the roof and fill the chimney with fuel so that it fed down into the fire. The whole lot often glowed dull red but never seemed to give out any heat. Under new management Max's Snacks is still open today and has recently been refurbished.

Next came the Tower Café at Beenham, a large purpose built place, there were other Towers at Towcester and Basingstoke. It became the Three Pigeons but having stood derelict for many years, was finally demolished in December '97.

On the left lay Aldermaston, starting point for the CND marches. A few miles on and also on the left at Colthrop was the depot of Thatcham Road Transport Services. In my Noble days I loaded several loads of cartons through them, hundreds of bundles all handball. In Parker Morris times it was 20 tons of Kraft liner or fluting into the Reed Corrugated Cases works opposite, by which time TRTS had been demolished and had become an industrial estate.

The receiving foreman at RCC was Wally, the most awkward, cantankerous man you could imagine. His name was notorious the length and breadth of Britain. How some hot-tempered person never brained him with a reel bar I don't know?

Newbury was the crossing point for the A34, the main Midlands-Southampton route. This had been much in the news for the by-pass protest. I never stayed in Newbury, but I had a mate who was a gambling fanatic. He made a point of stopping there; he used to drink in a pub used by jockeys and lads and reckoned he got red-hot tips. The pub was on the right coming in from Reading and may have been called The Greyhound.

On through Hungerford (another name which will never be forgotten) to the Golden Arrow at Froxfield. This was a traditional style café, for many years a BRS changeover point. The Grays-Newport service used it, as did Brentford-Swansea.

Through the Savernake Forest and down the hill into Marlborough round the sharp right hand bend. On that bend I discovered the road holding capabilities of Michelin X tyres. Noble's was trying a set when they first came into use. In a daydream I went down the hill too fast, but the old Dodge took that bend like it was on rails. I stayed at Marlborough twice, once on a cycling holiday, once when I broke down. The digs were a very tall Georgian house. The ground and first floors had electric light; the second floor had gas brackets. On the windowsill on the stairs were a candlestick and a box of matches for the third floor.

The town was noted for the extreme camber where the road formed part of the Market Square. I had just been promoted to an eight-wheeler and was on an early start to Bristol. As I got to the square there was a furniture van stopped, with the driver standing at the back waving his arms. I asked what was wrong, he said "I can't go any further, the van is falling over". I could not persuade him it was always like that. It finished up with me driving his van and him in my Bristol crawling all the way round to the wide bit by the school in second gear. When we had a cuppa at The Ridgeway it transpired that this was his first trip, he had never before driven anything bigger than a CF Bedford.

The Ridgeway was my favourite café in that area; I cannot remember when I first went there, probably 1940. I first knew it as a white weatherboard building, with snow blowing through the chinks in winter. It always smelled of paraffin, which was the cooking medium, the daughter of the family that ran it, served and cleared the tables. A funny little girl with nickel rimmed glasses, one rasher short of a full breakfast. It was on the brow of the hill, getting off the park westbound was dodgy, most westbound drivers pulled off onto the verge, which was later made into a proper lay-by. As a child I used to hop over the wall for a pee. Many years later it was discovered that, the place was an archaeological site connected with Avebury. The café was rebuilt as a brick building. The new owners wanted to rebuild yet again as a tourist trap. The National Trust put the kibosh on that and it is now a grass site. The Iron Age Ridgeway came out just to the east of the café.

Today, where the A361 crosses the A4 is Beckhampton roundabout. I first knew it as a crossroads with Halt signs. Drivers going to Bath and Bristol usually turned left to go via Devizes and Melksham to Box avoiding Calne and Chippenham and what was regarded as a bad road. There were two cafés on the A4. The White Horse at Cherhill, which was well used by young RAF men training as Wireless Operators at Yatesbury Camp. The other was in Calne; it only seemed to sell products of the nearby Harris Bacon Co., that area is now a car park.

There was a useful teashop/café in Devizes. The first digs I used were The White Hart, just behind Wadsworth's brewery. This was run by Mrs Ruxton a formidable lady, with a very hen-pecked husband. On more than one occasion she laid him out with a blow from an empty beer bottle. However, she was sweetness and light to drivers. That was demolished to expand the brewery.

The BRS digs was The Old Crown, another pub, by the cattle market. It was a home from home family run place and very popular. There was another official digs in Melksham, Mrs Hankin, but if possible we always went to The Old Crown.

There was a small café in Bathampton, I think called The Green Lantern and another near Sparrows' yard in Bath. Both roadside places with not much room to stop.

From Bath it was through Keynsham. Readers old enough to remember Radio Luxembourg will recall Horace Batchelor and his Infra-Draw method of winning the pools, write to K-E-Y-N-S-H-A-M. On the way into Bristol was Brislington, home of the Western Transport depot, which received all those Carrera's cigarettes from Basildon. It also stored and delivered soap powder for Proctor & Gamble.

When I started going to Bristol much of the town centre still showed signs of the war. It was possible to find ships loading at the Broad Quay almost in the shopping centre. It was rather odd to find gangs of dockers with mobile cranes working cargo by the roadside. Then to go round under the bows of a ship, down the other side of the dock to pick-up what was actually a straight through route. Watching 'Casualty' I finally worked out that that bit of the dock had been filled in.

In my early days I was delivering imported furniture in the Hotwells district off Hotwells Road, site of many Regency brothels. I asked the way and was told to take the seventh on the right; the job was at the top. I duly turned up a road that looked like an entry between two terraces, it petered out into an unmade track. After a struggle I turned round, just as I emerged the helpful pedestrian came along, he said "What are you doing up there? The next one is the seventh, we don't count this one, motors never go up there".

Bristol had two BRS depots, Spring Street and Day's Road which lay behind Temple Meads station, an area littered with low bridges. Outside Day's Road depot was the Bridge Café, a rough and ready place, but a good digs for all that, clean beds and plenty of food.

I'm going to jump back a hundred miles to Hanger Lane and go A40 past the Hoover building now a Tesco's. Past the War Memorial to the Poles who served in the RAF, Northolt aerodrome with its ultra-short lamp posts and the lay-by so popular with 'plane spotters. Annis had some load spreading plates stashed there for dropping loaded knock-out trailers. In fact anyone with a heavy load to park used them. Two or three minute's walk away, there was a first class café tucked away beside the embankment for the railway bridge. This was a dustmen's café. Before the 7.5 tonne weight limit we used to cut through past that café to get into Uxbridge.

The café I always made for was at Loudwater, it might have been called The Marsh, the café was on the left, the park on the other side of the road. Before the M40, it was right through the shopping centre of High Wycombe to the tight right and left bend at the Market Hall. Picturing the Market Hall brought back an almost forgotten incident from 1940. Dad decided to get out of London before the sirens went and sleep in the van. When we got to High Wycombe he decided to pull up in the market place. As we got off the road on to the cobbles there was a bang. When we got in the van, hanging down in the Luton was an inn sign. He had hit it in the blackout, it had swung round its bar and knocked a hole in the roof. He got out the hacksaw and sawed off the eyebolts. When we left in the morning the sign was leaning against the pub, while the roof of the Luton bore a tea chest lid for a patch.

Going out of the town on the Oxford Road was the BRS digs. An Ebbw Vale driver was boasting to his mates about "having it off" with the landlady while her husband was up the road. Unfortunately, the husband was sitting at the next table; said driver was very surprised to get a good thumping. Further along was the BRS depot, which backed onto the railway.

One weekend a gang emptied all the fleet out into the road and then used a couple of empty wagons to haul away the Victorian platform canopy from the closed station. They even put the motors away again.

Through West Wycombe the A40 is on an embankment. This was built by unemployed men under the auspices of Sir Francis Dashwood's, very early "workfare" scheme. Obtaining the chalk created the noted West Wycombe Caves, which became connected with the infamous Hellfire Club. At the top of the hill was the famous Chris's of Stokenchurch; still going. At one time it was only shut from Saturday evening to Sunday afternoon. Along on the left was the Black & White which was used as a tea stop by long-distance coaches.

I had done a late delivery in Oxford and was on the way home. At Tetsworth I was stopped by the police, there were a couple of other BRS motors already stopped. The copper said, "I see you're from Grays, do you know a driver called Joe Bloggs (obviously not his real name) these other BRS men think he comes from your depot?" I knew him; he was on night trunk, so I asked what was wrong. I was told that he had put his whole week's wages (it was Friday night) in the fruit machine in Chris's without getting a penny back. He had then gone berserk and run off and they had tracked him to a garden in the almshouses and were trying to persuade him to give himself up. He was a notorious gambler and after a long chat we persuaded him to come back to the café with us. With a little persuasion the manager gave him most of his money back, we filled him with tea and sent him on to changeover.

Today, near Wheatley is a modern cabin café in a lay-by, which is usually so full you, can only pull-in with a bit of luck. On the Oxford ring road there is the infamous service area at the Pear Tree Roundabout which forbids entry to LGVs.

In the old days I can't remember a café in the Oxford area, there was one in Witney which had two famous products, blankets and Pam Ayres. When I was young the sun naturally bleached the former. I can still picture them all spread out on the bleaching frames.

The Windrush Café at Windrush was another must in the old days. A BRS changeover point, with one of the garden shed offices. It is much loved by my friend Alan Spillett the painter and features in his picture of me hauling the fibreglass spire for Tuffley RC School.

Though Northleach (the musical museum is well worth a visit) it's up over the Cotswolds to Andoversford. At its edge was the station, which was converted to a café when the line closed and is now a smart house. Today, much of the traffic for Gloucester forks left before Andoversford to go via the much-improved Birdlip Hill. A road we used to avoid, it was hard on the brakes going down, hard on the engine going up.

We always went via Cheltenham, turn right at the bakers for Evesham, turn left after the Pump Room for Gloucester. Going out of the town was The Golden Valley café, which did digs. From there it was into Gloucester past the aeroplane works. We saw the first experimental jet fighter there and thousands of prefabs waiting for delivery when its product was changed after the war. In the town, the A40 came to a T-junction; sharp right took you to The Bridge Café, which I used regularly. Just over the Severn was another popular café, The West End, easier to use going east.

Out of Gloucester and turn left on to the A48 through Minsterworth. At one point the road runs alongside the Severn and there is a parking place to watch the Severn Bore. I saw my first bore at the age of seven.

From there it was through Chepstow. No one who has gone that way can forget dropping down beside the Wye to that right angle turn over the bridge. Many wagons whose drivers ignored the "low gear" sign went straight on at that bend; eventually a trap was built. Over the bridge was a left turn into a one-way system which came out just below the then famous Chepstow Arch (l3' 6" in the middle) one of the old (15th Century) gateways beyond which was a well used tea stop.

Late one night, as I turned left there was a waving torch; it was the local bobby who told me to take it easy round the next corner, as there was an ingot in the road! As I turned I could see a 16-ton dropforging ingot partially bedded in the road. Coming back the next night, outside the teashop I met the bobby and asked him how they had got on with the ingot. He told me that then the day shift had arrived with a lorry and a crane it was gone! Whoever had dropped it had gone back in the early hours with their own crane. The red lamps and signs were neatly stacked on the kerb and the people in the nearby houses had "never heard a thing?"

There was a place called Stormy Down (which has disappeared off of the map along with Nately Scures and Pauncefoot Slemming) which was notorious for getting snowed in. There was a very good café on the left overlooking the Severn. One of its specialities was home made custard tarts. Not the two bites and they are gone kind; these filled a tea plate and needed a spoon.

From here it was into Newport, generally turning right by Wynn's yard to BRS Newport which had a good canteen. From there we were sent to Rogerstone to load ally. Cardiff lay straight ahead through the town.

There was a good digs in Cardiff. Mrs Ackman in Salisbury Road, near the Castle. I spent a week there doing an exhibition van job for Prestige Cabinets. That was another home from home place; Phil (Mrs Ackman) loved to tell of her sexual experiences as a pubescent girl growing up in the incestuous environment of a Welsh valley mining village. At one time she had three Italian migrant workers as permanent lodgers. One of them was a chef who regularly made spaghetti in the traditional fashion, whirling it round like a skipping rope.

When I did the exhibition job there was a furniture shop in nearly every valley village. But most of the valleys were cut in half by a low bridge, it was a case of going so far up and turning back, then later going to the Heads of the Valley route and coming down the other way. On Noble's I collected piano actions, cigarette papers and washing machines from Merthyr Tydfil. On BRS, Cardiff depot would send us to Merthyr for crated export washing machines or into Ebbw Vale for steel. In Merthyr was a digs known locally as The Singing Hall. It was still possible (late '60's) to see ex-miners with "The Dust" walking a few steps then sitting on a windowsill to get their breath.

From the top of the valleys it was usual to come back to Gloucester via Monmouth, English Bicknor and Mitcheldean. In '66 Smiths of Bicknor and George Read's of Mitcheldean were taken into BRS to form Forest of Dean Branch, regarded as the most picturesque depot in Britain.

Going west from Cardiff the next town was Cowbridge. By the time I started to go there regularly it had been by-passed, there was a good café at the end of it as I remember. It was the place to turn right for Llantrisant, initially with raw material for the building of the Royal Mint. Later to collect two shilling piece planchettes, or blanks, to be struck at the Mint in Mint Street in London.

I never stopped in Bridgend. It was on past the steelworks at Margam, Port Talbot and Briton Ferry into Swansea. Reporting to Swansea depot usually resulted in being sent back to one of the above to load steel, occasionally to be sent on to Llanelli. The only digs I stayed at regularly was Mrs Edward's in Carmarthen Road. She was another widow with a homely private house place. Due to delayed loading at Margam I was sent to a digs on a nearby council estate. It was only the second place that I have ever been to where I vowed to sleep in the cab rather than go there again. Three beds crammed in to a small room and a tribe of unruly kids, the food was horrible too.

Very occasionally I ventured to Milford Haven, Pembroke Dock or Fishguard with ships' stores. These were imported from Holland via BRFS and often included fresh herrings and ice folded up in a plastic 'tarpaulin'. These trips were the result of the ship sailing from Cardiff or Barry before we arrived and we chasing it to its next dock. One of my mates missed his ship at Barry, chased it to Pembroke, where he was told it had been diverted to Bangor. When he had finished his overnight (over hours) dash to Dee-side, he was met with blank looks. The Harbour Master's office finally told him he was on the wrong side of the Irish Sea. He had to trek round to Preston and put the trailer on the Irish Ferry.

Thinking about South Wales, I realised that despite really good digs in Cardiff and Merthyr we always thought about getting into and out of it quickly. Since the Severn Bridge, even the authorities charge you to get in and let you out free. Since '74 it is an area I have only been to seven times. Four times at work and three socially. On one of the four working visits, I saw one of the finest forklift truck drivers I have ever seen. It was at the big brewery at Magor. Delivering a load of cartons, I had to wait for a trailer of beer to be loaded. The girl had a truck, which picked up two pallets at a time; she put on a forty-eight pallet load double-decked, in seventeen minutes. No second goes, no pushing into place. Off the ground and on to the lorry in one continuous, skilful manoeuvre.

There was a surprise on each of my social visits. My wife and I visited Alan Spillett in his rural retreat at Aberaeron. Coming home through mid-Wales, what had been barren hillsides, were covered in dense alien softwood plantations, almost a mini-Canada.

There was a road haulage surprise when we visited her brother who lived in Blaenwaun, which is in the middle of nowhere. There was a steady flow of immaculate modern artics past his cottage. He told me that Mansell Davis, one of the biggest hauliers in Wales, had its depot and HQ in the next village.

The most severe shock was when we went to the Garden Festival at Ebbw Vale. We stayed in Pontypridd, which I remembered as an industrial town, but now seemed to be a tourist centre. Going up Merthyr Vale I realised that the dual carriageway we were travelling on was on the opposite side of the valley from the road I remembered. The tragic village of Aberfan was a cluster of houses in the distance. When we came into Ebbw Vale it was incredible. No vast steelworks; slagheaps hardly visible; so clean and smoke free. Different from the dismal, noisy, fume filled place, with the roads covered in black slurry, which I recalled, from loading steel for export. A lot of it for countries, which now sent vast quantities to us, no wonder the steelworks, were all gone.

CHAPTER 24
LONDON

Transport cafés in London were like fleas on a hedgehog. I've picked out the ones that I used regularly and had a little story. For years there were many, often called 'dining rooms' more like pubs. Acid etched windows; mahogany booths and marble topped tables with iron legs. Even a few with scrubbed tables, forms and sawdust on the floor. Bill May's, mentioned later immediately comes to mind. It smelled like a carpenter's shop. Some bore the sign "A good pull up for carmen". Today, the carman has a job to pull up to deliver his load, let alone have a cuppa or a meal. Any area with a cluster of factories or warehouses generally had a selection of cafés of varying styles and qualities. The modern collection of industrial units, seems to be served by a quilted aluminium van, playing *"I wish I was in Dixie"* at full volume, plus the ubiquitous tea, coffee, chocolate machine, which serves a universal brown liquid tasting of soup or onions. It does not seem possible that there was a time, when no matter where you were at mid-day there was somewhere to get a cooked meal.

Now, thanks to town planners? Yellow lines and Red Routes, the transport café is a fond memory. The transport catering of the late 20th century, is a trailer caravan or an old bus parked at the side of the road or on a bit of waste ground. Even these are getting up the planner's collective nose and being closed at the least excuse.

One of the most famous of the roadside places was Bill May's, outside what was Regent's Canal Dock, now the Limehouse Basin. It was noted for saveloy sandwiches and taking your tea mug away half full, which we reckoned was a ploy to sell more tea. I spent a lot of time (and money) in there while waiting in Lowell Street to get into the dock. Even today in my home, if anyone goes to take half drunk tea they will be asked "who do you work for, Bill May?" On the Narrow Street side of the dock in Northey Street used to be The Lock Café, a very good place. There was a canal boat repair dry-dock across the road and a lock, which allowed lighters and canal boats to enter the Limehouse Cut to get into the Lea Navigation, this has now been filled in. The main ship lock, which connects with the Thames, still exists, as does the main lock flight, which connects the dock to the Regent's arm of the Grand Union Canal. Which is beside Bill May's.

At the side of the Blackwall Tunnel approach Robin Hood Lane used to lead down to Poplar High Street, now gone with the Docklands Development. On the corner was a good family run Italian café. I had a bit of luck there. I went in by chance, to find spaghetti Bolognaise on the menu, very rare in a working class café in the late '50's. The waitress asked what I wanted with it, "chips or boiled, peas or cabbage?" I told her on its own with a lot of Parmesan and a spoon and fork would do. When it came, it was a big dinner plate full to overflowing. The waitress said, "Momma says anyone who eats their pasta properly deserves a proper helping". After that I made a point of going in there. The waitress would call into the kitchen; "It's for the proper pasta man". She was a beautiful Italian girl, thinking about her now, I wonder if she is as big now as her Momma was then.

Going east still further was the (then) newly built Silvertown Motel in Silvertown Way. This advertised food, beds and secure parking. It was run by a couple of real East Enders who had been boxers or wrestlers. George Burroughs the RHA Security Officer went to check out the parking. He was assured "There'll never be nuffink nicked orf our park guvnor, the lads know that if anythink goes from 'ere we'll be round their drum breakin' a leg or two". The last time I passed by it looked almost derelict.

Further down Silvertown Way is George's Diner, now a purpose built place with a car park and plenty of on-street parking. Years ago it was further down the road, the other side of the Silvertown By-Pass, which was the first all cast-concrete bridge in London now sadly demolished.

On the Chelsea Embankment was a little roadside tea stall, just by the entrance to the Duke of Grosvenor's Canal (now the Chelsea Refuse Dock). It was only a little shed but well used. The shed still exists as a builder's office. In the same class, on Clerkenwell Green was a really small tea stall, which always had the cheapest cup of tea in London. I first remember it as being "The last "1d cup of tea", the last sign I can recall was "The last 3½d cup of tea".

In Seven Sisters Road was Bill and Rose's. Bill was an ex-Hay's Wharf driver who had suffered in an accident and bought the café with his compensation. He did real drivers dinners; the local side roads were always full of parked wagons. Nowadays you can't get a wagon down those streets which are full of cars parked both sides.

In Hornsey Road near the railway arch was a café where I had a funny (ha ha) experience. I had steak and kidney pie for dinner and ordered mince tart and custard for dessert, as I took the first mouthful I found another helping of steak and kidney pie, this time with custard! My wife and I used to laugh about it, she was my girlfriend then, and I had picked her up and taken her to lunch.

In Tooley Street at the corner of Joiner Street was Romano's (commonly known as the I'ties) well patronised by Hay's Wharf dockers and the many drivers collecting and delivering at the numerous wharves and wine vaults in the area. Mrs Romano was a wonderful woman with a typically large, close Italian family who all worked in the café. It was one of the few cafés where you could get suet pudding and treacle (the proper black stuff, not cissy golden syrup) plus steak and kidney pudding done in a cloth straight in the water, not in a basin.

One day a young driver came in accompanied by a young 'lady of the road'. She was as black as the ace of spades (dirt, not skin colour), all her assets on show as her tee shirt was torn down to the waist. Mrs Romano shot out the back and came back with soap, flannel, towel and needle and cotton. She said in her very fractured English, "Even the dockers wash before they come to dinner. No one sits in my café with their tits hanging in their plate. Go round the corner (to the toilets in Joiner Street) wash, sew up, then I serve you," and she did. In the uproar the driver crept away. Tooley Street was beginning to run down when her eldest son was killed in a car crash. The shock sent her funny (she worshipped her kids) the family sold up and it became a chrome and plastic snack bar.

Down Tooley Street in to Tower Bridge Road there was the only digs in London which would take Billingsgate fish drivers, who unloaded themselves (wet fish in wooden boxes). This became a down and out's hostel. It was featured in a TV programme where a reporter became a down and out. It probably smelled better in the days of the fish men. It is now a listed building, while behind it where Mark Brown's and Tower Wharf used to stand and the Polish bacon (see page 14) was unloaded stands that weird glass building which houses the G.L.C.

Bray's Café in Liverpool Road, Islington was another well-known and very popular place. Fred turned out good food and did beds for day and night sleepers. His ad. in the Headlight described the place as being "..as quiet as a country lane". Poor old Fred suffered for the Islington revival. The large Victorian houses (with servants) which were opposite gradually moved down market, first to flats finally to cubicle bed-sits. Then they went full circle back to gentlemen's houses. The in-coming middle class complained about lorries being parked in the street. They set the public health and fire officers on to him. He would have had to rebuild, from the damp course up. Instead he sold up.

In Creek Road, Deptford, until very recently there was an old-fashioned café run by two elderly chaps. Good food at very low price, they ran it for the company and to have something to do. They were hauled up by the Inland Revenue for being on the fiddle, not paying enough tax. After an examination of the books they were told that their meals were far too cheap, they should charge more and pay the amount of tax expected from that kind of business.

On the A2 at Blackheath, on the corner of Long Pond Road is one of the smallest tea stalls in London (about 8' x 4'). It has been there as long as I can remember, Long Pond Road must be the last place in South London where it is possible to park without hassle (if there is room).

I had not long started work one morning when I did not feel too good. I parked up, had a cuppa and got my head down. I was woken by banging on the door; the tacho clock said 10:30. It was two PCs, one asked, "Are you all right driver, you were here when we started and hadn't moved every time we passed?" I told them I was all right, but could they give me an escort for the rest of the day as I was now three hours late.

On Putney Heath was one of the oldest tea stalls still in use. It was a pony van, with shafts and proper wooden wheelwright wheels. When I used it, an émigré Austrian lady, Charlotte, ran it. In its early days it had been hauled into place every day by the pony. When that died it had become static. The local Council was obliged to let it stay, so long as it was in no way altered. I was there the morning that a gas explosion destroyed a nearby block of flats. You could not move for firemen and policemen until the Sally Army's mobile arrived. The Council must have changed its rules, it is now a portable building and the area in front is a bus turn-round.

In New Southgate High Street, was a café, George's which I used on and off for years. After dinner, a mate came in for a quick tea and a cake. We got into conversation and walked out together. When I was getting up'I realised I had not paid, George was all right so I thought I would pay him next time (he would not forget). I was up the road for about three months, then had a delivery that way. "Breakfast and pay up" I thought. When I got there, it was not only shut, but also demolished. The re-building that had been threatening for years had arrived.

Going to the West and Wales I stopped at Brentford Market. I should have gone over Kew Bridge; Kew Green is both sides of the road. The road round the left hand half finishes in Waterloo Place, which ends at the bridge abutment. In that corner was the best 9-to-5 café in west London, Ron's. He was an ex-Navy chef who really knew about good food. There was plenty of parking round the green; it was a quiet place for a kip. The residents of the 18th Century houses that faced the green began to acquire cars and got shirty about parking. That was the end of another "good pull-up for carmen".

Down the road to the lights you forked left into Mortlake Road for the Dodge works, now the Public Record Office. Keeping on Kew Road the next left was Kew Gardens Road, following that through all its different names took you past the Lass of Richmond Hill pub and the Star & Garter Home and into Kingston avoiding Richmond town completely. That was until the local brains put a weight limit on it.

Thinking about Ron reminded me of another good café, run by a former Merchant Navy cook. This was by the gates of Croydon BRS Parcels depot. At the Five-Ways on Purley Way was the Aero (another place with a propeller). That is now painted blancmange pink and part of the Hungry Horse chain. Neither of these can be used by transport because of parking problems.

Before leaving London there are two cafés, which deserve a mention because they both still exist. The Four Oaks at Dagenham and The Noake. The Four Oaks does digs as well as good food. It used to do a good trade with drivers from the Midlands who were delivering into Ford's. The Noake is just outside the London boundary but was well used by London drivers going to Tilbury Docks, VDJ, Procter's and the cement works of West Thurrock. It has been recognised as the ideal place to park for a dodgy night-out for as long as I can remember. Now the A13 diversion is completed both of these will be just off the new road, one at either end.

CHAPTER 25
GOING SOUTH

I didn't start going south on a regular basis until very late in my working life. By which time a lot of the cafés with which I had had a passing acquaintanceship were shut. The late '70s was the start of the flask and sandwiches era with the transport café fast declining. Thus many of the comments are dredged from the dark recesses of memory.

The Merry Chest on the old A2 near Greenhithe still exists (in 2000). It used to be one of the landing grounds for things that 'fell of the back of a lorry.' It was a weekday transport café that catered for tourists at weekends. Late one Saturday there were a couple of us on our way back from delivering urgent material to the building of Richborough Power Station (now shut and derelict). It was a warm summer evening, inside the café it was two high and a binder, so we got our tea and went and sat in the cab.

A gang of motorcyclists, who had just come in, sat down on the grass bank opposite us and proceeded to turn out all their pockets. After a confab one of the girls got up, pulled up her skirt and took off her knickers, which she hung on the handlebars of one of the bikes. Then she went round the park chatting to other male motorcyclists who she led away into the bushes beside the park. We sat for about three-quarters of an hour watching the goings on. Finally she recovered her underwear and tipped a large quantity of coins onto a hanky. After a quick count up they all set off into the café.

Before the Dartford Tunnel and the M2, we used to have nights out in Rochester. The big old mock Tudor house on the outskirts of Strood still reminds me every time I pass it. In Rochester itself was a 24-hour, 364-day a year café. It is still there, but with the dual carriageway bypassing the High Street it is no longer possible to park outside. All along the A2 were several small cafés. The only one that comes to mind was just past Wood's depot near Hartlip; this is now a Little Chef. The next one of note was a small but very good place at Dunkirk. For years a lone Tate and Lyle driver used it as a changeover point. For a short time it survived the improvements to the A2, which left it, marooned.

A little further on was the Gate Café; this was difficult to access coast bound because of the dual carriageway. Then its ethos changed to cater for the car driver, I am sure that last time I was past it was a Little Chef. There were a couple of lay-bys with proper portable buildings as cafés; these seem to be an official effort.

On the A20 there used to be a café at West Kingsdown, which was well used by young motorcyclists. They seemed to regard the lady who ran it as a surrogate mother. There was another more conventional transport café on the other side of the road, which, I believe is still there. At the foot of Wrotham Hill there used to be two cafés. One became a restaurant, which closed and has been demolished. The other is still going strong although parking is restricted somewhat.

Where the A20 and M20 converge at Eythorne stands a contemporary motorway services, built in the late nineties.

At Harrietsham was the Roebuck, behind the pub of the same name. This was another transport through the week-trippers-at-the-weekend place; the main part was a huge wooden shed. It was sold and demolished and a housing estate now extends over the site. The same fate was suffered by the place I can't remember the name of (may have been Truckers at the end) near the low bridge. That stayed open, becoming more and more run down finally closing about the time the last bit of the M20 opened.

Near Lenham was the Rose of Tralee which when I first knew it was indeed run by an Irish lady. At the time it was said that her husband built it and named it for her.

At Ashford is the purpose built Lorry Services I understand it has everything including Customs facilities. I can't say too much, I have never been there.

Round to the west and onto the A21. Starting with the now defunct Badger's Mount. Lorries on weekdays; motorbikes at the weekend. There are two things that make that place stick in my mind. When I started driving I was shown a lorry parked there, it had had a minor rear end shunt into another wagon. The driver had been thrown forward and banged his head. Despite getting out and walking away he died as a result of that blow. Many years after it was the start of a really hair raising long distance motorcycle trial in which I participated.

Next was the Retreat, Polhill, always and a heavily used place, which did accommodation. Including in latter years, welcoming sleeper cabs. It stayed open for a considerable time after it was by passed by the M25, from where it can be seen if you know where to look. Just down the hill from the café a mate of mine had a lucky escape. He went off of the road and down the bank. The wagon went between two huge trees with so little clearance that it knocked off both mirrors and door handles. He escaped unscathed.

Through Sevenoaks, about halfway down River Hill on the right is Morley's Farm Hut. I first went in there during the war with Mum and Dad. I clearly remember falling down the steps and raising a large bump on my head. As I said much earlier I can remember roast goat dinners and goat meat sandwiches at that time, as goat meat was not rationed in wartime. I mentioned to an old driver that I was going to put a bit about Morley's in a book. He promptly said "Don't forget to mention the goat meat, I can remember the herd of goats on the slope behind the café". That's the embankment on your left as you go down the new A21, you can actually see the café. It is now a posh brick built place, Morley's Motel the last time I passed. When I first knew it, it was just a hut built around two old railway carriages. Dad had his brush with the Ministry man at the bottom of that hill.

Going up the hill from Robertsbridge was a very successful modern place, The Sizzling Saveloy, it did sleeper cab parking as well. Then the oil company that owned it decided it would make them more money as a motorist's haunt. So the rent was raised to a figure the operator could not afford and that was another good place gone. There was a nice little old-fashioned place at John's Cross, just before the turn for Mountfield and the British Gypsum Works and Battle. That burned down and was replaced with up-market pseudo country cottages. That was your lot before the town cafés in Hastings.

Going the other way from Tonbridge, heading for Eastbourne is a road devoid of cafés, tea stalls and lay-bys. There was one very small place with a tiny park, just past Hailsham, but even that shut in the late '80s. The alternative route to Eastbourne the A22 via East Grinstead and Uckfield to Hailsham is as bad. After leaving the M25 at Godstone there is a tea stall in the lay-by just before New Chapel. In fact that is the only lay-by before the Ashdown Forest's picnic areas.

The A23 Brighton Road was at one time well provided with cafés. There is still a couple just past Coulsdon and another at Hooley, if you can get in the lay-by going north. There used to be a really good one at the start of the original Crawley By-pass that went when Gatwick was expanded and spread across the old road. There is the motorway services at Pease Pottage, which hasn't got much room for lorries. There was a proper place at Handcross, which even survived being left on a service road, which was created building the new road alongside the old one. That has now gone.

Back in the late '60s we found a good place by accident. A whole gang of us (four or five wagons) had been doing a big exhibition job at the Conference Centre in Brighton; we were on the way home on a

Saturday afternoon. We were desperate for a cuppa and something to eat. Just past Hickstead I spotted a place with an "open" sign and an empty car park. It had the look of a middle class motorist's stop but "any port in a storm." In I went closely followed by the rest, filling the car park. The lady behind the counter had a really 'counties, cut glass' accent, but she welcomed us like long lost sons, nothing was too much trouble. The lads from Grays called it 'The Dowager's' and used it regularly when using that road. My Bristol regularly shared the car park with Rolls' and Bentleys while I sat beside men in Saville Row suits receiving exactly the same service as they did.

Going into Brighton, just after you got to the County Pillars was an old style café, which became a Little Chef. It has gone back to being a transport café of the old style now called Robbo's. There used to be another almost opposite that has totally vanished with the road improvements.

By the time I started going into the areas covered by the A24 and A29 the era of the transport café was over. It was well into the era of the flask and a packet of sandwiches from home, or the mobile tea stall in a lay-by. Fortunately patronised by lorry drivers who had become immune to all known germs. Their standards of hygiene are variable to say the least, even to someone as unfussy as me.

The A3 was always a bad road for cafés once you were outside London. The first place I can think of after the Kingston by-pass was in Ripley. There was and still is a good café in Guildford, it is just off what was the original by-pass, on the road into the town centre. Before the advent of the M25, we used to go from Grays across the A25, through Reigate and Dorking. Thus, going right through Guildford east to west only, just missing the town centre and passing its front door. It's a park on the road place.

Going to Eastleigh and Southampton meant turning of the A3 onto the A31 (The Hog's Back). On that route there is one place worth a mention, Bert's at Runfold. That is another place by-passed by road improvements and dual carriageways. The dark recesses of my brain hint at a place in Alton, but I can't remember details. Anyone going that way and picking up the A32 to go to Fareham would have found a good place at West Meon. You've guessed, - now another Little Chef!

Back on the A3 the only place I can think of is the National Trust café at Hindhead. After serving lorry drivers for donkey's years, the middle classes have got their way and instituted a ban. From there I can recall a place near Butser Hill, gone with the road straightening. But to some extent replaced by a good, popular lay-by tea stall.

Three things stick in my mind about Portsmouth. In the winter of '55 I had a night out there in a digs just a little better than the one at Cheetham Hill. It was warm! When I got back to the wagon in the morning (it was in a waterfront lorry-park) the cooling system had frozen despite a full quota of anti-freeze. It was full of something, which looked like that children's treat "Slush Puppies." I was going to start up and let it thaw, but the diesel had waxed up as well. So I finished up with a fire under the tank, and the fuel filter and radiator (removed), thawing out by the stove in a friendly garage whose fitters were inundated with non-starting wagons.

Much later in my BRS days I had a night out in a new digs with one of my mates. Les, an ex-Navy man who was a terror for the ladies. The landlady told which bus to take to find a good pub. When we came out we stood at the bus stop on the other side of the road to go back. No buses with our number came along. A woman we had spoken to in the pub came out and asked what we were waiting for, we told her the bus number. She said, "Didn't you know? Buses going in have odd numbers those coming out are even, if you came on a 19 you want a 20 to go back.

On that job we were delivering cartons lined with greaseproof paper for Smith's family sized crisps; a load a day. One day I had to wait for the potato wagon (a 10-tonner) to pull out. I remarked to the driver that I hadn't seen him before although he must be in and out a lot. I was surprised to learn that his load lasted them for the week.

On the A33 there was, and so far as I know still is a well-used café. Across the road was a pub called The Lunways which was a place used by So'ton men for a "dodgy". Talking of the A33 brought back a memory from the '50s. In those days the original Winchester by-pass used to run under a cast concrete arch bridge. A common sight on motorways today, but then it attracted architects from around the world. Just before the bridge was a transport café, I was in there having my dinner when in walked the rep. from a very famous meat pie firm. The proprietor reached under the counter and came up with one of its pies, which he pushed into the reps. face, just like a music hall act. It transpired that one of the regulars had bought a pie and taken the top off to put in some brown sauce. The filling was covered with a layer of green mould, hence the café owners reaction. "A cup of tea and a meat pie" was a very common money spinning order at the time.

On BRS sometimes we got sent into Eastleigh to collect cable or scrap copper from the Pirelli Cable works. The latter was worth a lot of money at the time, you were supposed to eat and drink in the factory, then leave and go straight through to the metal merchants in Watford. The digs there was the Delhorn Guest House, it was what used to be called a commercial hotel. A place where commercial travellers (now called company reps.) used to stay. That was a pleasant place. When I again went into Eastleigh in the '80s I found that the guest house and the nice Victorian houses which adjoined it had all been demolished and a supermarket built on the site.

In the city of Southampton were three digs. The Sergeant Major's, run by Amy and her husband who had been an RSM in the Guards. He was a very interesting man, on retirement from the Army he had gone to Australia driving Land Trains, which certainly gave him some tales to tell. He was a stickler for locking up at half-past-ten. The young driver involved in the Kelvedon incident was a ladies man who liked to stay out late. He carried a knotted rope in his case; if he wasn't in when we went to bed; we tied the rope to the bed leg and dropped the end out of the window.

Just round the corner was Mrs Brown's a very popular place. Old man Brown was another teller of tall tales; he had been a chef on liners, finishing up on the Queen Mary. He always swore he had worked with Mr. Smith when he invented the potato crisp and that R. J. Mitchell had lodged with him while working on the forerunner of the Spitfire. I've never been able to verify either story.

Mrs Davies's in Regent Park Road was the digs that the depot booked if you did not specify Brown's or the Sergeant Major's. All the drivers said that the Vehicle Foreman had something going with Mrs Davies. Some thought financial, others thought more personal. She was notorious for two things. If you booked late you could find yourself sleeping in a boat on a trailer in the garden. If you wanted a second cup of tea after your evening meal she charged for it and did not pour it until the cash (1½d) was in her hand. She also refused to take black drivers.

In Poole was a real home from home place, run by the elderly lady who owned the Poole Pirates speedway club. I understand that it now lies under the RNLI's HQ.

There is no specific chapter for the east. I only ever stayed in Ipswich or King's Lynn. In Ipswich it was always at Mrs Mayhew's, the wife of the BRS shunter. A big Victorian house with a lot of bedrooms, a real home from home place.

There were odd times when I had to stay in King's Lynn. The digs there was run by a pair of gay' men, it was absolutely spotless and the food unbeatable with a lot of dishes cooked Norfolk style, very reminiscent of my Grandma's cooking. Just a point of interest, my Granddad always ate his dinner

Norfolk style with meat on one plate and vegetables and gravy on another. It must be genetic; I can't stand gravy on my meat and only have a tiny splash on potatoes. In those politically incorrect times that place was always known as "The Queers'".

Two nostalgic views of the A1 trunk road, long before it was modernised. In Dad's driving days it was still as shown above, from a photo taken probably in the 1930s at Eaton Socon. Below, is a later picture from the 1950s showing the filling station and cafe at Stilton.
(Photos: The Ratcliffe Collection)

CHAPTER 26
GHOSTS

The roads of Britain must be littered with ghostly apparitions. I thought readers might enjoy a few stories I have come across over the years, including an experience I actually had. In the beginning are a couple of tales involving a driver with an over-vivid imagination.

On the first occasion I had changed over at Bromford Lane and decided to go to the Brickhill Café to look up some mates. Coming under the bridge and round the bend at Willoughby I came on an eight-wheeler parked on the road with the driver waving me down. I asked him what was wrong, as even in headlights he looked pale. He said that as he came under the bridge a ghostly figure leapt out at him and then disappeared. We moved the motors up a bit, off the road and started to walk back. As we approached the bridge one of Alfie Dexter's box artics went past at some speed. Something white shot out of the hedge and vanished. After much scrambling, swearing and searching, I finally found a plastic pallet wrapper snagged up in a hawthorn bush, as we watched another box motor went past and out it shot. That satisfied him and off he went.

Two nights later, same spot there was a Manchester Scammell parked up, same driver. This time the story was that the motor was haunted. Every time he picked up a bit of speed there was something white floating in the cab, when he stopped to look there was nothing. I took his motor, he took mine once we were over Braunstone and I could pick up speed something white started to float, I switched on my torch (my mate never carried one) it was a sheet of newspaper. When I stopped I could not find it at first. It was tucked away right under the passenger seat. Those old Scammells had lots of gaps in the floor. Obviously at speed the draught was blowing it up, stopping created a slight suction which drew it out of sight. I told him to buy a torch and not keep honest folk from their tea!

My personal experience was in 1955 and was answered in part in 1969. I was going to Worcester via Banbury and Stratford. Coming up to Sunrising House the engine gave a few splutters and died. I turned off the headlights to save the battery and sat pondering on what was wrong. Should I try to fix it, or chance coasting down Sunrising Hill with no vacuum for the brakes to get into the filling station at the bottom in case it was a long job? It was then that I heard footsteps approaching and a sound like a walking stick being trailed along. When I put the lights on there was no one. The footsteps carried on past the nearside. Even when I got down I could still hear them receding into the distance. The torch showed up nothing. I put the bonnet up and found that the two screws holding the float chamber had come loose, the float chamber was overflowing but there was no vacuum in the jets. A quick tighten up and I was away, still wondering.

In 1969 BRS was into Work Study, the Branch Manager, Johnny the Steward and I were going to a conference in Droitwich. We stopped at a country pub just past Upton House for a meal. There was a coach load of American tourists in there, the guide was telling them the story about seeing the lights and hearing the sounds of the Battle of Edge Hill at the anniversary of the battle. This prompted me to tell my story to my two companions. An old local sitting at the table said to me "You never saw him then? Most people who hear him see him". I asked who and he replied "Why the wounded Roundhead of course". He told us there was a local story that a Roundhead pikeman had been wounded at Edge Hill and was trying to get home, probably to Banbury. Many people had seen him plodding along that stretch of road trailing a pike. He reckoned that when they had improved that bit of road a skeleton and some Roundhead armour, including the remains of a pike had been discovered in what had been a ditch. Not far away on the A41 is Church Warmington. It was reputed to be the most haunted town in England; there was a time when every house had a light on all night long. Apparently it was a re-grouping place for both sides in the Civil War; many of the wounded died there.

On the A4 just west of Newbury is the village of Speen. West of the village the road runs between low stonewalls and is slightly sunken, an old hollow-way. It was a notorious spot for black ice as it was sheltered. Many old drivers tell of a little old man sitting on the wall waving. If the driver stopped to find out what he wanted, he would be gone but the road would be a sheet of ice. This happened to my old mate Rodney on three occasions when he was running nights for Western, he was (sadly now dead) a man who I believed implicitly. He was so intrigued that he made some enquiries locally. The story he was told was that the Old Man of Speen as he was known, was a lengthman in the early days of tarmac roads. One winter's night he was going out to grit the notorious icy patches when he was struck by a skidding lorry and killed. Ever since when the road is icy he goes out to give a warning.

The next story concerns Knightlow Hill on the A45 just north of the Fosse Way crossing (now a roundabout). I have never experienced it personally, but I have heard it many times from different sources, more especially the drivers of my Dad's era who started on solid tyres. It made the pages of the Coventry Evening Telegraph and is included in a book on British ghost stones.

The story is always in essence the same. It is a winter's night and there is some mist or fog. There has been a puncture, a breakdown or an accident partly obstructing the road. Until the building of the second carriageway, the road was not overwide and a notorious black spot. The participants are looking out for approaching traffic to give a warning when they hear a lorry approaching. As it gets nearer they see dim yellow headlights and some report a strange clip, clip, clip sound. Then they see an old lorry with a sheeted load. Some report the driver as staring straight ahead; wearing a big overcoat and a shiny-peaked cap. The lorry goes unchecked through the obstruction and disappears northwards.

Some of the old drivers have reported the headlights as being oil-lamps and the strange sound as being that of a solid tyre with a cut. The facts are that in 1926 a General Roadways Scammell four-wheeler went off the road at that point and overturned. The petrol tank was longways across the scuttle, the petrol ran out, was ignited by the lamps and the driver burned to death. Strangely, G.R.'s men wore a uniform of navy blue Melton overcoat and shiny peaked chauffeur's cap. I have not heard the story since the dual carriageway was opened, although these days the road is nowhere near so heavily used at night. Earlier I mentioned a bad road accident at Knightlow, I have often wondered if the driver saw the Knightlow ghost in his drunken state which caused him to swerve off into the telegraph pole.

This tale is of a 'fetch'. For the uninitiated a 'fetch' is an apparition which portends imminent death. In my ancestor's land of Norfolk, it is a big black dog called the Black Shuck. The one in this story is a coach and horses. In the 18th Century the Bath Road (A4) crossed the A361 further south than today's Beckhampton roundabout. At this point a stagecoach guard shot and killed an innocent wayfarer, mistaking him for a highwayman. From then on there were stories of a phantom coach travelling that stretch of road, it soon developed the reputation as a 'fetch'. When the road was moved, it continued on the old route. Coming over the downs to the east crossing the road and travelling west up what became Dorothy Paget's gallops.

In one early hours, Bristol depot received a garbled 'phone call from its wagon and drag crew, (which was running down from London), saying that the wagon was at the Beckhampton Gallops and they wanted a relief. A relief crew was sent and found the outfit in charge of another Bristol driver who had found it standing in the middle of the road, lights on, engine running and doors swinging open. The driver and his mate were found at the 'phone box in Bishops Canning. Their story was that they had seen the phantom coach cross the road in front of them and they were not going on the road again. They sold their cars and walked or cycled to work, where BRS found them jobs in the yard. This is another story, which I have heard from several sources. When I asked their contemporaries in Bristol about it all they would say was that the two men had had a "nasty experience" and did not go up the road anymore.

The final tale concerns the A41. Travelling south it passes through Adderbury, where it takes a sharp left. Before the turn there used to be a hard verge where drivers stopped for a kip. A couple of times I heard about drivers being woken by the sound of odd footsteps passing their cab, but not being able to see anyone. Then Joe Dalton, the Preston driver from the early days, told me the story. He had had the experience himself as a young man. He said the footsteps were those of a man with a peg leg as he had an elderly relative with one and he knew the sound.

I asked in the big transport cafe near the spot (now another Little Chef) when I got on to days. The story was that a local man was gassed in WWI, he was given an outdoor job as a lengthman. While doing his length he was hit by a lorry and lost a leg, subsequently being fitted with a peg leg and going back to his job. One night going home from work, he was run over and killed, just at the spot where the footsteps are heard.

That's two ghost stories concerning dead lengthmen. A job I have mentioned earlier in connection with Mickey's Mile, Foster's Booth and Kilsby's Hut. Sadly now a forgotten breed, although at one time a vital feature of our road network. In the beginning they were probably employed by the owners of the road who collected the tolls. Their job was to keep the hedges and verges trimmed (the original purpose of a verge was to stop highwaymen hiding); clear the ditches and the water run-offs; fill holes in the days of water bound macadam and in more recent times spread salt and grit. There were still a lot about when I was a child, my Dad would often stop to talk to them. They were a mine of information on country lore.

The last one I can remember was Cecil, who lived in the lengthman's cottage beside the A5 at Potterspury, I last talked to him in '63 or '64. He told me then that once the M1 opened and all the traffic went off the A5 it was so quiet that nearly everyone who lived near the road had to take sleeping pills. The last time I passed ('97) the cottage had been demolished and there was a big pile of salt on the site.

"They don't make them like they used to!" (Photo: Peter J. Davies)

CHAPTER 27
LADIES OF THE ROAD

Back in the dark old days of the '50s and '60s, there were many 'ladies' involved in road haulage. Not as drivers, although some could drive very well, but performing a much more basic female function. In the south they were generally called scrubbers, in the north floozies, but characters to a woman.

In those days things ran at a much more leisurely pace allowing time for those who were so inclined to make use of their services; there were many more all-night transport cafés. These were the regular haunts of some of them, many of whom I got to know (not biblically) over the years. There were two that I know of who married BRS drivers.

Merle, Edna, Flo from Granage, Brenda, Towcester Betty, Screaming Edie, Sadie, Eva and Kitty. The ones I knew well, all like me now in the bus-pass generation.

The first that I met in '55 was an Australian nurse Merle, who always used the Watling Street Café on the A5. The was my first run having just come out of the Army, I was running in early in the evening and having something to eat as it would be too late when I got home. She sat down at my table and said "Looking for business" (An expression still used on the street in 2006). I said "no", so she asked if I would mind just sitting and having a chat. As that was a regular Birmingham run I used to stop there often and made a point of seeking her out, as she was an interesting talker. It transpired that she was a lesbian and as she had no emotional feelings towards men it was a good way to supplement the miserable nurses' wages. When someone caught her eye to go out onto the car park she would say "Won't be long, just off to cash my horizontal cheque book."

The second run was also memorable; it was when I first met Sadie a real outstanding character. Further up the A5 at Loughton was the 48 Mile Café, better known as the Glue Pot (now under the Milton Keynes Bowl), which was her regular haunt. I knew the place well having often been in with my Dad, so I set off to the Gents' which was a lean-to at the back. It was also the wash place for the digs, with a row of sinks down one side and the slab and W.C.s at the far end. Anyway I walked in and there was this young woman, hem of her skirt under her chin, one foot on the washbasin. Not just airing her difference but giving it a good scrubbing. She said, "You're in the right place love, there's no hot water in the Ladies." I went down to the slab and when I came back she said, "You can have a go when it's dry." I said "No thanks I don't like the look of it." With that she twisted herself round and looked in the mirror over the basin. Then she said, "Do you know neither do I, I'm glad I sit on it", then we had a good laugh. Forever after that when I met her she would say, "It doesn't look any better."

Much later on, one night she went to the pub in Loughton, (the Coach and Horses I think) with drivers from the digs. They all came back very merry and decided it would be a huge joke to fill her 'earning capacity' with marmalade (there used to be big dishes on the table), which they did, to much laughter. Between giggles she kept saying, "Bugger me, crumpet and marmalade." They and we thought it even more hilarious when some innocent came in and used the same spoon to put marmalade on his toast.

Another night, a driver was selling those torches that showed different coloured light. Sadie bought one and went and sprawled on a table in the dark end of the café. She lifted up her skirt displaying all her assets (she never wore knickers) and shone the torch on them while changing the colours saying, "Look lads a Technicolor f***."

On another occasion she got into a terrible argument with a driver, he wanted her to do something she was not prepared to do. It must have been pretty perverted; she was game for most things. Next night, him and some of his mates grabbed her, turned her upside down and filled her with gear oil. What a state she was in when she came back into the café! We realised that with all the additives that were being put into oil it could be serious. One of the lads going north took her to Daventry Hospital sitting on a load of newspapers. (You could get an aching tooth taken out there in the middle of the night). The next night someone asked where she was, only to be told "Sadie's up at Daventry getting her gearbox drained." Some of her regulars put the ring-leader in Northampton General for a few days; his mates had a lot of trouble with flat tyres and water in the diesel (a filler neck is the same height as a urinal) and all went on to other runs.

There was another girl used to come down from Stafford (can't remember her name). At that time ('50s) there was an old wives tale which very many believed that if a woman had a pee immediately after sex she would not get clap, cystitis, or pregnant. This girl could not pee squatting she had to sit. On those old trailers the hand brake was up by the landing legs with a rod or cable running down to the axle. She used to squeeze under the trailer and sit on the cable (yes some pervs. had a torch). As the rod or cable was generally dirty prospective clients could see how many had gone before by the marks down her thighs.

Edna was a mystery, she worked the Meriden and later the Stonebridge area. In those days the A45 ran through Meriden and pre–nationalisation the café had been a changeover for Fisher, Renwick. She was well-spoken, always well-dressed, - two-piece costume, matching shoes and handbag, rolled umbrella and gloves. Her opening remark was "You can't touch me unless you wear something."

At the Stonebridge changeover you would often find Flo from Granage, she was a good eight-wheeler driver and could handle a two-stick A.E.C. She was a scruffy as Edna was smart, she always wore a shapeless brown coat with a unique belt. This was a piece of rope with an eye splice one end and a back splice the other. The end was tucked through the eye and then wound like a timber hitch.

Towcester Betty worked the stretch between the Brickhill Café and the Towcester Towers. She was short and fat and often had a young lad in tow. He used to go and sit on the verge while she was working. There was a standing joke, "Never get weighed with Betty on board, your front axle will be overloaded."

Screaming Edie came from the St. Alban's area. She had a nervous disorder hence her nickname; she was a good lorry and trailer driver. One of her regulars, who carried high value loads, had to park in a specific depot for his break. He went in with her hidden on the passenger floor. While he booked in and had a cup of tea she put on a uniform cap and drove the motor out for it never to be seen again. She was also noted for another trick, some drivers would use her services and then not pay. She would bide her time and then let them have another go, right a the crucial moment she would pee, leap out of the cab and lock herself in the Ladies.

Eva lived in a caravan behind The Bell as you go into Hockliffe. A driver divorced his wife to marry her, only to later divorce her.

Kitty was getting on when I first met her she used Cyril's just off of the A45 Rowley Road roundabout. Pre-nationalisation she specialised in General Roadways and McNamara's men. I saw her many years later in north London; she was a very prim looking little old lady.

Brenda has one memorable story involving an A.E.C. Mammoth Major eight-wheeler. For the benefit of younger people I will explain that these had a small cab with a huge engine hump in the middle. The bonnet was thin sheet metal bent into a curve and sloping down from back to front. It rested on a ledge at each end and was held in place by the side panels with spring clips so that the fitters could take the lot off. The seats were hinged on the back of the cab so that they could be folded up out of the fitters' way. There was no horizontal athletics in those cabs; it was doggie fashion from the nearside. Brenda plied her trade at the Ace Café at the top of Weedon Hill and on this particular night Bill Bailey, (later killed in a crash with a mobile fish and chip van), was making use of her services.

Just as things were getting exciting, the bonnet slipped off the back ledge and crashed down on the engine. This tipped the pair of them over onto the driver's seat, which broke. They kept going and hit the driver's door; a wood framed door with the lock held on by four screws. These tore out and the door bust open pitching both of them out on to the grass verge of the car park (good job the motor wasn't parked facing the other way).

We were all on the car park chatting to the changeover men; the first we knew was the crash as the door hit the side of the cab and the screams. We grabbed our torches and rushed over and round the wagon. Georgie Wright from Parcels was first on the scene and he said, "Chuck a bucket of water over 'em." Brenda was moaning and Bill was twitching but not trying to get up. What we didn't know was that Bill had both hands inside her jumper exploring her other assets so that his arms were now trapped between her and the ground. He explained the situation and with a bit of pulling and lifting we got him off. I'll say this for him, even after the disaster he was still 'up' for action! Two of the other girls came over and asked Brenda if she was all right. All she could say was, "Me tits is squashed and me insides hurt." I wasn't surprised at the latter, they were still travelling forward when she hit the ground and stopped dead, she must have felt like a kebab.

The girls took her of to the Ladies and we tried to mend Bill's motor. We scrounged a lemonade crate and put it under the seat and roped up the door, leaving him to explain at Coventry Workshops. The girls came back and said Brenda was all right but, "You should see her tits, four bloody great bruises on each one." We bought her some tea and got her laughing (she was normally very jolly) and worked out what had happened. When the bonnet collapsed Bill hung on to something to save himself; obviously he hung onto what he had in his hands at the time. Bill came back from his changeover very pleased with himself. Apparently he told the foreman that the seat had collapsed when he hit a bump and he was lucky to be alive because the door had burst open. Foreman was convinced. Brenda was back at work after a couple of days and none the worse. However, whenever anyone approached for trade, her first words were, "Not if it's an A.E.C!"

On the A1 at Stamford was a Doctor's wife who was "turned on" by lorry drivers. She used to do it free for fun. She often appeared in a Russian Sable fur coat. Then in Nottingham was a nymphomaniac W.P.C. who, when she was on the two-to-ten shift, would patrol the Cattle Market Lorry Park looking for a driver she fancied and make a date with for later, after she finished her shift. She was another one who did it for fun; she would not take money, "It would not be ethical."

Just after the M1 opened I was going up by Junction 9 where there used to be two access slips. A Leicester eight-wheel coal tipper, (one of those economy ones, a Dodge four-wheeler with two added axles), came up off the A5 at speed and it turned over from the second slip into the first, putting coal all across the M1. We all stopped and started to run up. The nearside door opened as we were running up to it and the driver I was with said, "Bloody hell he's got a pet chimpanzee." Then as we got nearer we could see it was a teenage girl, stark naked and covered from head to toe in fine black dust, all you could see was white teeth and white eyes. We never found out if the nudity caused the accident.

When I got back on the Birmingham run in the late '70s everything was on the M1 and all the old girls had gone. For a little while there was one very pretty girl about nineteen or twenty. She was very well organised working between Watford Gap and Newport Pagnell. She carried a big holdall, clean knickers one end, dirty the other and washing kit in the middle, she washed after every customer. She didn't last long, one of the drivers did a bit of pimping and she went to London to work for him.

In the late '70s I also went on the A12 running to Harwich and there was one girl working that road even then. She was involved in one of the most hilarious events I have ever seen, far funnier than the Brenda episode. With all the things I have seen I always wonder what I have missed.

Anyway Sue decided to work the A12 to cash-in on all the drivers using the Haven ports. Her speciality was oral sex (we later found out that at nineteen she had had two abortions and still had a positive Wassermann, {i.e. syphilis test}).

There was also a group of parcels drivers who worked a tight schedule, but managed to take their break at the cafe, and always at the same time. They had a card school and when Sue was in she joined in. They played with a pack of pornographic cards and she would look at the pictures and masturbate under the table. She would go all dreamy eyed and one of the drivers would say, "don't lay any cards yet, Sue's coming". 'Mother' (in her late sixties) behind the counter would invariably say "I wish I had time for some of that!"

Then a real Jack the Lad started on that run, to hear him he could "see to" the Luton Girls Choir with the Dagenham Girl Pipers for afters. He had a *'Sex Instructor'* sun strip on his windscreen, and an *'I choked Linda Lovelace'* T-shirt. God's gift to women he thought. We decided that he and Sue should meet so we told them to look out for one another. Then one night they were both in the café together and finally went out to his cab, we crept round behind a trailer to watch. First thing he did was light a fag, he smoked fancy ones he got off of a sailor. When he turned off the cab light we could only see the fag glowing, then it started to go bright then dim, it was obvious when she sucked so did he. Suddenly there was a burst of flame and a hell of a hullabaloo in the cab. The door shot open and Sue jumped out beating at her head. He came out more slowly, clutching his face and when he got down, his wedding tackle, with the other hand. Sue was hysterical.

We got them into the café and the elderly lady we all knew as 'Mother' took charge of Sue. We had a look at our hero, his face was black, his eyebrows singed, his nose and top lip burnt. He kept saying "Oh me cock" and when we looked at that it was bleeding and beginning to swell. 'Mother' had got Sue calmed down and we pieced together the story. His fancy extra long fags had a filter tip. Unlike British filter tips this was a long piece of crepe like paper rolled up inside an extra long cigarette paper. In the excitement he had smoked right down to the tip and it had burst into flames and he had dropped it. He had put his hand down to protect himself, forgetting that this is where Sue's head was. Sue felt the hand on her head and thought he was one of those men who pushed the girl's head down as he ejaculated. (Several 'working girls' have been killed like that) So she did what she had been told by the "old hands" to do and bit him hard. When she jumped out she could smell burning hair and feel the pain at the back of her head, fortunately his slap had knocked off the burning fag end.

'Mother' sorted out Sue with the kitchen burn spray. But our hero had to go to Colchester A. & E., his nose was so swollen he couldn't see properly and the other end so swollen he could hardly walk. To crown it all, like so many 'same species' bites it turned into an abscess and he had to be circumcised. He tried to keep it quiet but got so much stick he left the firm; last I heard of Sue she had taken up with a Dutch driver and gone to Amsterdam to work in a club.

Artic An articulated vehicle. Which consists of a non-load carrying tractor with a partly superimposed trailer mounted on a fifth wheel. (q.v.)

Artic unit The tractor (cab) of the above.

A.T.S. Associated Tyre Services

Ally Aluminium (abv.)

Anthrax An extremely infectious and fatal lung disease, carried by airborne spores.

B.R.F.S British Road Ferry Services

B.R.S. or BRS British Road Services. The general haulage arm of nationalised road haulage.

B.T.C. British Transport Commission

B.T.C. British Trailer Company, Finchley and Trafford Park.

Back Scotch Specially for loading reels of paper. An eight-foot long triangular piece of timber with a rope fixed to each end. It is tied across behind the last reel.

Bank Part of a transport depot where the floor is the same height as a lorry floor, to facilitate loading and unloading.

Bill of Lading A document showing the exact details of the cargo loaded on a ship.

Bogie A small very heavy trailer to carry one end of a long load. Also Dolly (3)

Bolster A wooden beam mounted on a turntable to carry the end of a long load. It can be fitted to an artic. unit or a specially adapted rigid vehicle usually eight-wheeler. Together with the above forming a "lorry and bogie."

Bolster (2) A strong frame fitted to the front of a rigid so that it's cross bar carried long loads over the cab. Sometimes a loose trestle like arrangement usually called a "floating or rolling bolster", considered by many as very dangerous as it would rollover under heavy braking, dropping the load on the cab.

Boxes I.S.O. containers. The 20' and 40' shipping containers everyone knows.

Bristol Vehicle built by Bristol Commercial Vehicles Ltd.

Brum Birmingham (Local abv.)

Bump stops Rubber blocks fitted to a vehicle's chassis above the road springs to stop metal to metal contact on full deflection.

Bosky glen	A dip on the road sheltered by trees. Borrowed from fairy stories.
C.B.	Citizen's Band radio
CMDE	Constant Mesh Direct Engagement. A gearbox using helical gears which can't slide and so need dog clutches to engage the gears. But without synchromesh. so needing skill to change gear by double de-clutching, similar to an old straight tooth sliding 'crash' box.
CMR	Certificates Merchandise Routiers. An insurance convention laying down the rules and paperwork for the carriage of goods on international journeys.
CPC	Certificate of Professional Competence. A formal qualification required by Transport Managers.
C.T.I.	Container Transports International (a company)
Carriers licensing	A system of licencing to control the numbers of vehicles allowed to carry goods. Originally conceived to limit competition with the railways. Three categories: 'A' to carry anyone's goods anywhere: 'B' to carry certain good within a defined area: 'C' to carry one's own goods. Now replaced by the ' 'O' for Operator's licence governed by quality as opposed to quantity.
Changeover	The type of long distance service where drivers exchange vehicles or trailers allowing each to return to his own depot. The location where this takes place.
Clamp truck	A fork lift truck fitted with hydraulically operated curved jaws instead of blades. Generally used to pick up reels of paper or stacks of tyres.
Corner boards	Pieces of fibreboard or wood placed under a rope to protect cartons etc. from being damaged by roping down.
D.E.R.V.	The type of fuel on which diesel engines run, originally called light oil. Hence the "oil engine" badge on some old vehicles. Stands for 'Diesel Engined Road Vehicles' originally marked on dispensing pumps at filling stations.
De-nationalisation	Taking road haulage out of public ownership in 1952.
Docker	A dock worker employed to work on the quay or in the shed, loading and unloading lorries. Receiving cargo unloaded by the stevedores (q.v.) or sending cargo to the ship to be stowed by them.
Dolly	This has three meanings. (1) A type of knot used to help tighten a rope when loading. (2) A wheeled device to support the front of a semi-trailer (making it into a trailer). (3) See bogie.
Diff.	Differential (abv.) found in the middle of a drive axle. Allows the wheels to revolve at different speeds when cornering.

Digs	Overnight accommodation; a café or private house which provides beds and meals for payment.
Double drive	Applied to six and eight wheelers when both rear axles are driven. Compare <u>trailing axle.</u>
F.L.T.	Fork lift truck.
Fifth wheel	A turntable fixed to the chassis of an Artic Unit (q.v.) it forms the coupling and hinge of an articulated vehicle.
Foreign base	A British Road Services expression. It defines men, machines and depots other than those from 'home base'.
Furniture bumpers	A nickname (generally thought to be derogatory) for drivers delivering new furniture.
G.I.T.	Goods in Transit. The insurance cover which applies only to the load.
GV9	A vehicle defect notice issued by a Ministry of Transport vehicle examiner.
H.G.V.	Heavy Goods Vehicle. Now changed to L.G.V., Large Goods Vehicle.
I.S.O.	International Standards Organisation.
J.I.T.	Just in Time. Of deliveries made as goods are needed, thus reducing the need for reserve stocks to be held in factories or shops.
Jack-knife	An articulated vehicle folding-up when braking due to a brake imbalance.
Jack Johnson	A type of crowbar fitted with tiny rollers to make it easy to "inch" heavy items.
K.G.V	King George the Fifth. One of the London Docks.
L.A.D.	Leyland, Albion, and Dodge: of components shared between the three makes.
L.T.S.	London, Tilbury & Southend Railway.
Lancashire flat.	An early type of vehicle body which could be lifted off of a vehicle complete with its load. Possibly named from early use sending loads from Preston to Northern Ireland.
Locals	Collections and deliveries close to the depot.
Log sheet	A driver's written record of his hours of work. Now replaced by the tachograph.(q.v.)
Luton	On a furniture van, the part of the body extending over the driver's cab or a van body with a Luton.

M.o.T.	Ministry of Transport.
Max. Cap.	Maximum capacity. BRS description applied to artics when m.g.v.w was 24 tons.
Mermaids	The men from the Weights and Measures Dept. <u>The ones with the scales!</u>
Night out	Spending a night away from home. I.e. "That trip involves a night out"
Nuts & bolts	The M.o.T.'s vehicle examiners involved in roadside checks.
Ops 4, 6, 12 (et al)	All BRS forms had a number. Those beginning Ops. were to do with operations. 4 was a request to workshops for a repair. 6 was a vehicle's "running sheet". 12 was a driver's daily log sheet.
P.D.Q.	Pretty damn quick!
P.H.O.	Public Health Officer.
P.L.A.	Port of London Authority. The controlling body for the docks and the river.
P.o.W.	Prisoner of War.
P.X.	Post Exchange. The American equivalent of the NAAFI.
Pole truck	A forklift truck with round poles instead of flat blades. Some times with just a single very long pole to handle objects with a hole in the middle.
R.D.C.	Regional Distribution Centre. Mostly used by supermarkets.
Re-bar or Rebar	Toothed steel rod used in reinforced concrete.
Roll-ups	Hand made cigarettes.
Ro-ros	Roll on-roll off ferries.
Scotch	A heavy wooden wedge. Generally a 4" x 5" x 6" triangle about 3" wide.
Scotching up	The act of using scotches to hold cargo (usually reels or barrels) in place.
Showboat	The familiar name for a type of Scammell eight-wheel high capacity van operated by Fisher, Renwick Ltd.
Shunter	A driver loading and unloading vehicles or trailers brought by long distance or night trunk drivers. Returning to his depot each night. (See Locals)
Side-loader	A special type of fork lift truck. The lifting forks work at 90degs. to the side allowing long loads (usually timber) to be carried front to back as they would be on the lorry.

Skein	Rope wound round the arms in a figure of eight into a hank.
Skeletal trailer	A trailer which is just a bare chassis with twistlock fixing points for an I.S.O. container.
Stevedore	A dockworker employed to stow and unstow cargo in a ship's hold.
'Suit'	A managerial, office or administrative worker. Someone who normally wears a smart suit to work.
T.D.G.	Transport Development Group. An operating group of associated companies.
T.G.W.U.	Transport and General Workers' Union. The Union of most drivers and dockers.
T.R.R.L.	Transport and Road Research Laboratory. A Government organisation researching into all aspect of road and vehicle safety.
Tachograph	Device for mechanically recording drivers' hours of work, linked to the speedometer.
Telex	A teleprinter or the message sent by it.
The Met.	The Metropolitan Police.
Tilt	A waterproof cover fitted over a fixed framework on a lorry or trailer body. Also applied to a trailer with such a body.
Traffic operator	The member of the office staff that allocates loads or jobs to the drivers.
Trailing Axle	On a six or eight-wheeler. The second rear axle has no driving gear and is only for extra weight capacity purposes. An economy measure to save initial cost and increase carrying capacity by reducing unladen weight.
Tramp	A driver who goes from depot to depot taking whatever load is available not necessarily going back to his own depot.
Trouncer	The traditional name for a driver's mate on a brewer's dray.
Trunk	A regular service run between two depots, most often at night.
Trunker	A driver involved on a trunk (q.v.). At one time the older and more experienced drivers, when the emphasis was on getting the trunk through in any situation.
Tugmaster	A specialised artic unit (q.v.). The fifth wheel (q.v.) is raised and lowered from the cab by hydraulics, making it unnecessary for the shunter to raise and lower the landing legs manually. Reducing the effort of moving many

trailers.

W.I.   Women's Institute

Whisper   A method of controlling a fractious horse by whispering into its ear. A strange and unexplained ability naturally enjoyed by certain people.

Also useful equivalent weights/measures.

£. p. One pre 1971 pound is equal to 240 pence (d) or 20 shillings (s). One shilling = 12d.

T. C. Q. lb. One ton = 20 hundredweights (cwt.). One cwt = 4 quarters (qtrs.) or 112 pounds (lbs)

One kilogram (kg) = 2.2lbs. 1,000kg = 1metric tonne or 2,200lbs

One inch = 25.4mm

One foot = app.30cm

Three feet, three inches = app. 1 metre.